The Book that provoked these
shocking headlines:

"MP ASKS: WAS SIR ROGER A KGB DOUBLE
AGENT? IS THIS ANOTHER COVER-UP?"

—*The New Standard,* March 23, 1981

"PREMIER ORDERS URGENT PROBE INTO
PINCHER'S SOURCES."

—*The Daily Mail,* March 28, 1981

"THE PRIME MINISTER CONFIRMS THAT
MI5 CHIEF WAS A SPY SUSPECT."

—*The Daily Mail,* March 27, 1981

"HOW MANY *MORE* TRAITORS ARE THERE
STILL IN OUR MIDST?"

—*Winston S. Churchill, Tory MP*
The Sunday Express, March 29, 1981

THEIR TRADE IS TREACHERY

**THE SENSATIONAL TRUTH
ABOUT THE MOST DAMAGING SPY
IN HISTORY!**

THEIR TRADE IS TREACHERY

Chapman Pincher

SIDGWICK & JACKSON

LONDON

First published in Great Britain in 1981 by Sidgwick and Jackson Limited

Copyright © 1981 Chapman Pincher

First paperback edition 1982
Reprinted (twice) prior to Publication

ISBN 0-283-98847-9

Printed in Great Britain by
Cox & Wyman, Reading
for Sidgwick and Jackson Limited
1 Tavistock Chambers, Bloomsbury Way
London WC1A 2SG

To the loyal members of the
Security and Intelligence Services,
on whom so much depends

Contents

Foreword

Their Trade is Treachery was originally the title of a booklet prepared in 1964 by the Security Service (MI5) for restricted circulation among Whitehall officials with access to secret information. The booklet's purpose was to describe, by means of genuine case records, the ruthless methods used by the Russians and their allies to trap the unwary into serving as spies and saboteurs.

Though, after securing a copy, I regarded it as a feeble effort, ludicrously restrained by Foreign Office sensibilities about offending the Kremlin, I believed that it should have a much wider circulation because—as this book will show—the most dangerous spies tend to be recruited long before they secure any official position of trust. Whitehall put so many obstacles in my way, however, culminating in resort to threat of prosecution under the copyright laws, that I was able to do little more than mention the booklet's existence in the newspaper for which I then worked.

I decided then that, one day, I would produce my own version of *Their Trade is Treachery*, giving the general public the fullest possible details of the appalling penetration of Whitehall, including the security and intelligence services, by Soviet spies and saboteurs. Where relevant, I thought I should include details of the penetration of the comparable services of Britain's allies. Here it is.

I sincerely hope that the facts that I have checked at every available point and which have been studiously suppressed by authority will alert thinking people to the true extent of the Communist conspiracy against them. It is my belief that through Whitehall's exaggerated zeal for secrecy, even senior ministers have been kept in ignorance of the extent of the penetration of what is our first line of defense. As the former home secretary, Merlyn Rees, said in the parliamentary debate on the Anthony Blunt affair, "My view is that security is a matter for the nation." It is also mine.

Though much that I shall disclose is bound to generate criticism of the past history of the security and intelligence services, making both look like a mountain of "mole hills," that is not my purpose. They are bastions of the nation's freedom against an opponent growing more dangerous and more daring day by day; for, in an age of nuclear stalemate, the threat from subversion is probably greater than that from direct attack. Therever Soviet-style communism has been imposed on a nation, it has been accomplished by very small minorities, a few thousand zealots, backed and often controlled by Soviet professionals, who secretly undermine a few key objectives—the security and intelligence services being top-priority targets.

If one nation can penetrate the security and intelligence services of another, it can then control them like puppets on a string. During World War II, by means of brilliantly contrived deception techniques and double agents, the British were able to do just that to the Germans. Since then, for many years and with equal skill, the Russians have penetrated and exerted control over both MI5 and the Secret Service to an extent that has been so successfully suppressed that the public is scarcely aware of it. The facts disclosed here will speak for themselves as regards the extent of the cover-up.

I have taken professional advice on the security aspects and am completely satisfied that while many of the events that I reveal may anger those who wished them to remain secret, none can prejudice current or future operations. The security aspects of the various situations are outdated. It is the truth that is new.

Furthermore, some of the formerly sensitive information originates from American sources—the Central Intelligence Agency (CIA) and the Federal Bureau of Investigation (FBI) being both intimately concerned—who have been involved in the investigations into the Soviet penetration of the British security services. Such information is not subject to official secrecy restrictions.

I also risk being accused of censuring dead men who are unable to defend themselves, but it is the facts that do that, not I. All the allegations made against the men that I name

arose *from their own colleagues,* who were witnesses to
secret events that infuriated them.

Researchers looking for source references will find few
here, for in the main this book deals with prime source
material, collected over the years from people who insisted
on remaining anonymous in their lifetime. I am confident
that the reader will be able to assess the truth of the
statements from the detail with which they are presented. As
far as possible, I have avoided drawing on published material,
so much of which is inaccurate and tends to be perpetuated
from one book to the next, for the security services eschew
correcting published errors on the principle of "keeping the
waters as muddy as possible."

There is some confusion in the public mind between the
Security Service (MI5), concerned with counterespionage,
mainly in Britain, and the Secret Intelligence Service (MI6),
concerned with intelligence gathering and espionage, mainly
abroad. In this book, therefore, I shall generally refer to the
Security Service only by its well-known initials, MI5, and to
the Secret Intelligence Service by its simpler and better-
known name, the Secret Service. (There is no direct American counterpart of MI5 because its work is shared by the CIA
and the FBI. The CIA also carries out the functions of the
Secret Intelligence Service.)

For similar reasons, I shall refer to the Soviet espionage
and security organization by its well-known name, the KGB,
though it has had different names in the past. There are
currently other lesser-known arms, like the GRU, the military branch, to which I will refer only when necessary.

After thirty-five years of investigative journalism, I have
seen many intelligence and security officers and senior civil
servants go to their graves with secrets that are part of the
fabric of history. I do not propose to make that error.

1
Supermole?

On March 26, 1981 Mrs. Margaret Thatcher, the British prime minister, announced that her government was to set up an inquiry into the defenses of the security and intelligence departments against penetration by spies. It would be the first independent inquiry into this situation for twenty years, and it would also cover the Foreign Office, Home Office, Defence Ministry, and other departments of state harboring sensitive information.

The prime minister made this announcement as part of a long statement about the original British edition of this book, which had been published that day, and as a direct consequence of various disclosures it contained. In her statement, the prime minister confirmed that Sir Roger Hollis, a long-serving director general of MI5, had been deeply suspected by some of his own colleagues of having been a Russian agent, perhaps for nearly thirty years. The suspicion was so great that Sir Roger had failed to dispel it when called back from retirement in 1970 and fully interrogated. So, in 1974, a further inquiry, to settle the issue if possible, had been set up in great secrecy. A former secretary of the Cabinet, Lord Trend, had been asked to undertake it and had spent a year doing so. Before the publication of this book, the public had known nothing of what has since become known as the Hollis Affair or of the Trend Inquiry.

The choice of Lord Trend had not pleased those security and intelligence officers who had been pressing for a further inquiry. Formerly Sir Burke Trend, he was very much a Whitehall Establishment figure, having held the Cabinet secretaryship for ten years between 1963 and 1973, the period when the suspicion against Hollis had grown and reached its climax. It was greatly in Whitehall's interest to have Hollis cleared, and while not impugning Lord Trend's integrity, the security officers would have preferred a man who had been less involved and more detached.

The pile of evidence facing Lord Trend indicated that there had been at least one "Supermole" and possibly two with the unrestricted opportunity of burrowing into secrets and undermining the entire counterespionage organization.

All the relevant files recording long investigations by a joint team from MI5 and the Secret Service, along with tape recordings of the dramatic interrogation of Hollis by men junior to him, were made available to Lord Trend. He questioned witnesses and visited MI5 headquarters, spending many days there reading documents.

Understandably, Sir John Hunt, the reigning Cabinet secretary, and the few Whitehall chiefs who knew of the inquiry hoped that it would clear both men, Hollis in particular.

Witnesses who had carried out the original investigation came away convinced that Lord Trend agreed with them that there seemed to be a *prima facie* case that MI5 had been deeply penetrated over many years by someone who was not Anthony Blunt, the art expert who had been exposed as a spy during his wartime service in MI5. They believed that he also agreed that the circumstantial evidence against Hollis was so weighty as to demand explanation. Hollis had not cleared himself during his interrogation. His answers to searching questions had been unconvincing and his memory had been at fault only when it had suited him. Furthermore, the evidence showed that Hollis had consistently frustrated attempts by loyal MI5 officers to investigate the obvious penetrations of their service. His behavior during the Blunt investigations had been particularly suspicious as I shall show.

The other senior officer who had fallen under suspicion while the apparent KGB penetrations of MI5 were being internally investigated was Mr. Graham Mitchell. Until his retirement in 1963, Mitchell had been Hollis's deputy. So, for several years, both the director general of MI5 and the deputy director general had been under deep suspicion of being Soviet spies—a truly appalling circumstance for any security organization whatever the eventual outcome. (In her effort to allay public disquiet over these disclosures, Mrs. Thatcher tried to suggest that the inquiries into these two men were almost routine when, in fact, they were unprecedented and calamitous in their impact on morale.)

Lord Trend quickly cleared Mitchell, agreeing with the advice of witnesses that he had virtually cleared himself by his convincing responses when he had been resolutely interrogated in 1967, as I shall describe in chapter 3. He delayed a decision on Hollis for almost a year. I shall deal with that decision later because it did not become known to more than a very few people until Mrs. Thatcher made her statement to Parliament following publication of this book in March 1981.

In the meantime, early in 1980, Mrs. Thatcher was warned about the politically explosive nature of the Hollis and Mitchell affairs by a Conservative member of Parliament, Mr. Jonathan Aitken, a great-nephew of the late Lord Beaverbrook. He had learned of moves by former members of MI5, the Secret Service, and the American CIA to secure a searching inquiry into the security and intelligence services because of the mass of evidence that both had been penetrated by the Russians to an extent unsuspected by Parliament or the public. In a long letter to the prime minister, Aitken outlined some of the most spectacular evidence that had been given to him by MI5 sources and CIA sources who feared that Hollis, who died in 1973, may have recruited Soviet agents who might still be "in place."

Whether Mrs. Thatcher was first informed as a result of this letter or knew beforehand, she soon became fully aware of the situation concerning Hollis and the general penetration of the security services by the KGB. Her predecessor as prime minister, James Callaghan, had also taken steps to ensure that the heads of MI5 and the Secret Service briefed him fully on the matter. Sir Harold Wilson, another former Socialist prime minister, was given the basic facts but was vague when I questioned him. He said that while he had been told about the suspicions concerning a former director general of MI5, he had not heard Hollis's name mentioned in that connection. Immediately prior to Mrs. Thatcher's statement, however, he had been allowed to refresh his memory by consulting Cabinet papers, including the report of the

Trend Inquiry. He then confirmed that there had been serious leakages from MI5 and that some of them could have originated from Hollis. He also went on record, both in Parliament and outside, as claiming credit for having set up the Trend Inquiry!

Soon after Wilson had resigned as prime minister in March 1976, he had made some sensational charges concerning his doubts about the loyalty of MI5, charges that many deplored as unworthy of a former prime minister. While these remarks had been conditioned by his belief that members of the organization had been plotting against him in an attempt to bring about his downfall and undermine the credibility of the Labour government, they were to some extent a *cri de coeur* by a very tired man, horrified and baffled by what he had learned about the penetration of the security services.

I had known about the cover-up of the Hollis situation for several years and in 1978 named him as suspect in the paperback edition of my book *Inside Story*. Since then, I have had confirmed details of most of the evidence against him, together with the sinister events and the strange aspects of Hollis's behavior that eventually led to his dramatic interrogation. They point to a situation so menacing to national security that the nation should be made fully aware of it. The view of the loyal MI5 officers who uncovered the evidence is that the Russians penetrated both the security and intelligence services so deeply and for so long that they not only neutralized them but effectively ran them.

I have established that this is also the view of senior officers of the CIA, who had to be alerted to the facts. The confidentiality between the American and British security and intelligence services is always close, but when KGB penetrations are involved, it tends to be total because a "mole" in any of them could prejudice them all. Some of the CIA officers, past and present, seem satisfied that the main culprit was Hollis, in which case he may have been the most damaging spy in history, for the director general of MI5 is not only responsible for counterespionage, countersabotage, and countersubversion but for protective security. This last, which is regarded as more important than the catching of spies, is the prevention of espionage by physical security precautions, the investigation of leakages, and the weeding out of those who are unreliable. A head of MI5 who happens to be a

Soviet agent is also in a crucial position to assist in any attempted Communist coup or Russian attack.

As Hollis died in 1973, I may be charged with defaming a very senior public servant who can no longer defend himself. I accept that risk not only because I believe that the seriousness of the implications for national security justify it but because all the allegations against Hollis originated *from his own colleagues inside MI5* and from the Secret Service. None has been concocted or embroidered by me or anyone else outside the security services. Furthermore, Hollis was given ample opportunity to defend himself during his interrogations and made a feeble, unconvincing show of it.

There is the additional factor that had I, or anyone else, undertaken a biography of Hollis, it would have been dishonest to have omitted what must have been the most traumatic period of his life, when he knew that he was suspect and was recalled for a quite hostile interrogation.

If Hollis was a Russian spy, the odds are that he was recruited before he wormed his way into MI5, as I shall describe. So it is small wonder that Whitehall covered up the situation even, I suspect, from prime ministers. Sir Harold Wilson was prime minister in the late 1960s when the evidence against Hollis assumed frightening proportions, yet he did not hear about it until 1974, when he agreed to the Trend Inquiry and was told in the following year by Sir Michael Hanley, the reigning director general of MI5, that one of his predecessors seemed to have been "a renegade working for the other side." It was at that stage, according to Lady Falkender, his political secretary, whom he had elevated to the peerage, that Wilson emerged from a meeting and said, "Now I've heard everything. I've just been told that the head of MI5 himself may have been a double agent." Ironically, Wilson had angrily called the meeting with Hanley to discuss false rumors, believed to have come from MI5—which they had not—that he and Lady Falkender were running a Communist cell in No. 10!

As with the rest of the prime source material in this book, the official evidence against Hollis is presented with the main objective of demonstrating the scale and effectiveness of the threat both from Soviet espionage and subversion and from British agents whose trade is treachery. I have no personal animosity toward Hollis or any member of his family.

During the whole of the decade from 1951 to 1961 MI5 had achieved no major success against the Russians who, following the defeat of the Germans and the advent of the Cold War, had become Britain's main adversary. Counterespionage operations against other countries trying to penetrate the national security screen had been more than reasonably successful, but almost every one mounted against the Soviet subversion effort had fallen flat; certain senior officers were wondering why.

The public had been led to believe that the arrest in 1952 of William Marshall, a Foreign Office radio-operator who had been recruited to Soviet Intelligence while serving in Moscow, had been a counterespionage triumph. In fact, it had been an absolute fluke.

An MI5 surveillance man, alighting from a bus while off duty, had spotted a Soviet Intelligence officer, whom he happened to recognize, in intimate conversation with an Englishman. He followed the Englishman home and noted his address. The latter turned out to be Marshall, who was then watched and eventually prosecuted for revealing secret information.

Balked of their share of routine successes, a few officers took the initiative and tracked back to try to discover what was going wrong. They discovered that in 1945 a defector from the Russian Embassy in Ottawa, Igor Gouzenko, had alleged that there was a major Soviet spy inside MI5. Gouzenko, whose evidence led to the exposure of a large spy-ring in Canada, and to another in the United States, still lives, incognito, in Canada. He has recently described to me how he had learned of the existence of a most valuable Soviet spy inside MI5 while he had been working in the main cypher room of Soviet Military Intelligence (GRU) in Moscow. "I had a desk in what had been the ballroom of a pre-revolutionary mansion. There were about 40 of us at a time working in three shifts. I sat next to my friend Lieut. Luibimov and one day he passed me a telegram he had deciphered from the Soviet Embassy in London. He said it came from a spy right inside British counterintelligence in England. The spy's code-name in the secret radio traffic between London and Moscow was "Elli."

"Luibimov told me that the spy was so important that he was never contacted personally but through 'duboks'—secret hiding places where messages were left and collected. The favorite hiding place was a split in a stone tomb belonging to some person called Brown."

As Gouzenko told the Canadian security authorities the word "Elli" was also a code-name for a British woman spy called Kathleen Willsher in the High Commission office in Ottawa. "The Russians often use the same code-name for spies in different rings," Gouzenko explained. "There would be no confusion in secret telegrams between an "Elli" in Ottawa and an "Elli" in London."

Gouzenko had also revealed that when a senior MI5 officer, Guy Liddell, had decided to travel to Ottawa in 1944 to discuss security issues with Canadian Intelligence, this had been leaked in advance to the Russians there by a warning from the Centre in Moscow.

Nothing had been done about these tips, and when Gouzenko was questioned about them again in 1952 he said that it had been a mistake to give them to MI5, where "Elli" himself had probably smothered them. In fact, as I shall describe in greater detail later, the MI5 officer sent out in 1945 to deal with the British aspects of Gouzenko's defection was Roger Hollis.

The suspicious MI5 officers did not know in 1952 about the treachery of Anthony Blunt, who had spied for Russia inside MI5 from 1940 to 1945. Since then, however, they have proved that Blunt was not "Elli." Blunt worked for the KGB while, at that stage, "Elli" operated for the GRU. Furthermore, according to Gouzenko, "Elli" was able to bring out MI5 files on Soviet intelligence officers so that they could see exactly what was known about themselves. During the war, these files were held at the MI5 out-station at Blenheim Palace, near Oxford, while Blunt was located in London.

When Blunt was eventually interrogated in 1964, he said that the Russians had specifically instructed him not to ask for personal files on Soviet intelligence officers unless he had a pressing reason to see them for MI5 purposes, the object being to avoid drawing attention to himself. This was confirmed by the MI5 registry records which showed that Blunt had rarely consulted them. Hollis, on the other hand, had been evacuated to Blenheim along with his department and, through the nature of his work, had every reason to consult the personal files regularly and did so, as the registry records showed. During his interrogation Blunt accepted that Hollis could well have been "Elli."

The investigators discovered further disconcerting leads hidden in the records.

In 1946, a Russian intelligence officer of the GRU had approached a representative of the British navy in Japan and offered to defect. Eventually, he gave contact arrangements to enable him to be met in Moscow in case of emergency. Two reports concerning the case had been sent to MI5, where they were handled by Hollis, who instructed a junior officer to make a special file on it and put it away in the registry.

No more had been heard of the intelligence officer until the early 1950s, when another Russian called Rastvorov defected to the West in Japan. He insisted on being taken to Australia because he said he knew that British intelligence was penetrated by the KGB and he was frightened to go to Britain or any British-controlled territory. While waiting in the airplane at a Japanese airport to take him to Australia, he discovered that it was going via Singapore. He immediately fled to the American embassy and was flown to the United States. There, when debriefed, he explained that he knew that British intelligence was penetrated because a GRU officer who had planned to defect a few years previously had been blown by a source in British intelligence and had been caught and shot.

When this news reached Britain, it was assumed that Kim Philby, the Secret Service man already strongly suspected by MI5 of being a KGB spy, had been the source of the leak, but a different explanation emerged when another Russian defected to the CIA. He claimed that he had been the case officer in KGB counterintelligence who had handled the attempted defection of the GRU man in 1946. He said that copies of both the reports sent from Japan to MI5 had been available to the KGB and that the details of the arrangements for contacting the would-be defector in Moscow had enabled him to be caught. Two KGB officers, posing as British Secret Service men, had approached the Russian, who had given himself away and had then been shot. The defector was certain that the information had reached the KGB from London. When shown the two documents in the MI5 registry file, he said that they were identical with those he had seen in Moscow, where they were stapled together in the same way. Checks showed that MI5 had been the only place where the two documents had been held together.

Finally, when Philby was eventually interrogated in Beirut, as I shall describe in the next chapter, he strenuously denied having any knowledge of the case. He had no conceivable reason to lie about it and seemed to be taken by surprise by the question. It would, in fact, have been in the KGB's interest for Philby to have taken the blame.

As the MI5 investigators were only too aware, the dismal records showed that whenever they managed to secure a double agent to work against the Russians in London, his identity was quickly "blown." Retrospectively, they examined more than fifty attempts to penetrate the KGB assault in Britain and could not find one that had been run for more than a few weeks without being blown. All these operations could have failed as a result of leaks, and the failure of many of them could be explained in no other way. Sometimes, when the KGB tried to recruit a university student, he would report the fact to MI5 and offer to accept but really to work against the Russians. Whenever this happened, the Russians found out so quickly that they must have been in touch with an MI5 officer with access to that very secret information. Hollis was the head of the branch dealing with anti-Soviet counterespionage.

Similarly, whenever MI5 secured advance information about a meeting between a Soviet intelligence officer and one of his British agents, the "watchers," as the surveillance experts are called, would be carefully stationed, but the meeting would not take place. The cause of these persistent failures appeared to be so obvious that even the young daughter of a retired MI5 officer, who was herself working in the organization, told her father that there must be a spy in it.

One of the most suspicious incidents concerned what has become known as "the Arago Affair." In the autumn of 1957, a cypher clerk in the Czech embassy in Washington, who had been recruited as a spy by the American FBI, gave some intriguing information that was passed to MI5. The clerk, known by the code name "Arago," said that during a visit to intelligence headquarters in Prague, he had talked at length with Colonel Oldrich Pribyl, the Czech military attaché in London. Pribyl maintained, because of something that had recently happened to him, that the Russians must have had a marvelous spy in MI5 who was always on tap. He described how he was debriefing one of several British traitors he had recruited; to avoid being overheard, this took place while driving his car through London. He had become aware that he was being followed by what he thought was an MI5 vehicle, but after taking evasive action, he believed that he had outwitted it.

Pribyl then told "Arago" that he was so concerned that MI5 might know the identity of his agent, he decided to consult the Russian military attaché in London. He saw him on the Friday of a bank holiday weekend, and the Russian explained that, because of the holiday, it might take a little longer than usual to find out exactly what MI5 knew, but he expected to have the answer by Tuesday. Sure enough, on that day, the Russian told Pribyl that MI5 watchers had indeed been following him but had given-up the chase because they had decided that he was only giving a colleague driving instruction. This information horrified MI5 because it was correct.

Further facts provided by "Arago" strengthened the belief that there must be a very active spy inside MI5. Pribyl had also related how the Russian had warned him that the MI5 men who tailed Soviet bloc cars had just changed their tactics. Instead of waiting near the Communist embassies, where they could be too easily seen, they were waiting by the main Thames bridges that the Soviet bloc spies were likely to use. This ruse, which had been immediately betrayed to the Soviet embassy, had been abandoned within a fortnight because no Russians came near the bridges.

The talkative Pribyl had also told "Arago" about a British spy for the Czechs, Brian Linney, who was providing highly secret information about a new RAF missile that he had picked up while working as an engineer in a factory at Shoreham in Sussex. In conjunction with the police, MI5, which by itself has no power of arrest, wanted to swoop immediately after Linney had handed material to Pribyl and to arrest them both. They knew all the arrangements for the crunch meeting, but while Linney turned up, Pribyl never left his office. Linney was eventually convicted in 1958 only because he was bluffed into confessing the details of his treachery. This cost the RAF 8 million pounds, as they were forced to make necessary changes to the missile to counter what the Russians knew.

The investigators were driven to conclude that the Russians knew where the MI5 watchers were going to be stationed wherever they were sent. Also, when the surveillance men decided in advance to vary the frequencies of the radio network they used to keep in touch with each other, the Russians seemed to know and were always able to listen in.

On one occasion, all the watchers in London were sent to the Midlands to assist in a most secret operation, which turned out to be a fool's errand, almost certainly organized by Russian disinformation so that the KGB could have a free hand in London for a few days. On the day that the watchers left London, the Russians turned off the radio-listening equipment on the roof of the Soviet embassy, which they normally used to tune into the watchers' walkie-talkie sets! When the watchers returned, in as unobtrusive a way as possible, the Russians switched it on.

The director general, Sir Roger Hollis, was informed of these disturbing events but seemed unimpressed.

Having access to an ingenious device, new at the time, called the probe microphone, MI5 was keen to use it in counterespionage work against the Soviet consulate in Bayswater Road, which was known to harbor several dangerous KGB spies. Knowing the details of the building, MI5 technicians were able to bore a hole through a party wall so that it came out behind a moulded leaf in the high frieze of a specially selected room of the consulate. The hole, where it emerged behind the leaf, was no wider than a pin and there was no way in which it could have been detected by accident. The microphone operated successfully for only a short time. At a later date, when a chance opportunity presented itself to an inside agent who is no longer active, examination of the pinhole showed that it had been plugged up with plaster, rendering the whole apparatus useless. The MI5 officers involved in the operation were in no doubt that it had been betrayed by a source that could only be inside MI5.

As the investigators continued the analysis of their failures into the 1960s, they were particularly angered by the frustration of a most important operation by what they interpreted as yet another high-level leak. They had been convinced for many years that the British Communist party was in regular receipt of substantial sums of money from the Soviet government. That was the only way that the party and its widespread activities could be kept going; the various appeals were merely a cover.

It was also known that the Russians were careful not to use their Narodny Bank for such transactions but delivered the money in cash to a senior party member who served as paymaster. Transfers of cash in shoe boxes had been observed, but what MI5 wanted to see were the ledgers showing how the Russian money was dispersed and whether any was used for espionage and subversion purposes.

In the early 1960s, the current paymaster lived in a two-story house divided into two single-floor flats. One day, it was seen that he was advertising for a tenant for the bottom flat, so the security men applied for it through an agency and installed a "granny," as such women agents are called.

Soon afterward, at Christmas, when the paymaster went to stay for two days with another Communist in the country, the MI5 men decided to search his flat. They were unable to do so because he left the house where he was staying and was lost by the watcher following him. In fact, he did return to his friend's country house, but by that time the search had been called off, and the flat was never entered.

Nevertheless, the moment the paymaster returned home, on the day after Boxing Day, he gave the "granny" a week's notice, refusing to give any reason. The MI5 top management had been told about the projected operation only two days beforehand, its approval being necessary before the flat could be entered.

It was considered most unlikely that any of the paymaster's neighbors could have told him about the preparations for the raid on his flat. Watchers had been stationed to forestall this, and the presence of the extra people in the flat below had been covered in the guise of a Christmas party given by the "granny" for friends and relations.

The "freelance" investigators compiled a list of about forty instances, strongly suggesting that MI5 had been, and might still be, seriously penetrated. Much more impressive evidence was to accrue later. The list was shown to Hollis, by

then director general of MI5, but he adamantly opposed any
investigation of members of his staff, saying that the idea of
setting up a special internal team to check on the leaks was
"intolerable and would break morale."

One of the officers had the temerity to tell him that such a
team would be welcomed by loyal members of the staff, with
nothing to fear. Hollis, who had previously declined to introduce regular positive vetting of the MI5 staff, a routine that
had become mandatory for other secret departments, ignored
the remark. It could be argued that Hollis was motivated by
loyalty to his service, but there are many who believe that his
loyalty lay with another service.

Suspicion of continuing Soviet penetration was strengthened
in 1962 after Anatoli Golitsin, a senior KGB officer with a
mass of documents and other information, defected to the
CIA from the Soviet embassy in Helsinki. Among the many
leads he provided (which will be discussed later), he revealed
that the Soviet embassy in London had no "SK" (for "Soviet
Colony") department. This is a group of KGB officers installed in almost every Russian embassy to ensure that there
are no defectors from the ranks. Golitsin explained that the
Russians had such an excellent source in MI5 that they could
be confident of being warned of any likely defection in
London. So, no SK officers were needed.

He also reported that in the British department of the
KGB in Moscow he had seen an index that had a section
entitled "Material from the British Security Service." It was
recent material, secured long after Blunt or any spy previously
suspected had left MI5.

The detailed evidence of various spy cases, such as those of
William Vassall and the Navy Spy Ring, provided further
indication of day-to-day penetration of MI5 by Soviet intelligence. But it was not until a spectacular event in January
1963 that the suspicious officers were convinced that the spy
they were seeking was still inside their organization and as
active as ever. This event was the defection of Kim Philby
from Beirut to Russia in circumstances that have been rigorously
concealed in spite of all that has been written about it.

2
The Truth about Philby

Soon after the "runaway diplomats," Donald Maclean and
Guy Burgess, who had both served in Washington, defected
to Russia in May 1951, senior officers in MI5 suspected that
their Cambridge University friend, Kim Philby, was the
Third Man who had provided the warning that Maclean was
about to be interrogated on suspicion of being a Soviet spy.
Their hunch was shared by the CIA, whose chief, General
Bedell Smith, demanded Philby's removal from Washington,
where he had been the British Secret Service's officer responsible for liaison with the CIA and, even more so, with the
FBI.

Philby's colleagues in the Secret Service regarded the
suspicion as quite unjustified and essentially an expression of
MI5's overall distrust of its sister service. They were dismayed
when the director general of the Secret Service, Sir Stewart
Menzies, seized on Philby's tentative offer to resign and
continued to believe in their friend's innocence for another
decade.

In MI5, however, suspicion was strengthened when an
opportunity to subject Philby to hostile interrogation arose in
the autumn of 1951. Philby was told that a judicial inquiry
into the Maclean-Burgess Affair had been ordered and that
he would be required to give evidence. The MI5 men,
including Arthur Martin, an outstanding interrogator eventually named by Philby in his book *My Silent War*, could not
wait to get at him.

The main "judicial" interrogation was carried out by Helenus
Milmo, now a High Court judge, and the impression has
been given that he made a hash of it, crudely blustering
while Philby, ever the professional, remained relaxed, using

14

his stammer to gain time to think. The tape recordings, which still exist, tell a different story. Milmo, who was a wartime MI5 officer, threw questions at which Philby spluttered, as well as stammered, while he so obviously tried to evade them.

Milmo's insuperable problem was that MI5 had no real evidence, only supposition, and Philby knew that so long as he continued to deny everything, however unconvincingly, he was safe. Philby continued this stonewalling when questioned by Jim Skardon, the MI5 interrogator who had broken Klaus Fuchs, the atomic spy. But though he has been almost admired for his bland evasions, his performance was poor compared with that of the fragile-looking Anthony Blunt, who far more persuasively withstood eleven interrogations, starting in 1951.

Philby was also assisted by friends, such as the late Sir Richard "Otto" Clarke, a Cambridge contemporary who became a Whitehall mandarin. Clarke knew that Philby had been a Communist, but when consulted in 1951, he told MI5 that he was sure Philby was "a calm, dependable Social Democrat."

Nevertheless, most of the MI5 officers with access to the results of what has become known as Philby's "secret trial" were satisfied that he was not only the Third Man but a long-term Soviet agent. The view at that time of the inscrutable Roger Hollis seems to be unknown. He must have been questioned about Philby because the two were opposite numbers for several years. Hollis headed the MI15 department responsible for overseeing Soviet and Communist operations in Britain and the colonies, while Philby was involved with Secret Service operations against Russia outside Britain.

As Philby recalled in his book, "We both served on the Joint Intelligence Sub-Committee and never failed to work out an agreed approach to present to the less well-informed representatives of the Service departments and the Foreign Office." Apart from such professional meetings, it is unlikely that Hollis and Philby saw much of each other during the war. While Philby was based in St. Albans and then in London, Hollis was at Blenheim Palace, in Woodstock near Oxford.

Philby, who, it will be remembered, was in the Secret

Service, not MI5, also suggested in his book that he had access to the MI5 archives at Blenheim—the registry where the secret files were kept. I have been assured that this was unlikely and that even if he had been allowed to see certain MI5 files, he would certainly not have been permitted to borrow them. Philby's suggestion could therefore be construed as a KGB insertion to protect Hollis, who, in 1968 when *My Silent War* appeared, was still alive and had not then been interrogated. The Soviet defector, Gouzenko, had stated that the spy in MI5 called "Elli" had been able to take out certain files from the registry. In 1968, Hollis was officially suspected of having been the culprit, but Philby's claim offered an alternative explanation likely to be seized on by anyone anxious to clear Hollis.

There was a further link between Hollis and Philby that has only recently come to light. Hollis had a brother called Mark who worked in Philby's section, R5, dealing with overseas counterespionage operations against the Soviet bloc. I have been assured by officers who knew Mark Hollis that no suspicion was ever attached to him. Perhaps it was because of his Secret Service work that Mark was never mentioned publicly when portraits of Sir Roger appeared after publication of this book. It was generally believed that Sir Roger had only two brothers, one a member of Parliament, the other a bishop.

The MI5 men lived in hopes that evidence against Philby would reach them one day, and the case remained open, if static. The Secret Service was reluctant to take any action, but it was eventually required to institute positive vetting— independent checking on the background and activities of new entrants—and this was made retrospective to cover existing officers and other staff. In the process, which did not begin until 1954, several officers were required to leave for such offenses as having failed to declare previous connections with communism or for consorting with people they knew to be active Communists. In 1955, a parliamentary question, posed by one of those MPs who seize on any subject likely to get their names into the newspapers, forced the foreign secretary of the day, Harold Macmillan, speaking on behalf of the Secret Service, to say that there was no evidence that Philby had been disloyal. I have investigated the background to this statement. It was based by the law officers on the

results of a "comfortable" interview with Philby carried out
by old colleagues from the Secret Service who were convinced that he was not a spy and wanted him cleared not only
in the service's interest but also for his own sake. The tape
recordings show that he parried questions until acceptable
answers were put into his mouth.

MI5 also submitted a much more cautiously worded statement in which the word "evidence" clearly meant "evidence
which could be brought into a British court of law." I have
discussed this issue recently with Mr. Macmillan, who is
unrepentant about his speech, which effectively cleared Philby
so that he could threaten libel proceedings against any newspaper that might have suggested that he had been the Third
Man. Mr. Macmillan was told by the law officers that Philby
was almost certainly guilty, but he was unprepared, in the
interests of individual liberty, to use the privilege of Parliament even to suggest an unproven situation regarding Philby,
as MI5 wanted. He was not prepared to say in Parliament
what he knew he would not dare to say outside.

Consideration had also been given to the possibility that
Philby might have defected if any suggestion was made that
he might be guilty, for under the law the police would have
had no power to stop him from flying anywhere he liked. So
long as he remained in the country, MI5 could at least
continue with its inquiries.

The director general of MI5, then Sir Dick White, wrote
to his counterpart in the Secret Service, Sir John "Sinbad"
Sinclair, warning him that despite the parliamentary whitewash, the evidence against Philby still stood and that he
should never be employed again in any position offering
access to secret information.

The Secret Service responded by reemploying Philby as an
agent to secure information about Near East affairs from a
base in Beirut. As cover, they induced the *Observer* and the
Economist to use him as a foreign correspondent. Despite
this, MI5's warning was heeded, especially after White was
transferred to become director general of the Secret Service
in 1956. Philby was never given official access to secret
information, though he may have wheedled some out of
visiting colleagues, who still believed in his integrity.

Little was done on the Philby case inside MI5 because,
after the whitewash, no resources were made available. This

irritated those officers who "knew" that Philby was a spy
because of secret information that had reached them in 1949
following the brilliant deciphering of wartime coded radio
signals between Moscow and London by American cryptog-
raphers. This showed that in 1945 there had been three
highly valued agents in London with the cryptonyms (code
names) "Stanley," "Hicks," and "Johnson." After the defection
of Maclean and Burgess in 1951, it had become certain that
"Hicks" was Burgess. "Johnson" was almost certainly Blunt—
one of the reasons that he was repeatedly interrogated—
while MI5 felt confident that "Stanley" was Philby.

This lead was suddenly strengthened in 1962 when the
CIA sent over information it had secured from the debriefing
of the KGB defector, Anatoli Golitsin. The defector had
described what the KGB Center in Moscow called "The Ring
of Five"—five spies all recruited at English universities before the war and, contrary to usual practice, known to each
other as Soviet agents.

Golitsin had named Maclean and Burgess as two of them
and said that the third, known as "Stanley," had warned the
other two in time for them to defect. He had been unable to
name Philby in that connection but gave other clues to his
identity. He had also told of a major KGB operation against
certain "reactionary" Arab nations in the late 1950s that had
been based in Beirut. A former Secret Service man, called
Philby, had been deeply involved in it.

This regenerated interest in the case, but nothing could be
done until a couple of months later, in July 1962, when the
first real breakthrough came from a totally unexpected source,
which, for reasons that will become apparent, has been
concealed.

Mrs. Flora Solomon, a Jewish woman who formerly lived in
Russia, where she had been a close friend of Kerensky, head
of the provisional government of 1917, but was normally
resident in London, was attending a cocktail party in Israel.
She happened to say that she was extremely angry at the way
Philby was slanting his articles in the *Observer* against the
Israelis and in favor of the Arabs. He was supporting Nasser
and Nasserite nationalists in South Yemen and elsewhere in
the Arab world. "As usual, Kim is doing what his Russian
controller tells him," she said. "I know that he's always
worked for the Russians."

When this was overheard by another visitor from England, Mrs. Solomon was asked if she would make a statement to the security authorities in London. Reluctantly, she agreed, though she realized that her evidence would imply that she had known that Philby was a Soviet spy for many years and had failed to report it.

Mrs. Solomon, who is still alive at eighty-six, is well known in London as the founder of the famous welfare department of the Marks and Spencer chain store. Philby's second wife, Aileen Furse, was personal assistant to Mrs. Solomon, who probably introduced them and was a witness at their marriage, six years—and three children—later.

When Mrs. Solomon was interviewed by the MI5 head of Soviet counterespionage, she described how Philby, an old friend, had taken her out to lunch before World War II while on brief leave from his job on the *Times* as a reporter on the fighting in Spain. Philby had told her that he was doing "a very dangerous job for peace, working for the Comintern," while using his reporting job as cover. He needed help, and he asked her to join the "cause." While Mrs. Solomon said that she had refused to help him, she conceded that she had told him that he could always come to her for help if ever he was desperate and that she would keep his secret. Again with great reluctance, she agreed to give evidence against Philby if that became necessary.

Under pressure, Hollis, by then director general of MI5, had to concede that there was now hard evidence with which to confront Philby and hopefully force a confession. Sir Dick White agreed that the prime purpose should be to secure information about the Ring of Five and their activities rather than to wreak revenge on Philby. After the forty-two-year prison sentence imposed on the Secret Service spy George Blake after he had confessed, it was obvious that Philby would not volunteer to return to London. Beirut was outside British jurisdiction, and the possibility of kidnapping him was never seriously considered. So it was decided to try to interrogate him there.

The attorney general, the late Sir John Hobson, was approached and since Philby had been denied access to British secrets for eleven years, it was agreed that he could be offered immunity from prosecution, provided that he admitted to having been a spy, would provide checkable proof of his cooperation with the British security authorities during further interrogations in Beirut, and would then agree to return to London for long debriefing in detail. Because it was known that Philby had sent many British agents to their deaths behind the Iron Curtain, it was considered essential that the offer of immunity should always be kept secret, in view of the domestic political consequences, particularly in Parliament.

The MI5 officer most suitable for the task of making this offer was Arthur Martin, who had been present during the Milmo interrogations of Philby in 1951 and, as a Soviet counterespionage specialist, knew all the details of the case. Martin was therefore selected, but after Hollis had been to see White at Secret Service headquarters, he was told that a Secret Service man would be going instead. This was Nicholas Elliott, a former close friend of Philby who had previously believed in his innocence but had become convinced of his guilt. Elliott had volunteered to confront Philby, and White had supported him, Hollis explained.

The Secret Service was anxious to keep the Philby affair away from MI5 and within its own confines as far as it possibly could. Hollis, who had put up no resistance on MI5's behalf, explained to his men that Elliott, an old colleague who was very angry at having been betrayed, might induce Philby to confess by playing on his sense of decency. This produced guffaws from Hollis's officers, who knew of Philby's sense of decency. This was typified by his behavior when called to the telephone from a cocktail party in Beirut in December 1957. Aileen, the wife he had abandoned, had been seriously ill in Britain, and Philby returned to the throng with a wide smile and the announcement "You must all drink to my great news. Aileen's dead!"

It was decided that Elliott should stage his interrogation in January 1963. He himself took every precaution to keep his mission secret, and only seven others were supposed to know about it. Nevertheless, there is no doubt that Philby was forewarned of it. Inquiries showed that of those who knew of the plan to confront Philby, only two were under suspicion in connection with previous disasters. They were Hollis and Mitchell.

A check made by MI5 later showed that a very special KGB officer had visited Beirut in May 1962, shortly after the news that Golitsin had strengthened the suspicion against Philby. His name was Yuri Modin, and during his service in London before 1951, he had run the Ring of Five. His visit to Beirut was his first time outside the Soviet Union for eight years, and there is little doubt that he saw Philby and told him about Golitsin's statement, which he could only have heard about from a British or a CIA source. Neither Philby nor Modin needed to worry much at that stage because both knew that the defector's evidence was thin and inadmissible in a British court even if Golitsin was willing to appear as a witness, which was most unlikely. But the evidence given by Flora Solomon was a different matter, and it could hardly be a coincidence that soon after the British security authorities had received it and decided to act on it, Modin returned to Beirut, presumably alerted via a British source, for the CIA had not been told about it.

His mission was almost certainly to warn Philby of the new and more potent danger and to discuss plans for dealing with it. This could not possibly have been left to the local KGB chief in Beirut, who would then have been able to surmise that there had been a leak to Moscow from London. This could have prejudiced the London source, and the Center would go to any lengths to protect that.

Modin's visit made sense in another direction. He happened to be the Soviet intelligence officer in London in 1951 who had supervised the defection of Maclean and Burgess and then, as we shall see, unsuccessfully instructed Blunt to follow them. The odds are that he brought with him to Beirut an escape plan for Philby.

If Philby had defected before Elliott interviewed him, it would have been obvious that he had been alerted, and the source responsible would have been thereby put at risk. So the best all-round solution for the KGB was for Philby to make a confession of old events no longer of consequence and use it to give misleading information to cover current operations. The confession would provide the reason for his eventual defection, the implication being that he would not trust any British promises.

As will be apparent, there is little doubt that Philby's confession, which was tape recorded, was written in advance under KGB control, most probably with Modin at his side. Philby's intense anxiety during the few weeks he had to wait for the showdown after Modin's warning can well account for his extreme drunkenness at the time. Donald Maclean had behaved similarly in Cairo in 1950, securing temporary forgetfulness from the bottle, after he first heard that evidence was mounting against him.

Elliott traveled to Beirut early in January 1963 and remains satisfied that no indication of the purpose of his visit came from him or from any officials in the embassy there. Furthermore, I have established that the CIA, which had a mission in Beirut, was not told in advance of the coming interrogation in spite of reports to the contrary.

Elliott telephoned Philby from a private flat, which had been hired and wired, and invited him around for a drink. The first thing Philby said was "I was half expecting to see you." In his diary, Harold Macmillan recorded that Philby had confessed "in a drunken fit." In fact, throughout his encounters with Elliott, he was sober.

Without delay, Elliott told Philby that new evidence had come to light and that both White and Hollis no longer had any doubt about his guilt. With some anger, Elliott accused his former friend of behaving abominably to everyone who had trusted him. He then invited him to confess his past, assuring him that no action would be taken against him if he told the whole truth and returned to Britain.

Without even asking what the new evidence was, Philby agreed to confess, and as though to cover his first, unguarded remark, he said, "This was bound to happen one day. There was bound to be a defector, a cypher clerk or a spy-in-place who would know about me." But at no time did he ask for any details.

He then admitted that he had been a Soviet agent since 1934, when he had been recruited in Vienna, that he had warned Maclean through Burgess, whom he had recruited in the same year, and that he had been responsible for sabotaging a succession of Secret Service operations, which had cost many lives. These included the betrayal of a would-be KGB defector called Volkov, the failure of a Secret Service operation to free Albania from communism by infiltrating Albanian nationalists into the country, and the sabotage of an operation called "Climber." The intention of "Climber" was the infiltration of secret agents operating for the CIA and the British

Secret Service into the Soviet Union via the Caucasus. At least twenty of these agents were never heard of again.

Philby denied that Blunt had ever been a spy. Instead, he threw false suspicion on an old colleague, which was proved to be an attempt to blacken an officer greatly disliked by the KGB. He also gave some information about his early Soviet controllers that turned out to be false.

The security authorities had been keen to establish the identity of a Ring of Five controller with the code name "Otto." Philby said that while "Otto" had never given his true name, he had discovered him to be a man called Arnold Deutsch, a Comintern agent whom he had met in Vienna, where he had been firmly recruited to the KGB. Deutsch had come to London in 1934 for so-called postgraduate studies, but he was certainly not "Otto." Philby said that he had recognized "Otto" after he had seen a photograph of Deutsch in the FBI files in Washington. A check showed that the FBI files had contained no photograph of Deutsch before Philby defected. Furthermore, the detailed description of "Otto" later given by Blunt in his confession did not fit Deutsch. As with much else in Philby's "confession," this was a KGB move to cover the truth. Finally, Philby offered to write a summary, which he would sign, for Elliott to take back to London but said he needed more time to think about the immunity proposition. Next evening, he produced a two-page typewritten document, which he signed, but he still insisted that he needed a few more days to make up his mind about returning.

With Sir Dick White's agreement, Elliott flew direct from Beirut to Washington to brief James Angleton of the CIA about the confession. Only then was the CIA mission in Beirut told of it.

About ten days later, on January 23, Philby disappeared from Beirut, probably on a Soviet freighter conveniently docked there and, it is believed, with the connivance of the Lebanese police. The freighter is believed to have been the *Dolmatovo*, registered at Odessa. Modin may also have been aboard it.

Elliott strongly suspected—and still does—that Philby had been forewarned of his mission by an MI5 source, and in *My Silent War* Philby was to write, tongue in cheek, "Maybe I was tipped off by a Fourth Man." Nevertheless Elliott's colleagues at Secret Service headquarters tended to accept the confession as a reasonably true account, though incomplete. Philby had made no mention, for example, of his motives in opposing the circulation of papers concerning Admiral Canaris, the chief of the German Abwehr, which might have shortened the war. Canaris, who was opposed to Hitler and was eventually executed by him, seemed prepared to collaborate with the British Secret Service from late 1942 onward to expedite the Nazi leaders' downfall. Philby stifled the move, probably because the Russians wanted the war to continue; once they had the Germans on the run, they could communize as much of Europe as possible.

In MI5, however, both the signed confession and the tape recordings were judged to be KGB "confections," and it was concluded that the KGB had been able to follow the conduct of the Philby case from early 1962 onward. Among the possible lies listed by MI5 was Philby's admission that he had not only sent Burgess from Washington to London to warn Maclean that the net was closing around him but, a few days later, had given the final alert in the form of the precise date when Maclean was to be interrogated. It is considered possible that Philby never knew this date. Very few knew it, but among those who did were senior officers of MI5. As Geoffrey McDermott, a long-serving diplomat, commented, "Parts of Philby's confession could well have been bogus. He might have been protecting the real 'third man' so that he could continue his activities among us." Further evidence to support McDermott's hunch is presented in chapter 14.

Still, such was the Establishment's success in continuing to conceal the truth that not until five months after Philby's defection was the government driven to admit that he had been the Third Man and a Soviet agent. And, since then, the salient facts that I have described, such as the offer of immunity, have consistently been suppressed.

Lord George-Brown has assured me that when he was foreign secretary and politically in charge of the Secret Service, he tried hard to learn the full facts of the Philby case but was denied access to the files. D-Notices—advisory notices to the media requesting suppression of sensitive information—were issued in an attempt to suppress disclosures about Philby and his activities.

Philby has continued in his totally unprincipled way behind the Iron Curtain. He remains a drunkard and even stole the only consolation left to Donald Maclean in dismal Moscow, his wife Melinda. Yet had he accepted immunity, this traitor, liar, cheat, and accessory to murder might have remained "respectable" into old age, rejoining his old clubs, like the Athenaeum, unless tongues wagged audibly enough for some writer to expose him. But there was no way that the Russians would have permitted him to face full interrogation in London out of their control. Maclean, who might have cracked under relentless questioning, had been required to defect to protect Philby so that, hopefully, he could remain an active spy. Perhaps Philby, a burned-out agent showing signs of instability, was forced to defect for a similar reason.

Like the rest of the Philby story, his defection was covered up to the maximum possible extent, though the authorities were in no doubt that he was in Russia. The Secret Service was anxious to avoid any suggestion that it had staged the interrogation in order to induce Philby to defect and so save the embarrassment of a trial. Both the Secret Service and MI5, as well as the government of the day, were determined to keep the immunity offer secret. They were also keen to prevent inevitable questions about Philby's continuing employment by the Secret Service after 1951, for though his missions may not have been of high importance, he had obviously betrayed every one of them to the KGB.

3
The Mitchell Case

The circumstances of Kim Philby's defection and analysis of the events preceding it profoundly dismayed those officers of MI5 who had been delving into the previous penetrations, which had nullified the counterespionage efforts of their organization. They felt so certain that a deliberate leak to Philby had originated in MI5 that it was a "moment of truth," as one of them described it, concerning their suspicions of the existence of a really high-level "mole." Knowing that they would get no effective support from their own director general, Sir Roger Hollis, they sought advice from someone more senior, whom they trusted, their former chief, Sir Dick White, then head of the Secret Service. Impressed by the weight of their evidence and appreciating the integrity of the men concerned, White advised them to continue with their inquiries and to report back to him before taking any action.

Comparing the tally of the suspected Soviet penetrations with the duties performed by all the senior officers, together with their known access to secret information, they produced a short list of five, including one woman. The investigators then fed these suspects "barium meals," specially doctored documents or verbal information that might enable them to ascertain if any of it was being leaked. This narrowed the suspects to three and then, quickly, to two—Hollis himself and Graham Mitchell, the deputy director general. Though Mitchell remained suspect for years, he was eventually cleared completely. To avoid a collapse of morale at lower levels, the inquiry into Mitchell was kept as secret as possible within MI5, and he was referred to by the code name "Peters." That was the name by which I referred to him in the first edition of this book, though I knew his identity. He has since admitted, both in writing to me and in public, that he was "Peters."

As Hollis could not be told that he was suspect, the investigators again sought advice from White. He was an old friend of Hollis's, had previously appointed him his deputy, and had then recommended to Sir Anthony Eden, the prime minister, that he should succeed him as director general, so he could not bring himself, at that stage, to believe that he could be a traitor. He advised that the alternative candidate, Mitchell, should be thoroughly investigated first, using all the facilities available to MI5. For this, Hollis's permission would be necessary.

When consulted, Hollis agreed that Mitchell had been behaving most peculiarly, a common symptom of a spy who believes that he may be under suspicion, as both Maclean and Philby had demonstrated. There was also a statement that Blunt had made during his interrogation to the effect that Burgess and he had taken Mitchell out to lunch at the Reform Club and that Blunt had assumed that Burgess was looking him over as a likely recruit.

The mode of Mitchell's entry into MI5 also appeared to be relevant. He had previously worked in the Conservative party Central Office, which was regarded as a likely jumping-off place for a newly recruited Soviet spy, as it provided a right-wing image. Hollis would agree only to a limited inquiry to be confined to MI5. It was pointed out that this would be impossible because Mitchell knew all the MI5 watchers who would have to be detailed to keep him under surveillance. Hollis then reluctantly agreed that watchers from the Secret Service, who were unknown to Mitchell, should be called in and that the whole operation should be a joint MI5-Secret Service exercise. It was to be controlled by Martin Furnival Jones, then director of security.

It is convenient, at this point, to dispose of allegations that have been made against a former deputy director general of MI5, Guy Liddell, because he may be confused in the minds of some readers with Mitchell. Liddell had left MI5 ten years previously, in 1953, because he resented being passed over when Dick White, his junior, was made director general. He may have been imprudent when talking socially to former colleagues, like Blunt, who turned out to be spies, but he was never suspected of disloyalty. Nor is there any truth in the allegation that he was demoted and transferred to a derisory job in the Atomic Energy Authority. As Sir John Hill, chief of the Atomic Energy Authority, has confirmed to me, Liddell, who at sixty-one was beyond retirement age anyway when he left MI5, was the authority's chief adviser on security. He could not have been appointed to a more sensitive post, especially in view of the poor state of Anglo-American relations on the interchange of atomic secrets following the cases of Fuchs, Pontecorvo, and the Maclean-Burgess defection.

All the allegations against Liddell, who died in 1958, have been generated *outside* the security services. Those against Hollis, Mitchell, and others I detail in this book were all generated *inside* those services by professional security and intelligence officers with inside knowledge.

Throughout his long and distinguished service in MI5, Liddell kept full diaries, which he dictated nightly, and I am told that nobody reading them could entertain the smallest doubt about his loyalty to Britain and his service. When he left MI5, he obeyed the rules and handed the diaries in for storage as a record. They were kept in the director general's safe, under the code title "Wallflowers," and when Hollis was about to retire from that post, he ordered that they should all be destroyed. By chance, they were intercepted on their way to the shredding machine by someone who suspected Hollis, and so a valuable history of the department, covering many years, has been preserved.

Hollis's strange behavior in that respect was marked down in the dossier against him. So was his refusal to allow the now-official investigating team to tap the telephone at Mitchell's home. It had been decided, in order to dispose of the case against Mitchell one way or the other and as quickly as possible, he should be given the full technical treatment. A mirror in his office was removed and made see-through by resilvering so that a television camera could be hidden behind it, the object being to allow the investigators to see if Mitchell was in the habit of copying secret documents. A check was kept on his office telephone, but when Hollis was asked to request the necessary Home Office warrant for Mitchell's home telephone to be tapped and bugged, he refused, saying that he did not want any outsiders to know anything about the investigation. Though the investigators were unable to tap the home telephone, they secured the help of post office security men in installing hidden microphones.

One "outsider" was kept fully informed of all the details, even including the see-through mirror: the then prime minister, Harold Macmillan. It was not only Hollis who told him but, also, Sir Dick White, with whom Macmillan has always been on close terms. (Though Hollis was director general of MI5 during the whole six years of Macmillan's premiership, the former prime minister, whose memory for contemporaries is remarkable, claimed that he could not recall Hollis when I mentioned him to him recently. Hollis had been such a shadowy figure that Macmillan confused him with Gen. Sir Leslie Hollis, a marine commander who had served on Churchill's staff during World War II.)

When Hollis tried to prevent the MI5-Secret Service team from using some of the technical facilities at their disposal to investigate Mitchell, they threatened to go over his head to Macmillan. Rather than face this, Hollis gave way. A meticulous search of Mitchell's office, carried out at night, showed that there was one locked drawer in an antique desk, formerly the property of Guy Liddell, that had been unused for years. Examination showed that unlike all the other drawers, the edges of which were dusty, the locked drawer had recently been in use. So, one evening, Hollis, whose office had a connecting door with Mitchell's, was asked for his permission for the drawer to be opened the following morning by means of a skeleton key. He agreed.

When, on the next day, the drawer was eased out, there was nothing inside, but from marks in the dust it was obvious that some flat object on four button feet had been in the drawer on more than one occasion and had been hurriedly removed from it. The investigators thought that it could well have been a tape recorder.

The purpose of such a hidden device was only too obvious. The decisions about where the MI5 watchers were to be used, and against which targets, were taken at a weekly meeting held in that room. Though Mitchell chaired the meeting, a recording of it would be of enormous additional value to any KGB men with whom he might be in touch.

The surveillance men reported that Mitchell was certainly behaving as though he knew that he was under suspicion or was taking precautionary steps prior to meeting a contact. He wandered about in parks, repeatedly turning around as though to check that he was not being followed. In the street, he would peer into shop windows, looking for the reflections of passers-by. He also wore tinted spectacles, which might enable him, from the reflections, to see anyone who might be on his trail. The "candid camera" in his office revealed that whenever he was alone, his face looked tortured as though he were in deep despair.

In the context of Mitchell, it is possible to explain a peculiar and quite unprecedented event that occurred in July 1963, when MI5 announced the name of a KGB defector currently in Britain as Anatoli Dolnytsin. In fact, it is now known that the defector was Anatoli Golitsin, who had been passed to MI5 by the CIA. So why the false name, which did not fool the Russians for an instant?

This is what had happened. Colin Coote (later Sir), then editor of the *Daily Telegraph*, had learned that there was an important defector in Britain and, being determined to run the story, demanded to know his name. He happened to meet Lord Home, the foreign secretary, and, later, the Foreign Office was instructed to put pressure on MI5 so that Coote could be given the name. The MI5 officers handling this defector, probably the most valuable ever, were loath to name him at all because he was so fearful of being assassinated by his former KGB colleagues. To those few in MI5 who knew of his existence, he was known only by the code-word "Kago." With both Hollis and Mitchell under suspicion of being in regular touch with the KGB, it was essential that they should not be told his real name or of his presence in Britain.

The MI5 chiefs were anxious to comply with the Foreign Office request because it appeared to have come from the foreign secretary. So, in some desperation, the men in charge of Golitsin falsified his name to something they could eventually claim, however lamely, had been a slip of the tongue. They chose Anatoli Dolnytsin because a Soviet diplomat of that name had once served in London. This name was passed to Mitchell, who arranged for it to be given to Coote through the proper channel—the D-Notice Committee, which then served as the link between MI5 and the media.

The MI5 officers, however, were determined to get some revenge on Coote for forcing the issue, which they regarded as dangerous. He wanted the name exclusively, so Col. Sammy Lohan, the D-Notice secretary, was instructed to put out the name over the agency tapes so that every newspaper got it, thereby depriving the *Telegraph* of its scoop.

The officers' fears had been fully justified. The day that the name "Dolnytsin" appeared in the newspapers, Golitsin packed his bags and returned to the United States on the next aircraft. Furthermore, he refused to return for several years, which meant that MI5 men had to fly over to see him and, for a long time, were denied the continuous interrogation they needed to extract the two thousand world-wide leads the defector eventually provided.

After patient surveillance, the only clue of any substance that was found against Mitchell was a torn-up map in his wastebasket suggesting some rendezvous, which was later satisfactorily accounted for. The team decided that they still wanted to interrogate him, especially as he was soon to retire. Hollis then told them that he had been to see the prime minister to secure permission for the interrogation, which he did not need to do, and that this had been refused because Macmillan thought that Mitchell might then defect, with dreadful political consequences, especially regarding Anglo-American relations on secrets' exchange. The MI5 officers believed that Hollis was lying, and Macmillan remembers so little about him, while recalling the Mitchell case in detail, that they might have been right. Whatever the truth, Hollis's statement triggered off the most extraordinary event.

Hollis was told that whether Mitchell was interrogated or not, the suspicion against him was so strong that the CIA and the FBI would have to be warned of it because of the damage he might have done to them. At first, Hollis insisted that the Americans should not be informed, but when he was told that Sir Dick White would then have to tell the prime minister about this strange decision, which would breach the Anglo-American agreement on security, he produced a bombshell. "Right, I'll go and tell them myself," he announced.

Normally, an MI5 case officer with full knowledge of the details would have been sent over to consult with CIA and FBI men at his own level. By insisting on going on his own,

Hollis automatically raised what was a thin case to the highest political level. This danger was pointed out to him but with no effect. Neither was he caring of the fact that Lord Denning was in the middle of his inquiry into the Profumo Affair, in which Hollis was deeply, and peculiarly, involved.

On arrival in Washington, Hollis went to see J. Edgar Hoover, head of the FBI. "I have come to tell you that I have reason to suspect that one of my most senior officers, Gosham Mitchell, has been a long-term agent of the Soviet Union." He then drove to the CIA headquarters at Langley, outside Washington, and gave the same message personally to the fiercely anti-Soviet chief, John McCone, in the presence of James Angleton, then the CIA's chief of counterintelligence. The Americans disbelieved him, especially when he was unable to provide the details requested by their aides. Hollis also took the unusual step—deprecated by McCone—of explaining his mission to the British ambassador, Lord Harlech. Harlech has no recollection of the meeting but told me that so much was happening at the time and that visits by intelligence chiefs were so frequent that he may have taken little notice of it.

Hollis returned to London in some anger and demanded an independent inquiry under another official of his choice. His objective was not only to clear Mitchell but to undermine any suspicion that MI5 had been penetrated at all, a motive he did not conceal from his officers. Mitchell was temporarily cleared, but in spite of further opposition from Hollis, Sir Dick White agreed that a fuller and more wide-ranging inquiry into all the aspects of penetration was essential. As White was senior, Hollis deferred to him, and a permanent joint MI5-Secret Service committee was set up in November 1964 to examine all the suspected penetrations of both services in the greatest possible depth. For want of a better name, it was called the Fluency Committee. There were three members from MI5, including Arthur Martin, three from the Secret Service, including Stephen de Mowbray, a particularly ardent and able young man, plus a chairman. Such was the urgency of objectives that it met every fortnight.

To dispose of Mitchell, at this point, he retired at his own request, somewhat short of sixty, the normal retiring age from MI5. Harold Macmillan believed that he had simply become unbalanced through being so many years in undercover work.

He told Sir Dick White that ten years in it was enough for any man, while fifteen should be the maximum. Mitchell had served more than twenty.

At the end of 1967, by which time Hollis had retired from MI5 and been replaced by Sir Martin Furnival Jones, Mitchell was brought to London for the interrogation that was so overdue. He had no difficulty in answering every question. He explained that he had always taken precautions against being followed as a routine part of his job. So far as his miserable demeanor was concerned, he said it was entirely the result of trying to work with Hollis, who refused to delegate work to him so that he had far too little to do. He would not admit that he suspected Hollis, but those who interrogated him think that this might have been at the root of his anxiety.

He had a simple and checkable explanation for the torn-up map and convinced his questioners that he knew nothing about the locked drawer in the antique desk, which later proved to have differ3nt significance.

The MI5 conclusion that Mitchell was clean was fully endorsed by Lord Trend when he studied the evidence along with that against Hollis. Nevertheless, for *four years*, there had been deep suspicion that the two most senior officers of the organization set up to catch spies had been spies themselves. And, as I shortly relate, for a short time there was a third senior officer suspect enough to be thoroughly investigated and interrogated.

The confusion and despair at the middle levels as one counterespionage operation after another went sour can be imagined. Everything possible was done to conceal the suspicions from as many of the staff as possible, but internal leaks in such a small organization were inevitable, and those specially trained to be alert to suspicious circumstances soon realized that something serious was amiss.

The interrogation of Mitchell had been almost routine to eliminate him from the inquiries because evidence of Soviet penetration continued to accrue after he had left MI5. On occasion, the Soviet intelligence officers were almost contemptuously impudent in the way they forced MI5 to waste time and money in following up bogus leads. Flats and houses were rented to watch spies who never appeared or, more likely, never existed. In one instance, a suitcase containing an old radio transmitter was deposited in a left luggage office. Counterespionage men were tipped off about it and set a long watch but nobody ever collected it.

The behavior of Hollis during the confession and continuing interrogation of Anthony Blunt in the spring and summer of 1964 helped to intensify the suspicion against him. The case officer who induced Blunt to confess happened to be the man who first suspected Hollis and was a prominent member of the Fluency Committee investigating the Soviet penetrations. This was Arthur Martin, who had been involved in interrogating Philby, not Jim Skardon, as has been reported. Hollis forced a row with him when he had barely begun to interrogate Blunt and suspended him from duty for a fortnight. Martin offered to carry on with the questioning of Blunt from his home, but Hollis forbade it. As a result, Blunt was left alone for two weeks, and nobody knows what he did, although the security authorities had their suspicions, as I shall describe.

Soon afterward, Hollis picked another quarrel with Martin, and though he was very senior, summarily sacked him. Martin believes that Hollis sacked him because he feared him, but his action did Hollis little good, whatever his motive. Martin's reputation was so high that he was snapped up by the Secret Service and, to Hollis's mortification, remained on the Fluency Committee investigating the leakages.

While the members of the investigating committee worked as quickly as their routine daily tasks permitted, Hollis reached the retirement age of sixty in December 1965. There is no truth in rumors that he was forced to retire early because of his handling of the Profumo case or for any other reason. Nor was Hollis "roasted" by Macmillan for his failure to provide adequate warning of the international implications of the Profumo Affair, as Macmillan himself has recently assured me.

The mistaken belief that Hollis was prematurely retired may have been given extra credence by the attempt by Harold Wilson, who had by this time become prime minister, to bring in a policeman, Sir Eric St. Johnston, as the new director general of MI5. The reason for this was that Sir Eric, then chief constable of Lancashire, had been friendly with Wilson, who held a Lancashire seat and thought a change might be salutary. Wilson was strongly opposed in this by

George Wigg, the security overlord, who eventually secured the appointment of Hollis's professional deputy, Martin Furnival Jones. Lord Wigg, as he now is, has assured me that he knew nothing of the suspicions against Hollis. Neither did Harold Wilson at that time.

Shortly before Hollis retired to Somerset, he called in one of the investigating committee and staggered him by asking, "Tell me, why do you think I am a spy?"

After swallowing hard, the officer gave his reasons and asked, "Do you dispute these undoubted facts?"

Hollis shrugged and said, "All I can say is that I am not a spy."

"But is there any evidence you can produce to swing the balance your way?" persisted the officer, warming to his opportunity.

"No," said Hollis. "You think you have the manacles on me, don't you?" he added with a derisive smile.

4
A Mistake
in a Shopping List

As soon as Martin Furnival Jones was fully installed as director general of MI5 at the beginning of 1966, the Fluency Committee produced a catalogue of two hundred examples of Soviet bloc penetrations of MI5 and the Secret Service, with assessments about each of them. It made certain recommendations, including the interrogation both of Hollis and of Mitchell, mainly with the purpose of closing the file on the latter, as I have already explained. Interest in Mitchell had been enhanced, to some extent, when Col. T. A. Robertson, a former much-respected member of MI5, happened to mention that when Mitchell had been discussing with him his forthcoming retirement, he had remarked that he would have more time to "play around with his wireless sets." Apparently, nobody in MI5 had known that Mitchell was a radio enthusiast, a common device adopted by spies who transmit their information that way. The situation was so desperate that no straw in the wind could be ignored.

The committee also recommended the interrogation of a defense scientist, indicated through a lead inadvertently given after 1964 by Anthony Blunt as possibly the Fifth Man of the Ring of Five. (This was not Dr. Basil Mann, the British atomic scientist living in the United States, who has previously been named but against whom MI5 has never entertained suspicion.)

No action was taken on any of these recommendations for nine months when it was found that they had never reached Furnival Jones, having been shelved somewhere at a lower level. Understandably, it is not easy for even a loyal officer to believe that the colleague who sat at the desk next door is a traitor, and it is even more difficult to credit that a long-serving director general was a spy. Still, this long delay was censured by Lord Trend in his eventual inquiry.

Once Furnival Jones saw the catalogue of penetrations, he ordered immediate action in certain directions, including interrogation of the suspected Fifth Man, as I shall relate in detail later. He refused to sanction the interrogation of his old chief Hollis unless the evidence could be strengthened.

Furnival Jones did, however, agree to the interrogation of a very senior officer, still serving, who happened to fit a description given by a defector, whose information had up till then proved fully reliable. This was such a sensitive opera-tion, as the suspect was in line to be a possible director general, that he was given the code name "Harriet" in the hope of concealing the situation from his subordinates. "Harriet" was fully cooperative, accounting during lengthy interroga-tions for every relevant part of his past life, including his entry into MI5, and he was fully cleared by the end of 1967.

Inquiries by the Fluency Committee into the origin of the defector's information suggested that it might have been a KGB plant. In that case, the KGB would have needed personal details about the officer being framed so that it could concoct the disinformation to fit him. It was noted that Hollis was one of only two officials with access to "Harriet's" personal file.

It is not unknown for genuine defectors to switch back to working for their former side because their relatives back home are being threatened or for money or even because of a change of heart: For this reason, they are always somewhat suspect unless their information continues to be accurate. As a former intelligence officer explained his attitude to defec-tors to me, "Only by their fruits ye shall know them."

The Fluency Committee renewed their efforts in Hollis's direction. One of their first steps was a reexamination of the so-called "shopping list," which had been handed in to British intelligence by a would-be Russian defector, Konstantin Volkov, in August 1945. Volkov had walked into the British consulate in Istanbul on a beautiful summer afternoon and asked to see

an official called John Read, who spoke Russian, having
served in Moscow. Mr. Read has given me a first-hand
account of the incident.

Believing, apparently, that Read was in charge of the
"anti-Soviet bureau," Volkov said that he was a senior KGB
officer and that he and his wife wished to defect to Britain.
He claimed to be of particular interest to the security authorities there because he had been employed for several years in
the British department of KGB headquarters in Moscow. He
said that he had deposited documents in a suitcase in a flat in
Moscow and would provide the address and a key if the
United Kingdom could arrange for his safe defection and the
odd figure of 27,000 pounds—probably a conversion of some
round sum in rubles—in cash. He insisted that no communication should be made with London by radio because the
Russians could read the Foreign Office cyphers.

Read asked him to put his offer in writing, and a couple of
days later Volkov returned with a typewritten document in
Russian. Read sat up most of the night translating it into
English. The document offered many things, including details of the current organization of the KGB and the identities
of hundreds of its officers serving abroad.

The crucial clause in the document read,

Files and documents concerning very important Soviet
agents in important establishments in London. Judging by
the cryptonyms [the code-names in KGB cables between
London and Moscow], there are at present seven such agents,
five in British Intelligence and two in the Foreign Office. I
know, for instance, that one of these agents is fulfilling the
duties of Head of a Department of British Counterintelligence.

With some excitement, Read reported the incident to the
British ambassador, the late Sir Maurice Peterson, who had a
deep-seated prejudice against the Secret Service, objecting to
having to house any of its representatives under diplomatic
cover. He declined to take any interest in Volkov's offer,
telling Read that the Russian's information was probably
unreliable. As a result the information and the translation
were passed to Secret Service headquarters in London at
relatively low level and the "shopping list" crossed the desk
of Kim Philby. He immediately identified the agent fulfilling

the duties of head of a department of British counterintelligence as himself. As he later confessed, he alerted his Russian controller in London, and Volkov was seized and removed from Istanbul to Moscow strapped to a stretcher. Nothing further was done about the other hints in the "shopping list."

The information that the British diplomatic cyphers were known to the Russians was ignored, though as events proved, Donald Maclean had continually compromised them, especially during his service in the British embassy in Washington.

To give the Russians time to deal with Volkov, Philby had delayed his arrival in Istanbul to "deal" with the defector for more than a fortnight. When Read asked him why he had moved so slowly, Philby shrugged and said, "It was a question of leave [vacation] arrangements."

With remarkable perspicacity the Fluency Committee decided that before the whole shopping list was investigated it should be translated again by an expert who had been concerned with decoding KGB traffic at the time and knew the jargon in use then. The expert translated the item which seemed to refer to Philby quite differently. The new translation read, I know, for instance, that one of these agents is Acting Head of a Department of the British Counterintelligence Directorate. This could only mean MI5—not the Secret Service, where Philby had been.

Two defectors from the KGB, Igor Gouzenko, the cypher clerk who had fled to the West in 1945, the relevant date, and Vladimir Petrov, who had defected in Australia in 1954—were also asked to translate the paragraph and came up with precisely the same result. Both said that Volkov could only have meant that there was an important KGB spy inside MI5. The defector Anatoli Golitsin, too, came up with the same solution.

The man inside MI5 who best fitted the description in 1945 had unquestionably been Hollis, who had then been responsible—as acting head—for the Department specializing in countering the Intelligence activities of Russian spies and Communist agents in Britain.

From that moment the investigation was concentrated on Hollis with new fervor. It was quickly realized that Hollis was also a good fit for "Elli," the spy indicated by Gouzenko as operating inside MI5 for the GRU section of Soviet Intelligence.

It had been Hollis who had been sent out to Ottawa to deal with the MI5 aspects of the Gouzenko revelations, so it could have been a case of "Elli" being investigated on the spot in Canada by "Elli" himself. While discussing this possibility with me recently Gouzenko disclosed new information which seems to strengthen it: "I was surprised that this man who, though only about forty, was so stooped that he approached me almost in a crouching way, asked me very little when I told him that the Russians had a spy inside MI5 in England known by the code-name "Elli." He took a few notes but did not show them to me."

Gouzenko then revealed that the original report about him put in to MI5 was read over to him twenty-seven years later in 1972, when he was questioned about it by a British counter-intelligence officer he knew as Stewart, though that may not have been his real name.

"Stewart was stationed in Washington and asked to see me at the Royal York Hotel in Toronto. He read me a long report—several typed sheets—paragraph by paragraph. I was astonished to learn that this was the report submitted by the man, who could only have been Hollis, because I could not understand how he had written so much when he had asked me so little.

"I soon discovered why because the report was full of nonsense and lies. For instance, he reported me as telling him that I knew, in 1945, that there was a spy working for Britain in a high-level Government office in Moscow. I knew no such thing and had said nothing like that.

"As Stewart read the report to me it became clear that it had been faked to destroy my credibility so that my information about the spy in MI5 called 'Elli' could be ignored. If the report was written by Hollis then there is no doubt that he was a spy. I suspect that Hollis himself was 'Elli' and he may have feared that I might recognize him if I had seen a photograph of him in the files in Moscow but as a cypher-clerk I had no opportunity to see photographs."

Public knowledge about Gouzenko's original revelations has been severely limited by a series of suspicious events. Crucial documents dealing with them have disappeared from the Canadian Archives. Extensive searches have failed to find the records of a high-level committtee set up to examine the ramifications.

Only one of the scores of diaries kept by the former Canadian Prime Minister, Mackenzie King, is missing. It is the very volume dealing with his account of Gouzenko's interrogation by MI5.

"It cannot be coincidence that these documents are missing," Gouzenko said. "They must have been removed on somebody's behalf." This suspicion was echoed by J. W. Pickersgill, a literary executor of Mackenzie King's estate—"If there is one volume that the Soviets would have liked to get their hands on it is the missing volume."

Gouzenko also gave me evidence suggesting that some similar "weeding" of embarrassing security files may have taken place in London: "Stewart, the British counter-intelligence officer, returned to see me again in 1973. He showed me six or seven photographs and asked if I could recognize any of them as the man who had first interrogated me—meaning Hollis, though he did not give his name. I picked one out but could not be sure because so much time had gone by.

"It seemed that the British were trying to establish the identity of the person who had interviewed me—as though they had no record of it. Perhaps someone had destroyed the MI5 records. It was all very odd and Stewart offered no explanation."

There were other aspects of the Gouzenko case which indicated that immediately after he had defected and the Canadians were trying to keep his movements secret the Russians were getting playback information from somebody involved in the day-to-day handling of the case. Mackenzie King, who handled the Gouzenko defection personally, was most anxious to ensure that the Russians, who knew only that Gouzenko had fled their embassy, should not learn that he was already in the hands of the Royal Canadian Mounted Police.

When Mackenzie King came to London soon after Gouzenko's defection to discuss espionage and other matters with the British prime minister, Clement Attlee, it was Hollis who went aboard the *Queen Mary* when it docked at Southampton with a message for him. It concerned a request from the U.S. president, Harry Truman, that the arrest of Nunn May, an

English atomic spy unmasked by Gouzenko, should be postponed. MI5 knew when and where Nunn May was scheduled to meet a Russian contact but once again there seemed to have been a tipoff and neither man appeared.

During Mackenzie King's visit there also occurred a strange encounter at an official function between him and the Soviet ambassador in London, Feodor Gusev. The Canadian suspected from their conversation that the Russian had inside information about the Western reaction to the Gouzenko business. Hollis had been present when Canadian and British officials had discussed the possibility of hushing up the whole Gouzenko affair in the long-term interests of East-West political relations, as Montgomery Hyde, who had access to prime source information in the form of King's diaries, records in his excellent book *The Atom Bomb Spies*.

Gouzenko had also reported that "Elli" had had access to files that turned out to have been located at Blenheim Palace, where Hollis was based during the war with his section of MI5. This statement also appeared to clear up a long-standing mystery concerning a professional Russian spy called Ursula Beurton—among many other aliases. She was an important agent and recruiter among the pro-Soviet spies who formed the so-called "Lucy Ring" in Switzerland during the war. She was an expert wireless operator, and though the Swiss spy ring was being prepared for what turned out to be a crucial intelligence role concerning German military intentions, she had been suddenly switched to Britain, where she arrived, in December 1940, in the guise of a Jewish refugee. She lived in Oxford, where her father had a post at the university.

It was known that she had served as a courier for the atomic spy Klaus Fuchs in 1942. Suddenly, there was light on what she might have done during the previous year and had continued to do, as well as transmitting the information provided by Fuchs. Fuchs joined the atomic bomb project in May 1941, when he then volunteered his information to the Russians on his own initiative. Until the end of 1941, he passed his secrets to a Soviet embassy official in London called Simon Kremer. Ursula Beurton did not become his controller until 1942, being chosen because Oxford was convenient for Birmingham, where Fuchs worked. Moscow could have had no knowledge before 1941 that Fuchs would become a valuable spy, so Beurton must originally have been sent to Oxford to assist somebody else. Hollis lived in Oxford while working at Blenheim Palace in nearby Woodstock.

One of Beurton's fellow spies in Switzerland, Alexander Foote, has recorded that he was led to believe that she had moved to England because she was disenchanted with working for Soviet intelligence. In fact, there is proof that she continued as an efficient and dedicated agent serving several spies operating in Britain. Her radio traffic to and from Moscow was discovered years later among the mass of material recorded during the war but could not be deciphered because she had been meticulous in using the one-time pad system (see page 57). Such an unknown "illegal" agent as Beurton with her transmitter would have been considered much safer for an important spy living out of London than regular contact with a "legal" controller with diplomatic cover, who would have had to make regular trips to Oxford with little excuse for being there.

In his description of "Elli," Gouzenko had said that he was so important to the Russians that he was not contacted personally but through dead-letter boxes. These were secret hiding places where messages could be left or gathered. One that was specially favored was a split in a tomb in a certain graveyard.

The Fluency Committee made a further study of the tape recordings of Nicholas Elliott's interrogation of Philby prior to his defection, and the circumstances of the confrontation were analyzed again. Hollis had been one of the very few who immediately knew about the new information against Philby provided by Flora Solomon and about the decision to send Elliott to Beirut. He could easily have passed the information to a Soviet controller in London.

It was also appreciated that Hollis had been perfectly placed to have informed Soviet intelligence about the precise date of Donald Maclean's interrogation in 1951. Though not even deputy director then, he had been one of five people fully in on the secret because of his special position concerning Soviet counterespionage.

Hollis had also known of the arrangements for the surveillance of Maclean. He could have told the Russians that there would be no surveillance after Maclean left Charing Cross station, in central London each evening, for his country home at Tatsfield in Surrey, a fact that Maclean appeared to know. I have been told that Maclean was not followed from Charing Cross to his home or watched there because officials of the Foreign Office had assured MI5 that he would never defect when his wife was so close to confinement. Someone in MI5 must have accepted this ludicrous advice and instructed the watchers accordingly. Hollis could also have told the Russians that secret microphones had been fitted in the Tatsfield house—information that would greatly have facilitated Maclean's escape with Burgess, as I will explain.

The CIA analysis of the Maclean case is that it was handled with a highly suspicious degree of incompetence. It would have been standard practice to keep Maclean under tight surveillance and even to warn him that he was to be interrogated with the object of forcing him into some panic measure that would help to betray him. Someone in MI5 must have countermanded the normal practice.

Officers who were involved with the Maclean case have always insisted that they did not want him to defect, as I and others have suggested. They urgently wanted to interrogate him, especially about the other members of the Ring of Five. But if Hollis was a spy, he would be under instructions from his Soviet controller to do all he could to ensure that the defection succeeded.

A survey of Hollis's behavior during the Profumo Affair, in which he played a major role, showed it to be so peculiar and, whether by design or not, so angled toward the Soviet interest that I shall deal with it separately in some detail. Suffice it to say at this juncture that the KGB may have "lit the fuse" that exploded the Profumo Affair and then exploited it ruthlessly and with staggering success.

There were other aspects of Hollis's behavior over the years that intensified the interest of the security investigators. His habit of remaining late in his office in Leconfield House, in Curzon Street, often until about eight P.M., when nearly all other staff had left, suggested some activity that he wished to keep private. In this context, the clue of the locked drawer of the antique desk fits in. As director general, Hollis did not attend the weekly meetings when watchers were apportioned to the various operations, yet a record of them would be a prime requirement for Soviet intelligence officers operating in London. There was no doubt, from marks on the lock and other clues, that the drawer had been in regular use. Hollis's office had a connecting door with Mitchell's, where the desk was located. He may have had the only key to the desk and stayed late in his office on the evening when permission was sought to open it the following day. So he had been given ample warning to whip out the tape recorder if that is what the locked drawer had contained.

His habit of walking home after staying late at the office was also noted in his dossier. Though he had a chauffeured car at his disposal, he would regularly walk to his house in Campden Hill Square, across Hyde Park, a convenient rendezvous if, by that time, he was in contact with a controller, and also offering a variety of places for leaving information if personal contact was still barred.

Hollis's attempted destruction of the diaries of Guy Liddell, several volumes of which gave a full record of MI5 activities throughout the war, could have been in the Soviet interest. Even odder was his behavior concerning the records of the early interrogations of Anthony Blunt, which began some eighteen months before he retired. The tapes were transcribed and then summarized. While the summaries were retained for the record, Hollis ordered the destruction of all the tapes and transcripts.

The strange insistence of Hollis that he must fly to Washington alone to convey the news about the suspicion concerning Mitchell to Hoover and McCone also began to make sense. It could have been the panic reaction of a man anxious to demonstrate that he could hardly be a traitor if he was so keen to unmask another. By indicating the nature of his urgent mission to the British ambassador in Washington, Hollis might have expected that this would be relayed to the foreign secretary and one day might stand him in good stead if ever he fell under suspicion. Hollis's stubborn refusal to allow Mitchell to be interrogated and to limit the inquiry against him was also explicable. If Mitchell went into retirement under deep suspicion that could never be resolved, inquiry might be diverted from himself.

The whole episode was reminiscent of Philby's behavior when he feared that the suspicion against Maclean might also extend to himself. He deliberately reminded his superiors of the tip given by the Russian defector Krivitsky early in 1940 that a young man "who had been educated at Eton and Oxford" had been recruited "in the early Thirties" and was working in the British diplomatic service. (In his book *My Silent War* Philby gives the impression that he was pointing a finger at Maclean to make himself appear clean. He was certainly attempting to divert suspicion away from himself but was also trying to *protect* Maclean. Krivitsky could not have known that Maclean was in the Foreign Service, which he did not enter until 1938, a year after the Russian had defected. Further, Maclean had not been either to Eton or Oxford. Philby's purpose—presumably with the agreement of his Soviet controller—seems to have been to implicate other diplomats who had served in the British Embassy in Washington and direct M15 on to time-wasting trails.

Though the evidence against Hollis was all circumstantial, it was strong enough to induce one of the Fluency Committee, Arthur Martin, to see Sir Dick White and say, "I'm sure it's Roger!" Martin had been firm in his mind about Hollis for many months. During the inquiries into Mitchell, he had secured a long session with Hollis, who was unusually nervous. Martin felt sure that Hollis believed he was cornered and that the rush flight to Washington, which followed soon afterward, was a symptom of his fright, as was Hollis's gratuitous sacking of Martin from MI5.

White was understandably appalled by Martin's charge and in a recent letter to me has expressed his revulsion at the requirement to investigate the man he had recommended as his successor.

The CIA and the FBI were duly informed, and soon there were few doubts in the mind of the CIA officer most experienced in counterespionage, James Jesus Angleton. On both sides of the Atlantic, a thorough backtracking investigation into Sir Roger Hollis's past was begun. In Britian the codename for Hollis used throughout this supersensitive operation was Drat—a typical British understatement for a situation in which the boss-man of the nation's Security Service was suspected of being a Russian spy.

5
Chinese Days

Hollis was born in 1905, the son of a clergyman—as was Blunt. His father later was appointed Anglican bishop of Taunton, while one of his three brothers also became a bishop. Another brother, Christopher, a Catholic convert, became an MP and was an eminent writer and historian as well as a frequent contributor to humorous magazines like *Punch*. The third brother, Mark, was also in intelligence work, in military field security during the war, and later in Philby's section of the Secret Service, as I have described.

Roger, who was a sickly child and suffered from inferiority feelings with respect to his brothers, was educated at Clifton College in Bristol and then entered Worcester College, Oxford, in 1924. At Oxford, he joined a circle dominated by the writer and esthete, Harold Acton. His political activity seemed to be confined to membership of the New Reform Club, but he was on terms of close friendship with Claud Cockburn, a sufficiently dedicated Communist to become diplomatic and foreign correspondent for the *Daily Worker* before and throughout World War II.

Cockburn was suspected by MI5 because he published a newsletter containing such accurate intelligence that it looked as though he must have good Soviet sources. When Hollis eventually entered MI5, he never recorded that he had been close to Cockburn, as he should have done, and held Cockburn's file in his own safe for several years.

Hollis was also a close friend of the late Maurice Richardson, the journalist and writer who for a time joined the Communist party. Another left-wing influence at Oxford was the extraordinary Tom Driberg, whose espionage career will astonish even his friends when I disclose its details in subsequent chapters.

After only two years at Oxford, Hollis decided to quit and get a job because he felt he was unlikely to do well in the examinations. Originally, he and Maurice Richardson decided to leave together and go to Mexico, but Richardson backed down. Hollis therefore left on his own, determined for some unknown reason to go to China. His parents, angry at his premature departure from Oxford, refused to finance his journey, so he worked for a year in the Standard Bank in London to save enough to pay his passage to China. He seriously underestimated the costs, and by the time he reached Penang, in Malaya, he was down to £10. He succeeded in securing a job there with the British American Tobacco Company (BAT) and was eventually posted to Shanghai where, according to old colleagues who are still alive, he worked in the advertising department.

Hollis's arrival in China was an expression of the dogged determination that was to characterize him throughout his life. Even his friends agree that he was not particularly talented. The MI5 backtrack revealed that in Shanghai Hollis became friendly with Agnes Smedley, an American left-wing journalist prominent in the English-speaking community there. Miss Smedley, who was officially correspondent of the *Frankfurter Zeitung*, was then in her middle thirties, had spent some time in Moscow, and had entered China on a forged American passport. There is no doubt that she was a dedicated agent of the Comintern, promoting world revolution, and was deeply involved with several Soviet spy rings in Shanghai, which, at that time, was a major center of the Comintern conspiracy.

One of these rings was created and run by Richard Sorge, a German who was a professional spy for the Fourth Bureau of the Red Army, first in China and then, with spectacular success, in Japan. Sorge's assignment in Shanghai was to set up a spy ring for operations inside China, but he also managed to recruit two of the most important members of his Japanese group there. In his memoirs, written shortly before he was hanged in Tokyo, Sorge recorded how Smedley had helped him by introducing friends, whom he was able to recruit, and allowing him to use her house as a rendezvous. Hollis was in Shanghai when Communists were being butchered by Chiang Kai-shek's troops, and his resentment at this as a young man might have facilitated his recruitment in the Comintern, as it certainly did with others, because Soviet intelligence was making a major effort to exploit the circumstances.

Sorge is also believed to have recruited a young German Communist of Slav origin who arrived in Shanghai as the wife of an architect. This woman, who later received intelligence training in Moscow and became a most productive Soviet agent, winning two Orders of the Red Banner, was none other than Ursula Beurton, whose real name was Ruth Kuczynski. As I mentioned in the previous chapter, she was to become a Soviet espionage courier in Britain during World War II and moved to Oxford just as Hollis arrived there with his evacuated section of MI5.

Before going to China, Beurton and her German husband had worked for the Red Army in Poland. By 1940, he was imprisoned by the Chinese for espionage activities, and his wife, then well established in Switzerland, decided to divorce him. Her purpose in doing this was to secure British nationality before moving on to Britain. On securing a divorce, she immediately married a British member of her Swiss spy ring and thereby secured the passport that enabled her to enter Britain, which she did with little delay, traveling via neutral Lisbon.

Richard Sorge left Shanghai for Moscow in 1932 before proceeding to Tokyo. It is not known whether Hollis met him, but he may well have done so because the European community in Shanghai was small and close socially. Miss Smedley herself was an active recruiter of Soviet intelligence agents for the Red Army. It is known that the spy "Elli," who may have been Hollis, worked first for Soviet Military Intelligence (GRU), probably before being taken over by the KGB, which usually acquires control of the most important spies.

According to the CIA investigations into Hollis's background, there was also a "particularly brutal" Soviet recruiter active in Shanghai at the time, and Hollis knew him. The "brutality" referred to the ruthlessness with which the Russian used bribery, women, and blackmail to secure agents. Hollis was certainly susceptible to sexual indulgence and developed a notable reputation as a ladies' man and a retailer of risqué stories. (It is almost certainly coincidental, however, that in the MI5 booklet *Their Trade is Treachery*, prepared while Hollis was director general, one of the Six Easy Lessons on How to Become a Spy is "Develop a few vices, especially abroad, so that with luck you can be compromised and blackmailed."

The investigators found that Hollis had been very hard up in China, where he also eventually worked in Peking, Hangkow, and Dairen. The recruitment of a young employee of a tobacco company would seem to make little sense, but as the history of the Ring of Five so clearly demonstrates, Soviet intelligence believes in backing long shots whom it can control and then push into positions of trust.

After about nine years' service in China, Hollis contracted tuberculosis and was sent by BAT to Switzerland for treatment. On the way, he traveled over the Trans-Siberian railway from Vladivostock and spent a little time in Russia. This could just conceivably account for a statement by Gouzenko, the GRU defector, that there was "something Russian in 'Elli's' background," though a relationship with the White Russian communities in the Chinese cities where Hollis worked would be a more credible allusion.

It could be coincidence that Hollis and Beurton were in Shanghai and Oxford at the same time: or they might both have been recruited in China and brought together in Oxford in the Soviet interest.

It is perhaps an even stranger coincidence that Hollis and Beurton should also have been contemporaries in Switzerland, while Hollis was there for treatment. Beurton lived in the Montreux area, but I have been unable to discover where Hollis was located. If Beurton recruited Hollis to the Soviet cause, it could have been accomplished in Switzerland, though the Fluency Committee regarded China as more likely.

The Swiss treatment was successful, but BAT regarded Hollis's health as too delicate for further employment, and he left the company. Though surprisingly athletic, he was to retain the look of someone who had been tuberculous and became progressively so round-shouldered that he looked almost hunched.

At the beginning of 1936 Hollis was basically a broken man. He had no degree, his health was suspect, and his experience in China was not likely to be helpful in securing a post in England. The only work he could find was as a clerk typist. Nevertheless, he was still able to afford to play a lot of golf, at which he was a devastatingly consistent performer, with a single-figure handicap, having secured a half blue at Oxford. He was also a good tennis player.

Through his tennis connections, Hollis met an army major and told him that he was keen to get a job in MI5. This in itself was odd because he had no special qualifications for the work. But when Soviet intelligence secures a promising recruit, he or she is urged to get a job in MI5, the Secret Service, Government Communication Headquarters (the radio-interception organization), the *Times*, the BBC, the Foreign Office, or the Home Office—in that order of preference. On the major's recommendation, Hollis was interviewed by an MI5 board, which rejected him but suggested that, with his foreign experience, he should try the Secret Service.

6
Entry with Intent?

When Hollis duly made his application, the Secret Service carried out its own inquiries and turned him down, ostensibly on the grounds that his health was not reliable enough for service abroad. Because of this, there must have been a Secret Service file on Hollis, but this was destroyed at some later stage. It may be that a known major spy, so far completely concealed from the public, but whom I shall identify later, was employed on "weeding" files for the Secret Service—removing documents no longer considered of use—and thus destroyed the record on Hollis.

In spite of these rebuffs, which would have deterred most normal candidates, Hollis persisted in his efforts to join MI5, and eventually, at a tennis party where he may have contrived an entry, he met Jane Sissmore, a woman officer of MI5. This woman, later called Jane Archer, was highly regarded in MI5, especially as an interrogator. On her say-so, therefore, Hollis was taken on the MI5 strength in 1936 with the understanding that he would work as her assistant.

There is no suggestion that Miss Sissmore took Hollis into MI5 for any other reason than that she believed he would be useful there when, with war in the offing, the organization needed to expand. His meeting with her may have been coincidental, or he may have been directed toward her by someone who knew her position, for in those days MI5 officers kept the nature of their employment secret. The director general at the time of Hollis's recruitment was the legendary Maj. Gen. Sir Vernon Kell, who had held command, with unchallenged integrity, from the inception of MI5 in 1909. Presumably, he approved of the recruitment, but at that time there was no positive vetting of candidates with a search into background and connections. The fact that Hollis's father was a bishop would be, in all probability, sufficient evidence of his loyalty.

Having engineered his entry into MI5, Hollis was to remain there for twenty-nine years without a break, almost always at headquarters and without experience as a field agent, though paying many liaison visits abroad. Eventually, more through time serving than outstanding aptitude, he occupied the post of deputy director general for three years and then, for nine years, the top position itself.

As assistant to Jane Sissmore, he was involved with those departments of MI5 responsible for overseeing Soviet and Communist operations in the United Kingdom and colonies. This meant that he had daily access to all known information about the activities of Russian espionage, subversion, and sabotage agents. He also knew of the MI5 efforts to penetrate the British Communist party and to monitor the activities of British Communists who might be assisting Soviet bloc agents.

The backtrack into the MI5 penetration produced one important item that might have implicated Hollis. For five years, in the late 1930s, British intelligence had been successfully decoding the Russian radio traffic to its Comintern agents in Europe. MI5 had access to the results, which were most useful, but suddenly the radio traffic ceased, the last message being an announcement that other means would have to be used for communication. This disappointing event occurred around 1938, after Hollis had arrived in MI5, but before Blunt joined.

Late in 1940, Hollis experienced one of several strokes of good fortune that were to speed his promotion. Jane Sissmore had a major quarrel with her superiors in which she insulted the deputy director general, Brigadier Harker and, at her own request, was transferred to the Secret Service. Hollis automatically succeeded her, and then became acting head of Section F. He and his department were soon moved as an evacuation measure to Blenheim Palace at Woodstock, the home of the Duke of Marlborough.

Hollis married in 1937, but, according to close friends, he chose the wrong wife, as they were temperamentally incompatible. He is remembered by a wartime woman colleague as being "very good-looking, in spite of his round shoulders,

dark, and of medium height." Others who worked with him
say that he was secretively quiet but dry and witty in
conversation, with an inexhaustible fund of smutty stories.
He was known as a good briefer, concise and clear with his
instructions. When he attended meetings of the Joint Intelligence Committee, he usually said very little unless questioned.
"He never believed in stirring things up: controversy was not
for him," George Young, a former deputy director of the
Secret Service, recalls.

He did, however, occasionally raise eyebrows in areas
outside MI5 concerning his judgment about the dangers of
communism. Col. Noel Wild, who had been in charge of
deception techniques at SHAEF during the war and was later
involved in cover plans in the Defence Ministry, told me of
an incident that had worried him. When he and Hollis had
been discussing a possible operation against extreme left-
wing trade union leaders, Hollis had predicted, "There will
never be a threat from communism to this country."

According to Sir Dick White, who eventually wrote Hollis's
obituary notice in the *Times*, "the hotter the climate of
national security the cooler he became." That, no doubt, was
an excellent temperament for a director general of MI5,
beset, as Hollis was, with an unprecedented succession of
security disasters. But, as Philby and Blunt showed, it was
also an essential attribute for a spy, invidious though the
comparison may sound.

Hollis was still in charge of Section F in 1944 when Philby
became his opposite number in the Secret Service, as I have
described. It is certain that Philby was then an active spy for
Russia, even, according to himself, an officer of the KGB. He
was under continuous KGB control and took no decisions on
any important issue without first consulting his Soviet superiors, using the excuse that he needed time for thought in
order to effect the necessary meetings. If Hollis was then a
penetration agent operating on a similar scale, as those who
investigated him believe, he and Philby formed a most
dangerous axis.

When Clement Attlee appointed Sir Percy Sillitoe, the
former chief constable, director general of MI5 in May 1946,
the prime task allotted to him was the investigation and
elimination of Communist subversion. He instructed Hollis
to brief him in writing, but all that Hollis did was to hand

him a description of the state of the Communist party, which
he had already compiled. Sillitoe's biographer, A. W. Cockerill,
records that Sir Percy was deeply disappointed because Hollis
provided little evidence of Communist subversion. Yet, by
1950, Attlee and his cabinet were convinced from their own
resources, that British Communists were behind a series of
crippling strikes and acts of subversion.

Sir Percy Sillitoe's son, Tony, has told me how the Secret
Service career officers reacted to the appointment of a policeman to direct them with a campaign of noncooperation
and personal hostility, which was not unconnected with the
fact that most of the senior promotions had been set back
several years:

> The campaign was led by Hollis, whom my father de-
> spised and distrusted. When my father called for files
> relevant to the defection of Burgess and Maclean in
> 1951, before flying to Washington to see Edgar Hoover,
> Hollis failed to produce them saying they had "gone
> missing" or were "unavailable." There was something
> about "dear Roger," as my father called him, that dis-
> turbed his policeman's instincts.

In 1947 Alexander Foote, a Briton who had been a key
member of the astonishingly successful Soviet espionage operation in Switzerland called the Lucy Ring, offered his
services to the West and was heavily interrogated by MI5.
Among many things he revealed were details of the espionage
activities of Ursula Beurton. He told them how Beurton, then
known to him only as "Sonya," had been detailed to train him
in operating "music boxes," as the KGB called radio transmitters. She had tried to convince Foote that she wanted to
leave Switzerland because she was so "shattered" by Stalin's
nonaggression pact with Hitler, but her previously total dedi-
cation to the Communist cause suggested a different reason
for the determination of this "demurely dressed woman with
black hair, good figure and even better legs" to reach Britain.

Hollis, still the key figure in Soviet counterespionage,
could not ignore Foote's information had he wanted to and
was obliged to take some action against Ursula, who was
living near Chipping Norton with her English husband, Len
Brewer, a Soviet agent also known as Leon Beurton. What

happened suggests that the approach to this woman spy was criminally soft. She was told that MI5 knew that she had been a Soviet agent in her early days but was convinced that she had been totally disillusioned by the unprovoked Soviet attack on Finland in November 1939—a year before she had arrived in England. This made no sense in view of her known participation in the Lucy Ring in 1940.

Naturally, she agreed with what the MI5 interviewers had been instructed to tell her, assured them that she had never spied in Britain but refused to cooperate any further. If MI5 had made routine inquiries in the area of George Street in the Summertown district of Oxford where she had lived, they could have found evidence that she regularly used a radio transmitter during the war, putting up an aerial from a neighbor's chimney for the purpose. They might also have learned of her regular visits to the Banbury area, where she had taken over the atomic secrets supplied by Klaus Fuchs, and of contacts with other agents living in the Oxford area, as Hollis had been during the time that she was active. The MI5 men made no effort to see her again and had little chance to do so, for Ursula and her husband moved to East Germany, where she still lives, aged seventy-four at the time of writing.

The team that eventually was to investigate Hollis discovered not only that Ursula Beurton had been a long-term professionally trained spy but that it was her brother Jurgen, another German taking refuge in Britain, who had first been approached by Fuchs when the atom scientist decided to betray secret information. Furthermore, her father, Professor Rene Kuczynski, an economist teaching in Oxford, also supplied secret political information that he secured from conversations with Sir Stafford Cripps, then a member of the War Cabinet.

Whatever the purposes of the MI5 visit to Ursula, the only one it served was to warn her that she was under suspicion and should get herself behind the Iron Curtain. The implications of her presence in Oxford, as regards Hollis, were not appreciated fully until 1967.

When the Attlee government decided to "purge" known Communists out of sensitive areas of the civil service in 1948 because they could be potential spies, Hollis was in charge of the drive. A few high-level Communists were removed from secret work, and the Communist party made maximum propaganda use of them. But several, who should have been detected in the more stringent screening measures supposed to have been introduced, remained in their trusted positions. A few, who had been transferred to nonsecret work, even managed to filter back during the expansion consequent to the rearmament program of the 1950s.

Sir Percy Sillitoe, who had become head of MI5 in 1946, was determined to apply the Communist purge to his own organization but met with considerable internal resistance and scant help from Hollis.

One Communist of historic significance, who was taken into top secret work during the period when Hollis was responsible for overseeing Communist activities in Britain, was Dr. Klaus Fuchs. His Communist past was known soon after he arrived as a German refugee in 1933, but MI5, which investigated him six times between 1941 and 1948, raised only vague objections, even after his name was seen on a captured copy of the Gestapo wanted list. An MI5 analysis in 1946 suggested that Fuchs might be a Soviet agent, but the report from Hollis's section rated the risk as slight, and he was cleared for work at the new Harwell atomic station.

Fuchs was not exposed as the result of any inquiries by MI5 but by a fluke, of which American cypher experts made brilliant use. Normally, the KGB used the safe one-time pad system for transmitting secret messages in code. In that system, the person sending the message and the one receiving it both have a small, identical pad composed of pages each covered with lines of letters chosen at random. The encoder uses the letters from one page to encipher a message, and the decoder, knowing which page was used, can decipher it. Since each page is different, the code is virtually unbreakable provided that any page is used only once. During the war, however, a Russian cypher section, possibly having run short of one-time pads, or through error, used some pages twice. In a superb and arduous operation code named "Bride" (later "Vanosa"), led by an American cryptanalyst, Meredith Gardner, many of the wartime Russian messages, including much information about Soviet espionage activities by more than two thousand agents, were deciphered. Among those decoded in 1949 were messages indicating that Fuchs had been a long-term Soviet spy.

The intercepts first indicated that there had been a major

leakage of nuclear bomb secrets from the Los Alamos laboratories involving a scientist there. A later deciphered message revealed that the scientist, whose code name was used in the traffic, had a sister studying at an American university. This made Fuchs the prime suspect.

That kind of evidence is not admissible in a British court, and, in any case, it could not have been used because at that time the American and British security authorities were most anxious to avoid giving any indication that they had broken the Russian codes, "Operation Bride" being under the highest security classification. So, though MI5 was convinced of Fuchs's guilt, the only way he could be prosecuted was by inducing him to confess.

In that operation, MI5 recorded a major success, partly through the skill and patience of the interrogator, Jim Skardon, but partly for another reason, not before disclosed. After Fuchs had repeatedly declined to confess anything, MI5 was about to abandon the task when a woman, who had listened in to Fuchs's replies to Skardon's questions and transcribed them, said that she felt "in her bones" that Fuchs was lying on four specific points and not very convincingly. She urged Skardon to try again and concentrate more forcefully on them. He did so, and Fuchs broke down. So, though Jim Skardon deserves all the credit he has been given, his success owed much to a woman's intuition.

As FBI records show, the KGB knew that Fuchs was in grave danger because one of the few people fully informed about "Operation Bride" and its findings was Philby, the Secret Service liaison man with the FBI and the CIA in Washington, whose duty it was to pass the information on to London. Indeed, one of his main functions was to assist in the interpretation of the results of "Bride." No attempt, however, was made to warn Fuchs or to retrieve him by an organized defection.

By that time, Fuchs had ceased to spy for Russia, so the KGB could "burn" him without much sacrifice, especially as his conviction would be guaranteed to do devastating damage to Anglo-American interchange of atomic secrets. However, the main reason for the KGB's failure to warn Fuchs was probably to preserve Philby's position, which was of such value to them. The defection of Fuchs would inevitably lead to a major inquiry into the source of the leak that he was under suspicion, and Philby, who was then above suspicion, might himself be endangered. The Russians knew, moreover, that if Fuchs held out and managed to avoid confessing, there was no way that he could be prosecuted.

The KGB also deliberately provides an agency that it has penetrated with an occasional success in the hope of averting suspicion against itself. In the Fuchs case, the success would appear to accrue to MI5, where there was a high-level KGB agent in need of protection, but it would also keep the spotlight off Philby in the sister service. All intelligence agencies play this game on occasion, but while MI5 regarded it rather as deliberately losing a piece in checkers, the KGB played chess—with checkmate the objective.

After Fuchs had been convicted and sentenced to fourteen years' imprisonment, he was interrogated in jail by both MI5 and the FBI. Aware that his controller, Ursula Beurton, whose name he knew, was safely in East Germany, he identified her from photographs and gave information against her. It was made to appear that other spies, who were eventually arrested, had been identified by Fuchs. Harry Gold, his courier when he was at the Los Alamos bomb laboratory in New Mexico, was picked out by him but only after being shown a film, when he recognized his walk. An American soldier called David Greenglass and the spies Julius and Ethel Rosenberg also appeared to have been tracked down by such clever detective work. But the truth is that all had been named repeatedly in the KGB coded traffic, and the secret of its decipherment had to be covered. Had the FBI been able to reveal the extent of this evidence, there would have been less opposition to the execution of the Rosenbergs. The FBI records show that Philby and his Soviet controllers must also have known about the intention to arrest the Rosenbergs, but again elected to avoid warning them.

"Operation Bride" also provided irrefutable evidence of the existence of a spy network in Australia based on the Soviet embassy in Canberra and involving civil servants and Communist union leaders. MI5 was greatly perturbed because of the decision to build rocket and atom-bomb test ranges in the Australian desert. The Americans told the British that the Australians were to be given no secret information until they set up effective security arrangements.

Sir Percy Sillitoe went out in 1948 to see the Australian

prime minister, Ben Chifley, and was soon followed by his chief security adviser in the shape of Roger Hollis. After talks with Hollis, Chifley agreed to a proposal by a senior Australian civil servant that a special surveillance and screening operation should be carried out on a big Russian delegation that was due to visit Australia. The operation, which involved scores of watchers and other people, produced no evidence whatever, and it was assumed that there had been a leak to the Russians.

A further public disaster in the atomic field, resulting in damaging publicity for MI5, occurred in October 1950 when another nuclear physicist from the Harwell atomic research station, Dr. Bruno Pontecorvo, a Jewish refugee from Mussolini, suddenly fled to Moscow with his wife and family. It quickly became known that Pontecorvo and his wife had long been dedicated Communists and that, while the former had been screened several times—most rigorously after the unmasking of Fuchs—the security authorities had never detected them.

Furthermore, inquiries revealed what seemed to be a dreadful misunderstanding between the Canadian security authorities and MI5. The Canadians believed that Pontecorvo had been cleared by MI5 before he reached Canada as a member of the British team in 1943, but MI5 claimed that he was never in Britain before he joined the Canadian project because, previously, he had been living as a refugee in the United States.

Pontecorvo had retained his house in the United States while he was away working in Canada, and the FBI, being suspicious of him, searched it. They found documentary evidence that both he and his wife were Communists and intensely anti-American and sent a warning report to the British embassy. The British liaison man in Washington at the time was Philby, so, once again, luck came to the rescue of those dedicated to the Soviet service. Philby sat on the report, which was found years later in the embassy records. Had it been forwarded to London, as the FBI expected, it is likely that Pontecorvo would have been refused permission to work at Harwell when he came to Britain after the war. Instead, a Canadian security clearance, which had never taken place, was accepted by MI5.

Pontecorvo, who was granted British citizenship in 1948 on the basis that he had lived five years in Canada, defected to

Russia with his family in October 1950. It is now certain that the journey and its concealment were organized by the KGB, which had induced Pontecorvo to leave Britain on short notice. His expertise was needed in connection with the crash development of the Soviet H-bomb. He was one of the few scientists in the world with knowledge of the type of nuclear reactor required to make the essential component of the H-bomb called lithium deuteride.

It is not known if Pontecorvo went out of ideological loyalty, the offer of more exciting conditions of work, or was blackmailed. Whatever his motive when he defected, the MI5 department of which Hollis was in charge appeared to have been taken by surprise.

When Cabinet and departmental papers relating to 1940 were released to the Public Record Office on January 1, 1981, under the thirty-year rule, those concerning Fuchs and Pontecorvo were withheld for a further twenty years, until 2001. I have been assured that there is nothing in those papers of genuine security value, in the sense that they would be of any assistance to a foreign power. It would seem, therefore, that the only purpose in extending their suppression is political. The papers might show that the Attlee administration had been warned by MI5, if belatedly, that Fuchs was a slight security risk and elected to take no action because he had learned so many American nuclear secrets while working in the United States that his services were essential. Until 1948, the Labour government's decision to make and to stockpile atomic bombs was an official secret. The arrest and trial of Fuchs would inevitably have revealed it—with loud outcries from the Labour left. Furthermore, it would have nullified the strenuous efforts then being made by the government to regain access to American atomic secrets denied under U.S. legislation.

7
Diplomatic Nonincidents

Another security disaster involving MI5 and Canada occurred in 1954 following the destruction, by fire, of the Russian embassy in Ottawa. During the fire, the Royal Canadian Mounted Police had been able to get someone inside the buildings and checked that the KGB setup had been exactly as described by the defector, Igor Gouzenko, nine years previously. When the Russians decided to rebuild it on a larger scale, they had to submit the plans to the Canadian planning authority. The Canadian intelligence chiefs thus realized they had a once-and-for-all opportunity to introduce eavesdropping devices into the sensitive areas of the new embassy. In this project, called Operation Dew-worm, they asked for and received assistance from MI5.

Gouzenko was consulted and helped with the decision as to where microphones should be placed. By working at night in the depth of the Canadian winter and using various subterfuges, the intelligence men were able to install the listening devices where, it was believed, they would remain undetected. (When the installation was almost complete and the wires all set deep in concrete, a worker inadvertently went through the main cable with a drill. It seemed certain that Dew-worm was ruined, but by ingenious improvisation six of the eight microphones were made to work.)

When the Russians moved in, it was clear that the intelligence men had chosen the right locations for the microphones. But the Russian ambassador was suddenly recalled to Moscow, and during the three months that he was away, a team of electronic "sweepers" from Moscow moved in, searched the area, and the KGB setup was moved to a different part of the building. The sweepers had failed to find the microphones, which continued to transmit useless information for eight years, when they were eventually discovered.

MI5 was in no doubt that the Center in Moscow had been told that the building had been "bugged." The leak could have emanated from Canada or from Britain.

Soon after the Canadian debacle, MI5 took part in a futile attempt to bug another Russian embassy, this time in Canberra. In 1954, the KGB chief in that embassy, Vladimir Petrov, defected to the Australian security authorities, taking with him evidence that the Kremlin was attempting to undermine the Australian government and people with a locally recruited network of spies and saboteurs, as it had done in Canada.

Reacting in its usual arrogant way when its activities are exposed, the Soviet government broke off diplomatic relations, evacuated the embassy, and left it in the care of the Swiss government. The KGB activities were no surprise to MI5 because the deciphered KGB radio traffic had shown that there were three locally recruited Russian agents in the office of Dr. Evatt, leader of the Labour opposition in Australia. The Australian security authorities, as well as the people, were shocked however by the findings of the Royal Commission inquiry into the affair and decided that they should take some precautionary measures against the day when the Russians might decide to return, probably before the Olympic Games were due to be held in Melbourne in 1960.

MI5 was called in and recommended the fitting of a device called a cavity microphone, which had been invented by the Russians and improved in Britain. This device, which had been intruded by the Russians into both the British and American embassies in Moscow, needed no battery because it was activated by a microwave beam generated outside the building. It could also be fitted quickly, which was an essential requirement because the Australian and British security men could only gain access to the embassy for two hours, when they could be sure that the caretaker would be missing.

Consultations with Petrov showed that the best place to install the device was in the room where the KGB chief spent most of his time. This was brilliantly accomplished by the Australians, led by Sir Charles Spry, after the instrument had been built, tested, and flown out by MI5. To lull the Russians, it was decided that it would not be activated for a whole year after their return. Meanwhile, the Australian security men secured a convenient building overlooking the embassy, from which the microwaves could be beamed.

When the device was eventually activated, it worked perfectly. They could hear a man entering the room, pulling up his chair, and rustling papers. They could even hear children playing in the embassy garden. But they never heard a single word of conversation. Whenever the occupant of the room wished to speak, he went outside and slammed the door. The operation was continued for a year until it had become clear that the Russians had known about it from the beginning and had refrained from removing the "bug" so that the Australians would go on wasting their time, manpower, and money. The leakage could have occurred in Australia, but it was considered more likely that it had originated in London.

Hollis became deputy director general when his colleague Dick (not short for Richard) White became the top man at the early age of forty-five on the retirement of Sir Percy Sillitoe, who had not pleased Churchill. Though Sillitoe tried hard, intelligence work depends on taking calculated risks in the hope of producing a dividend. If a project fails, the chief must accept the consequences, having agreed to it. Sillitoe tried to apply the police principle that any failure should result in censure or disciplinary action, so that officers became unwilling to take the necessary risks. However, as White's own brief reign in MI5 was to show, success was difficult to come by in an agency heavily penetrated by the opposition.

It is thought that Hollis may have given crucial assistance to ensure the success of the defection of Maclean and Burgess, as I have indicated. It is certain that he did everything he could to ensure that neither of them would ever return to Britain to undergo interrogations in which they might reveal information damaging to the KGB and dangerous to those who had assisted it. His strange behavior in this regard centered on a book about Burgess written by Tom Driberg. I shall reserve my account of this for chapter 21, which deals with the activities of politicians.

As Hollis and White, his MI5 chief until 1956, were of similar age and would be due for retirement at about the same time, Hollis seemed to have little hope of ever becoming director general, but like the members of the infamous Ring of Five, he had a charmed career. At no time was this better illustrated than by the tragic affair of Commander Crabb, the frogman who lost his life while carrying out a forbidden survey of the hull of a Soviet cruiser tied up in the dock at Portsmouth.

In April 1956, the joint Russian leaders Bulganin and Khrushchev were due to arrive in Portsmouth aboard the powerful cruiser *Ordzonikidze* for a good-will visit to Britain. Sir Anthony Eden, then prime minister, who had high hopes of establishing better relations and moderating the Cold War, issued a precise directive to all services banning any intelligence operations of any kind against the ship.

This directive was widely disobeyed. The navy asked the military intelligence authorities to secure a radar image of the cruiser as it sailed through the Channel. This was accomplished by a radar set installed in a cave in the cliffs near Dover so that it could not be seen by the Russians or by anybody likely to report its presence to the prime minister. A submarine was dispatched to lie on the sea bed in the cruiser's path to obtain records of the vibrations of the screws.

To Crabb, and to certain elements in the Admiralty and in the Secret Service, the directive was a challenge from a "wet" prime minister. Commander Crabb, a freelance frogman of great daring and experience, put up a proposition to a certain branch of the Secret Service, which was separate from headquarters. He gave an assurance that he could measure the pitch of the cruiser's screws, which was the main Admiralty requirement. The offer was accepted. A letter, of which a copy still exists, was sent to the Admiralty, which wanted no official knowledge of the operation but said that it would be grateful for any results.

Security for the Soviet visit was known to be extremely tight. The KGB chief, Ivan Serov, visited London in March with a team of electronic "sweepers" to check the security arrangements at Claridge's Hotel where, it was expected, MI5 would have installed hidden microphones. Because of his blood-stained record, Serov received a rough public reception, and it was made clear to him that he would not be welcome if he returned with the leaders in April. In spite of this, before leaving London, he had the brass nerve to ask the Foreign Office for facilities for a KGB "listening post" in Hong Kong to oversee China, which were refused. Furthermore, he did return with the Soviet leaders, remaining aboard the cruiser throughout the visit.

Crabb knew, as did the navy, that the *Ordzonikidze* had a "wet compartment"—a chamber below the water line from which frogmen could operate unseen. I have been told that Crabb had previously attempted to survey the ship while it was in dock in Leningrad, having been taken there by submarine, but had been chased off by defending frogmen. Nevertheless, Crabb booked into a small hotel in Portsmouth with a Secret Service officer, who signed the register "Bernard Smith" and gave his address as "Attached Foreign Office," the standard cover for Secret Service operatives.

It has been suggested that "Smith" was an American CIA agent who was actually a Russian spy. The truth is that "Smith," whose real name was almost as common, was a full-time British Secret Service officer sent down from the relevant branch in London. The next day, he suffered a slight heart attack but insisted on carrying on. On the morning of April 19, the two went, apparently unobserved, to the point of entry not more than three hundred yards from the cruiser. Crabb returned after a few minutes for an extra pound of ballast weight. Later, he took off and was never again seen alive by his colleague. He was forty-six and not really fit enough for the task.

That same evening, James Thomas, then first lord of the Admiralty, was dining with some of the Soviet visitors, one of whom asked, "What was that frogman doing off our bows this morning?" According to the Russian, Crabb had been seen swimming at the surface at 7:30 A.M. by a Soviet sailor. As he had been forced to return for more ballast, it is possible that he had surfaced, but in 1963 another possible explanation was given to MI5, which had known about the Crabb project and given minor backup support.

The KGB defector, Anatoli Golitsin, volunteered information to the effect that Soviet Naval Intelligence had known in advance of Crabb's intentions. As a result, frogmen may have been waiting for him in the cruiser's wet compartment, particularly as the ruthlessly efficient Serov was in active command of the security of the vessel. It is possible that Crabb was killed, though the evidence suggests that he died of drowning, perhaps during a struggle. The headless body washed up the following year was almost certainly his.

The Russians made the issue public and the Labour opposition forced a debate, which greatly embarrassed Eden. Understandably, he was furious with the Secret Service, and shortly afterward, its director general, Sir John Sinclair, who was near retirement anyway, was removed. The man chosen to succeed him was Sir Dick White, the director general of MI5.

The choice of Sir Dick, a career MI5 man, to head the rival organization, which considered itself more senior, was interpreted as an additional reprimand by Eden. As a side-effect, it meant that the top MI5 post fell vacant. White recommended that his deputy, Hollis, should fill it, and Eden agreed.

So, to use an official definition of MI5's task, Hollis took over responsibility for "the defence of the realm as a whole from external and internal dangers arising from attempts at espionage and sabotage, or from action of persons and organizations, whether directed from within or without the country, which may be judged to be subversive to the security of the State."

There was no way that the KGB could have foreseen the promotional consequences of the sad affair, but if the leak about Crabb to the Russians, alleged by Golitsin, had come from a high-level penetration source inside MI5, the resulting situation was piquant, to say the least.

8
Decade of Defeats

In 1960, Hollis received the knighthood, which is routine for the director general of MI5. It marked the start of an extremely harassing decade for his organization because of the exposure of a spate of spies.

The year 1961 opened with the arrest of the "Navy Spy Ring," headed by a KGB officer calling himself Gordon Lonsdale. In September of the following year, an Admiralty clerk, William Vassall, was arrested and later convicted for imparting an enormous amount of secret defense material to the KGB. In 1963 came the Philby defection, to be followed a year later by the revelation that Blunt had been a most damaging spy during his five years inside MI5. In 1965, an aviation ministry official, Frank Bossard, received twenty-one years for selling aviation secrets to Russia.

As Sir Martin Furnival Jones, Hollis's successor, admitted to the Franks Committee on Official Secrecy, the discovery of any long-term spy marks a defeat for MI5 because he should have been detected before he did so much damage. Nevertheless, the undercover detective work behind the cases I have mentioned was projected in Parliament and elsewhere as a triumph for MI5, as it was again by Mrs. Thatcher following her parliamentary statement about this book. The truth about all these cases, which to a large measure has been suppressed, reveals that MI5 had very little to crow about.

In the first place, *all* the spies concerned were detected only because of leads handed to MI5 by the Americans who had procured them from Soviet bloc intelligence defectors or other chance informers. Secondly, there are hitherto unknown aspects of the cases suggesting that the MI5 investigations that followed the tips were penetrated and, to some extent, even controlled by the KGB. In that context, I shall deal briefly with them here, introducing new material that has come to light during my inquiries. In 1958, a high-ranking Polish intelligence officer with strong liaison links with the KGB began to write letters to the CIA signed with a word that translated as "Sniper" and giving the names of many Polish agents operating against the West. For the best part of two years, until he eventually defected, "Sniper," whose name was Michal Goleniewski, supplied a mass of information including a statement that the Russians had a productive spy in Britain with a name like Huton. This spy was connected with the navy and had been recruited by Polish intelligence while serving in the naval attaché's office in the British embassy in Warsaw and had then been grabbed by the KGB.

MI5 had little difficulty in identifying the spy as Harry Houghton, a clerk in the Underwater Weapons Establishment at Portland, Dorset. The naval attaché in Warsaw had submitted an adverse report about Houghton's reliability, but he had, nevertheless, been posted to one of the most secret of all defense establishments. Houghton was placed under close surveillance, especially when he visited London on the first Saturday of every month, usually going by train to Waterloo. There he was seen to hand over a package to a man identified, from the number of his car, as Gordon Lonsdale, a Canadian running a business lease-lending juke boxes to cafés and pubs. Houghton's main source of secret documents was Ethel Gee, a filing clerk in the Portland drawing office, who was also his mistress.

Houghton's treachery was far more damaging than was publicly revealed at his trial. In addition to extremely secret details of antisubmarine warfare, he sold to the Russians sensitive facts about the performance of *Dreadnought* and other nuclear submarines.

Jim Skardon, who had been promoted from interrogation to being the officer in charge of the "watchers," mounted a massive surveillance operation involving scores of men and women, many cars, and, on occasion, helicopters. Lonsdale was followed to his bank in Marylebone, where he deposited a briefcase and an attaché case. The prime minister, Harold Macmillan, spoke to the chairman of the bank to secure permission for MI5 to examine the bags. The attaché case was found to contain a cigarette lighter mounted in a six-inch-diameter wooden block. When x-rayed, the block was seen to be hollow and contained one-time pads of the type used by the KGB spies. All the pages of Lonsdale's one-time pads were photographed, and the cases were returned to the bank.

Lonsdale had rented a flat in the White House in Regent's Park, and a search there revealed nothing except a radio capable of receiving morse from Moscow and a set of headphones for listening to it. His transmitter had to be located elsewhere. By clever surveillance, Lonsdale was followed to a house in Ruislip, the home of Peter and Helen Kroger, who were posing as booksellers. There, after a difficult search, the security men found the transmitter.

The MI5 men had rented the flat next to Lonsdale's in the White House, and by means of probe microphones they knew the times when Lonsdale was listening in to messages from Moscow. By entering his flat when he was out, they found that he had used some pages from his one-time pads, and from their photographs they were able to decipher the Moscow instructions, which confirmed that he was a spy.

For reasons too technical—and, I am told, still too secret—to be dealt with here, MI5 officers on the case concluded that the KGB had been alerted to the photographing of Lonsdale's one-time pads, a leak that could only have come from a source inside MI5. The radio traffic from Moscow to Lonsdale suddenly diminished, and the only messages sent to him concerned Houghton, whose code name was "Shah." Yet because of the complexity of the Lonsdale-Kroger setup, the investigators were sure that there must be other members of the spy ring apart from Houghton and Gee.

If the KGB had been alerted about the impending arrest of the known members of the spy ring, why were they not warned? Any warning to Houghton and Gee could have been very dangerous to the KGB's source, as a complete cessation of messages to Lonsdale would also have been. The KGB would know that there was already enough evidence against Houghton and Gee for them to be prosecuted, and they were relatively small fry who could be "burned," especially as they were not Communists and were spying purely for money.

So far as Lonsdale was concerned, it appeared that the KGB intended to withdraw him, along with the Krogers, in good time. As Hollis and a few others at the top knew, MI5 intended to run the case for a further three months in the hope of picking up more of the British agents whom Lonsdale was believed to be controlling. Instead, the case officers were driven to bring it to a close because, unexpectedly, Goleniewski had physically defected to the United States and it was argued that the KGB would assume that he would blow Houghton, and that the rest of the ring would be at risk and would be rapidly withdrawn to safety. In addition, they had become convinced that any other agents had been successfully switched to another, unknown Soviet controller. There was a last-minute move, the details of which are still secret, to catch some of these agents. It involved a forty-eight-hour suppression of the news that Lonsdale and the rest had been arrested. Regrettably, the police announced the arrests prematurely for MI5's purpose. Lord Wigg, who later had access to the facts, refers to this event in a couple of throwaway lines in his autobiography *George Wigg*, "Information about Lonsdale's arrest was leaked and heaven knows how many members of the Soviet spy gang took the tip and got out of England."

The case officers' decision to end the operation was taken only two days before they pounced. Fearing that Lonsdale and the Krogers had been warned of their danger, they were determined to give them no chance to flee the country.

There is intriguing evidence that the KGB chiefs in London were in no way surprised when first news of the arrest of Lonsdale and company was flashed on the TV screens, which they were watching at six P.M. on a Sunday. They made no attempt to get in touch with the embassy or with anybody else.

After Lonsdale was found to be really Konon Molody, a professional KGB officer (the dead male, Lonsdale, whose identity Molody had assumed, was known to have been circumcised, while Molody was not), he was interrogated in prison. He revealed little but when asked, "Were you taken by surprise when we arrested you?" he replied, "We did not think you would do it so quickly." The belief that there were other Britons in the Navy Spy Ring was later supported by defector evidence that Lonsdale had been replaced by another "illegal" controller who had never been detected. When the investigating team reported their suspicions that their operation had been "blown" soon after it had begun, Hollis ridiculed the idea, saying that he was not prepared to consider the absurd possibility that there was a spy at any level in his organization.

The arrest of William Vassall, the British traitor in the Admiralty later sentenced to eighteen years' imprisonment in 1962, was presented as something of a triumph for MI5 even though it demonstrated that a homosexual, quickly recognized as such by the Russians, had been able to pass extremely sensitive secrets to the KGB for seven years. Facts that have been concealed provided further evidence of a high-level traitor in MI5 and strong suspicions, never adequately followed up, of another inside the navy who reached the rank of admiral.

Though Vassall was a practicing homosexual, clearly living far beyond his means, there was no suspicion of the existence of a spy in the Admiralty until the defection of Anatoli Golitsin from the KGB office in Helsinki in December 1961. After Golitsin's big debriefing by the CIA, ten definitive allegations about KGB penetration of the British Security and Intelligence Services were passed to MI5. Later, when Golitsin came to Britain and was interrogated by MI5 officers, this figure rose to 250!

One of the early allegations, which I will call "No. 1," referred to the recruitment in 1955 of a man in the naval attaché's office in the British embassy in Moscow. This recruitment, Golitsin said, had been made under the personal supervision of Gen. Oleg Gribanov, then chief of the Second Directorate of the KGB, responsible for internal intelligence operations in the USSR.

Golitsin stated that Gribanov, a ruthless operator known to his colleagues as "Little Napoleon," had insinuated a man called Sigmund Mikhailski into the Moscow embassy staff as an interpreter and that he had been involved in the spy's recruitment. While serving in Moscow, the spy had handed over handwritten notes about documents passing through his office. When he had been posted back to London, he had been switched to an even more productive post in naval intelligence, Golitsin said, being run there by KGB officers located in the Soviet embassy in Kensington Palace Gardens.

In spite of this unusual detail, MI5 could not narrow the

list of suspects to less than four. One officer put Vassall at the top of his list, but another, more senior, put him at the bottom because Vassall was known to be "a devout Anglo-Catholic and seemed to be of high moral character."

Among Golitsin's first ten allegations was another, even more serious, which I will call "No. 2." He said that he was certain that there was another naval spy at much higher level because shortly before he had left Moscow for Helsinki, he had seen three extremely secret British documents concerning naval plans. These were not summaries but photocopies of the originals, and they carried the initials of the few British officials who had been allowed to read them, though he could not recall those initials.

One of the documents was stamped "Top Secret (Atomic)" and had dealt with the organization of a base on the Clyde for American Polaris missile submarines. The second concerned the reorganization of NATO dispositions in the Mediterranean. The third was a report of an extremely secret naval committee.

When the three original reports were withdrawn from the Admiralty files, interspersed among a wad of others and then shown to Golitsin, without hesitation he picked out the correct ones he had seen. The defector insisted that he knew the documents had come from another spy, much senior to the "No. 1" man, also believed to have been recruited while serving in Moscow.

A separate inquiry was set up to investigate the "No. 2" spy. The sole suspect was a naval officer who later became an admiral. When the time came for him to be interrogated in the hope that he might break down and confess, Hollis, the director general, refused to allow him to be approached. He argued that the suspect was within two years of retirement and was in a post where he could do little further damage. Even if he confessed his guilt, a prosecution would be unlikely because of the damage to American and NATO relations.

The case officers pointed out that the admiral could be offered immunity to induce him to yield information about his contacts and the extent of the damage he might have done over the years. Hollis remained adamant. The admiral has since died.

While the inquiry into "No. 1" continued, another KGB

officer, Yuri Nosenko, defected to the United States in June 1962. While remaining in his post as a KGB officer in Moscow and in the Soviet delegation to disarmament talks in Geneva, he gave more precise details of "No. 1," the spy who had been in the naval attaché's office in Moscow. He said that the spy had been "a pederast and had been recruited by homosexual blackmail." Nosenko then added, "He had access to the highest level in the British navy and gave us all NATO secrets, including documents which had to do with a lord." He confirmed that General Gribanov had been personally involved in the recruitment and said that he knew this because, as deputy chief of a KGB department, he was a close friend of Gribanov.

Vassall soon went to the top of everybody's list because inquiries quickly confirmed his homosexuality. He also had access to documents "to do with a lord" because he was working as a clerk in the office of the civil lord of the Admiralty. (Vassall was a classic example of the espionage value of a low-level agent who happens to be in the right place.)

Vassall's expensive flat in Dolphin Square was searched while he was at work. Cameras for copying documents were found in a bureau and cassettes of exposed film were discovered in a secret drawer in the base of a table. When developed, the films proved to be copies of *more than 170* classified documents—just one haul for Vassall's KGB controller.

Vassall was arrested, tried, and convicted after confessing that he had been compromised homosexually by KGB men, who had taken photographs of him while he was too drunk to appreciate what was happening, and had then blackmailed him into spying for them. He gave information showing that when he had returned to London, he had been run by the KGB top man, the "Resident," Nicolai Korovin, who had also been involved in the activities of the Navy Spy Ring. After Korovin hastily returned to Moscow following the collapse of the known elements of the ring, Vassall had been taken over by his successor, Nicolai Karpekov.

When interrogated in prison, Vassall described how, early in 1962, Karpekov had told him to stop spying and had taken his cameras away without giving any reason. To MI5, the explanation was obvious: the KGB had realized that Golitsin knew something about Vassall, so after he had defected to the CIA, the spy had to be deactivated.

If this situation had continued and Vassall had been strong enough to keep his mouth shut, he could not have been prosecuted because there would have been no legal evidence against him. Instead, as Vassall explained, Karpekov reactivated him a few weeks later, in May, by giving him back his cameras and insisting that he must produce more secret material than ever. This made it certain that Vassall would be caught.

By the time of Vassall's arrest, the MI5 case officers had come around to believing that he must also have been responsible for the leakage of the NATO documents attributed by Golitsin to "No. 2," the much more high-level source.

A more detailed statement by Nosenko, the later defector, had specified that the homosexual spy had given the KGB many more NATO secrets, so the investigators had assumed that Golitsin must have been mistaken. That was how the situation rested until the end of 1964 when James Angleton, the CIA's most experienced counterespionage officer, became convinced that Nosenko, who by that time had physically defected to the United States, was a KGB plant who had been sent over to offset the damage done by Golitsin and, later, for disinformation purposes connected with the assassination of President Kennedy. In that light, Vassall was questioned again in prison. He convinced his questioners that he had never seen two of the top-secret NATO documents, and it was quickly proved that they had never reached the civil lord's office.

If Nosenko was a disinformation agent still working for the KGB, he could have put the final finger on Vassall in such a way that he could be sacrificed to save the more valuable high-level spy whom Golitsin had described as "No. 2."

Under hostile interrogation in the United States, Nosenko admitted that he had lied about his rank in the KGB and that he had not really been a personal friend of Gribanov. Furthermore, there seemed to be no reason, from the type of KGB posts he had really occupied, why he should know anything about Vassall unless he had been told it for a KGB purpose before "defecting" to America. It therefore seemed odds on that Nosenko had been sent over by the KGB to induce MI5 to put the blame for all the naval espionage on Vassall, whose arrest had then been deliberately assured when Karpekov had ordered him to resume his spying activities.

Though Nosenko was eventually rated as genuine by the CIA after prolonged inquiries, the consensus in MI5 remains that he was a plant.

The MI5 case officers applied again for permission to interrogate the suspect admiral, but Hollis refused and declared the case closed. In the interim he had ordered all the papers on the "No. 2" case to be destroyed, a most unusual procedure.

The case officers were limited to concluding that, following Golitsin's disclosures, the KGB knew that MI5 had been conducting two separate inquiries. If they were right, that information could have reached the KGB only from a very high-level source because very few people knew of the suspicions concerning "No. 2." It could be significant that the MI5 officer who eventually came under deepest suspicion himself had doubly assured that "No. 2" could never be arrested.

There can be little doubt that while Vassall was the most despicable type of traitor, betraying his country through fear and for money, he was convicted of some offenses that he had not committed. Perhaps that was what he meant when, in his autobiography, he stated that he had been told that he had been "a pawn in the complex game of international strategy."

Exactly how much about the Vassall case the prime minister of the day, Harold Macmillan, was told may never be known but the publicity about it, resulting in a tribunal of inquiry through which two journalists were imprisoned for refusing to reveal their sources, sickened him. As his memoirs *At the End of the Day* show, he wrote in his diary—no doubt with his Birch Grove pheasant shoot in mind—his view regarding any captured spy, "Unhappily, you can't bury him out of sight, as keepers do with foxes."

Macmillan seemed to have a premonition that the Vassall case would be a political disaster according to information given to me by Lord Carrington. When Carrington, then first lord of the Admiralty, informed his prime minister rather triumphantly that the spy had been arrested, Macmillan responded by saying "Oh that's bad news! Very bad news! You know, you should never catch a spy. Discover him and then control him but never catch him. A spy causes far more trouble when he's caught."

I have already dealt with the defection of Philby so far as it involved MI5 and the suspicions concerning Hollis. In that same month, January 1963, MI5 had become involved in another mystery, with historic political consequences, the unexpected death of Hugh Gaitskell, the leader of the Labour opposition.

It had seemed certain that Gaitskell, who was only fifty-six, would become the next Labour prime minister but, in mid-December 1962, he was admitted to hospital with what was diagnosed as virus pneumonia. After little more than a week, he was discharged and pronounced fit enough to go ahead with a visit to Moscow at the personal invitation of Khrushchev. That same evening, however, he had a relapse and early in January was admitted to a different hospital, where he died on the eighteenth. Autopsy showed that his terminal illness had been due to a rare complaint called systemic lupus erythematosus affecting the heart and kidneys, though it was not recorded as such on the death certificate. I am now in a position to add some new information concerning this event.

When the KGB defector Anatoli Golitsin arrived in Britain for thorough debriefing by MI5, one of the first things he volunteered was a statement that, before defecting, he had heard from the chief of the Northern European section of the KGB that the organization was planning to murder a leader of an opposition party in his area. On being told of Gaitskell's death, he asked if the Labour leader had been to the Soviet embassy just before his illness. He was told that, in fact, Gaitskell had visited the Russian consulate in search of a visa for his projected trip to Moscow. Though he had gone by appointment, he had been kept waiting half an hour and had been given coffee and biscuits.

One of the doctors who treated Gaitskell was so puzzled by his symptoms that he contacted MI5 to report the fact that the disease that killed him was very rare in temperate zones, especially in males and particularly so in those over forty. It transpired that Gaitskell himself may have had his suspicions because he had told the doctor about the coffee and biscuits. The police were also sufficiently perturbed to contact MI5.

As a result, a security officer was sent down to the Microbiological Research Establishment—the so-called Germ-warfare Station—and then to the Chemical Defence Establishment at Porton on Salisbury Plain, but experts there could offer no information suggesting that the Russians knew how to induce the disease which is not an infection but caused by the victim's own antibodies.

By that time Golitsin had rushed back to the United States following the publicity over "Dolnytsin," as I have described. There he discussed the circumstances of Gaitskell's death with James Angleton, who appreciated that the elimination of a committed right-wing, genuinely democratic Socialist would have been in Russia's interests, particularly as his likely successor, Harold Wilson, was believed to be of the left.

Angleton therefore commissioned a thorough search of all the published medical literature on the fatal disease and came up with the startling information that Soviet medical researchers had published three academic papers describing how they had produced a drug that, when administered, reproduced the fatal heart and kidney symptoms.

Calculations showed that the dosage required was too large for it to have been administered surreptitiously in coffee and biscuits, but the research was already seven years old, so there could have been developments that had reduced the dosage. And if the KGB had decided that the drug was useful for their assassination purposes, no further papers would have been published.

The case officers concluded that Gaitskell might well have been murdered, but failing the arrival of some new defector who knew all the facts, the truth would never be known in the West. Hollis showed scant interest in the inquiries, but his successor, Sir Martin Furnival Jones, remained concerned about the circumstances of Gaitskell's death and its long-term consequences. Gaitskell's widow and most of his colleagues are satisfied that he died a natural death, which may well have been the case, but it is generally conceded that whatever its cause, the Labour leader's death was the single most important historic factor in the party's continuing swing to the left.

9
Hollis and Profumo

While it was Gaitskell's untimely death that brought Harold Wilson to the leadership of the Labour party, it was other factors that brought him to the premiership. One of these was the so-called Profumo Affair, a minor sex scandal that was expertly exploited by the Labour opposition and even more brilliantly manipulated by the KGB.

History is likely to agree that the Conservative government's apparent mishandling of the Affair hastened, and perhaps occasioned, the premature retirement of Harold Macmillan as prime minister in the autumn of 1963. When Macmillan's much less charismatic successor, Sir Alec Douglas Home, went to the polls in October 1964, Wilson beat him by only four seats. Without the burden of the Profumo Affair, which in the less permissive climate of that time was ill received by many voters, the Tories might have won, especially as Macmillan might still have been at the helm.

In Wilson's first six years of office, the Labour party slid progressively to the left, with leaders of trade unions, known at least to have been Communists in the past, exerting increasing influence on policy. At the time of writing, this slide has resulted in the election of Michael Foot as Labour leader. Foot's stated determination to pursue nuclear disarmament and the party's stated intention of eliminating American defense bases in Britain have the Kremlin's total support.

But not even the KGB could have organized the Profumo Affair, which originated from the chance meeting of the war minister, John Profumo, with a young call girl, Christine Keeler, and the fact, unknown to the minister, that she was

79

also on familiar terms with a senior member of Soviet intelligence, Capt. Eugene Ivanov, officially the assistant naval attaché at the Soviet embassy. But the KGB made the most of it once the intriguing situation had been brought to its attention.

There is even a possibility—some MI5 men would put it higher—that the KGB "lit the fuse" that ensured that the private affair would become a momentous public scandal. On November 11, 1962, George Wigg (now lord), who interested himself in all matters concerning the army and had recently crossed swords with John Profumo, the war minister, in Parliament, received a mysterious telephone call at the home of his party agent in his Dudley constituency. In what appeared to be a deliberately muffled voice, the caller said, "Forget about the Vassall case. You want to look at Profumo," and then hung up.

Wigg was immediately interested but remained baffled not only by the identity of the caller but how he had discovered where he was. There is evidence in the files of MI5 that the call was organized by the KGB and may have been made by a KGB officer. In the period shortly before the Profumo Affair became public, Vitali Lui, better known as Victor Louis, a long-serving KGB officer who still travels widely under the cover of being a journalist, visited London. He was under surveillance and is now known to have been in touch with Tom Driberg, who could have provided the information about the bad blood between Wigg and Profumo. As I shall show later, Driberg was an inveterate peddler of parliamentary gossip and was in the KGB's pay as a double agent at the time.

Whether Louis made the call himself or not, MI5 officers concerned with the case believed that he set the events in train. Wigg was the mainspring in Labour's exploitation of the situation, and it was the telephone call that wound him up. (This mysterious call was almost a carbon copy of the event that triggered off the publicity about the defection of Maclean and Burgess in 1951. A *Daily Express* journalist, sitting in a restaurant in Paris, received a telephone call from someone who knew his name, had a foreign accent, alerted him to the story, then hung up.)

It is not my intention here to rake over the cold ashes of the Profumo case but, as with the other cases I have discussed, to present new aspects, particularly with respect to the handling of the situation by MI5 and the KGB.

Without Ivanov, the Socialists could not have pursued the alleged security aspects of the affair and would not have attempted to censure Profumo on moral grounds. Wigg has repeatedly told me that there were too many with similar problems on his own front bench for that to have been practicable. Ivanov, therefore, is central to the whole episode, but the course that it took right through to its tragic finale was conditioned by the behavior of MI5 and, in particular, of its director general, Sir Roger Hollis. As the reader can judge for himself, if the director of the KGB at the Center in Moscow had been controlling the case day by day, he could hardly have handled it more effectively to Russia's advantage than Hollis did.

It is what Hollis repeatedly failed to do rather than what he did that calls for censure. That censure was made at the time inside MI5 but not in public. Instead, the long report on the Profumo Affair by Lord Denning, made after it had run its course at the request of Harold Macmillan, went out of its way to make excuses for Hollis, though the facts as reported by Denning do not support them.

The first fact that has not been properly appreciated is that by the spring of 1961, MI5 had received confirmation of their suspicion that Ivanov was no ordinary sailor but an officer of the GRU, the military arm of the Soviet espionage and subversion apparatus. This confirmation had come from the defector Oleg Penkovsky, whose debriefing had begun in April, three months *before* Profumo chanced to meet the call girl, Christine Keeler, at a party at Cliveden, the home of the late Lord Astor.

For some undisclosed reason, the Denning Report stated categorically that Ivanov never became Keeler's lover, though on at least one occasion "there was, perhaps, some kind of sexual relations." This was not the view of MI5 officers involved with the case. After Penkovsky's tip, Ivanov had been placed under surveillance not only in London, where he was known to visit the home of Stephen Ward, with whom Keeler was living, but also when spending weekends at Ward's cottage on the Cliveden estate, where there were also other prostitutes engaged in general promiscuity.

MI5 also had informers inside this group, including Ward

himself. They knew that Ivanov was a "ladies' man" and a big drinker. They also knew that he was a dedicated Communist who would do anything to promote his own career and would have no compunction about going to bed with Keeler or anybody else if it served his professional purposes.

Once Profumo had taken up with Keeler, as happened soon after their meeting at Cliveden, it is inconceivable that Ivanov would have been permitted not to take maximum advantage of the piquant situation, which he knew all about and would be expected to report on daily to the Soviet embassy.

Nor is there any doubt in MI5 that once the potentialities were appreciated, the KGB took over the operation from the GRU and controlled everything that Ivanov did. There was quick evidence of direct Kremlin interest, including that of Khrushchev himself, who was then the Soviet leader.

One of Ivanov's first moves was to ask Ward if he could find out "from any of his influential friends" exactly when the United States was going to arm Western Germany with atomic weapons. Though this request was played down by the Denning Report, it was of supreme interest to the Kremlin. For emotional as well as strategic reasons, Russia was totally opposed to the deployment of nuclear weapons by the regenerated Luftwaffe. The secret decision to place Russian nuclear missiles in Cuba had already been taken in Moscow, and if this leaked, the American decision to give the Luftwaffe atomic bombs for use on the East-West border could be a weighty political counter.

MI5 had almost immediate knowledge of this request by Ivanov because within a few days, on July 12, 1961, Ward telephoned MI5 to say he had some interesting information. He told them of Ivanov's requirement. He also mentioned that Profumo had been at the Cliveden party on the previous weekend and had met Ivanov and Keeler.

There is confusion as to whether MI5 was told, at this stage or later, that Ward had suggested that Keeler might try to get the information out of Profumo. Ward insisted that he had told MI5 about it either then or at a later meeting. Keeler also said that she had been asked by Ward to sound out Profumo, though she did not do so, as the war minister ended his relationship with her. Lord Denning seemed to be convinced that for more than a year MI5 had no knowledge of any relationship between Profumo and Keeler that would have made such a request feasible.

There has also been a tendency, even on the part of Harold Macmillan, to ridicule the idea that any professional intelligence officer would dream of trying to get information about atomic weapons from Profumo. "What would the war minister know about atomic weapons?" Macmillan once asked me rhetorically.

The point is that Ivanov was not after detailed information about atomic weapons but only the date when the Luftwaffe might be getting them. The war minister could well have had access to this date because the project had important consequences for the British forces in Germany, of which he was political head.

Of course, as Denning pointed out, Profumo was not the type of man to tell anybody anything of a confidential nature, but that difficulty has never deterred the KGB from trying.

As Lord Denning based his report on the evidence of witnesses, one or more of them must have convinced him that Ivanov's request about the atomic weapons was of little consequence. The chief MI5 witness was Sir Roger Hollis.

Because of the mention of the war minister, the MI5 officer's report on his interview with Ward was drawn to Hollis's personal attention. His reaction, or lack of it, was quite remarkable. Ivanov was an accredited diplomat and was clearly overstepping his proper function by trying to induce a friend to suborn influential people to secure secret NATO information. Hollis should therefore have reported the matter to the Foreign Office, either directly or indirectly through his proper channel, the Home Office. Instead, he sat on the information and did not warn the Foreign Office even that Ivanov was a Soviet intelligence officer until a year later, in June 1962!

Even then he seems to have moved only because he found out that the Foreign Office was being informed independently, and at the highest level, about Ivanov's activities. Ward had secured a meeting with the head of the Foreign Office, Sir Harold Caccia (now Lord), to promote Ivanov as a medium for discussing Anglo-Soviet problems such as Berlin and the Oder-Neisse line.

Later, in October 1962, during the Cuban missile crisis, Ivanov used Ward to try to contact Caccia again to suggest that Britain should take the initiative by calling a summit conference in London. Ivanov was prepared to assure Caccia that Khrushchev would attend such a conference. He would never have dared to give such an assurance without Khrushchev's agreement, so this was fair evidence that the game was being played at the highest levels.

Rightly, the Foreign Office refused to do business with either Ward or Ivanov, but no thanks were due to the director general of MI5, who had neglected to warn it that Ivanov was a professional spy for more than a year.

If the Foreign Office had been properly warned in good time, the Soviet ambassador could have been advised of Ivanov's excesses, and if these had continued, Ivanov could have been expelled as *persona non grata*. In that case, the Profumo scandal might never have reached such horrendous proportions. That Ivanov was still active in Britain while Wigg was making his inquiries and the story was breaking greatly exacerbated the security implications.

To return to the germination of the scandal in the summer of 1961, the only quick action Hollis took on receiving the case officer's report on the interview with Ward was to pass the buck to Scotland Yard by suggesting that Special Branch should make some inquiries about Ward and Keeler. After this had produced no results whatever, Hollis then decided that Profumo ought to be warned to be careful about what he said to Ward. In addition, he initiated action that showed incredible lack of judgment or something worse.

Avoiding any direct contact with the war minister or any other, as was his wont, Hollis went to see the secretary to the Cabinet, then Sir Norman Brook. He asked him to warn Profumo, then followed it up with the suggestion that, at the same time, he should ask Profumo if he would help in inducing Ivanov to defect to the West.

By any standards, this was an outrageous suggestion. No minister of the crown should ever be embroiled in espionage or counterespionage. Nothing would have served the Soviet purpose better than for Profumo to have agreed to cooperate and to have made a personal pass at Ivanov to encourage him to defect. Ivanov could have reported it to his ambassador, and then all kinds of political capital could have been made out of the situation. Profumo might have found himself under

threat of blackmail, the KGB being prepared to withhold
publicity about the incident if he agreed to be "helpful." Or it
could have been leaked to the Labour opposition, which
could have used it to savage effect.

It is a tribute to Hollis's quiet powers of persuasion that he
was able to induce the normally cautious Sir Norman Brook
to raise the possibility with Profumo, who rejected it out of
hand. Brook would have served his prime minister, and his
country, better had he told Macmillan that his director general of security was seriously lacking in judgment.

Hollis's motive in trying to embroil Profumo in the defection attempt is made all the more suspicious by the fact that
the reports from Ward, from the MI5 case officer, and from
the Secret Service in Moscow, all showed that Ivanov was a
totally committed Communist, as is underlined in the Denning
Report. The chances that he might defect were minimal.

Ward's willing cooperation with MI5 is also a matter for
conjecture. He admired the Soviet regime and sympathized
with Communists in Britain, advocating their cause to his
friends so intensely that some reported him. He was personally fond of Ivanov and was relying on him to provide facilities
for a visit to Moscow. Could it be, therefore, that Ward was
feeding information into MI5 on Ivanov's instructions as part
of the KGB's exploitation of the situation?

If Hollis's delay in informing the Foreign Office about
Ivanov was reprehensible, his consistent failure to inform
ministers, in spite of warnings from junior officers, was little
short of criminal. As director general of MI5, he had a
personal responsibility to the home secretary and right of
access to the prime minister. He carefully avoided exercising
either until the Profumo situation was beyond repair. On
March 21, 1963, George Wigg, who had received further
evidence indirectly from Keeler, including the atomic bomb
allegation, raised the matter in the Commons. From that
moment, a public scandal was assured, especially after Profumo
foolishly denied his intimacy with Keeler.

Though Hollis had been put in the picture in the summer
of 1961 and had been intimately involved ever since, coldly
watching the tragedy unfold day by day, he had given no
information whatsoever to the home secretary, Henry Brooke.
The home secretary was in the embarrassing position of

knowing nothing about the matter that Wigg had raised. Only on March 27, 1963, was Brooke given the background, after *he* had taken the initiative and sent for Hollis.

By that time, as a result of a tipoff, as Denning records, Ivanov had skipped out of Britain on January 29, and Hollis skillfully used his absence to excuse his lack of action on the case. He said that all security interest had ceased as soon as Ivanov had left Britain and argued that if Profumo had been sharing a mistress with Ivanov, there could be security interest, but as Ivanov had gone, all risk had disappeared with him.

This was a specious argument because it is standard practice to continue inquiries into the activities of a known KGB agent long after he has left the country—as witness the interrogation of Anthony Blunt about his Russian contacts, who had been out of Britain for at least ten years.

Hollis told Denning that he did not learn of Profumo's sexual association with Keeler until the end of January 1963, which, by strange coincidence, was exactly the time that Ivanov was warned and scurried to safety in Moscow. From discussions with senior officials intimately concerned with the Profumo case, I have reason to believe that Hollis's statement was untrue. It would be difficult to believe if only because MI5 had such close contact with Ward and his entourage. Whether MI5 watchers had seen Profumo with Keeler or not, there was plenty of talk about their relationship in the Ward households, as Keeler testified, and much of this was retailed to MI5. Hollis made much of his belief that it was none of MI5's business to involve itself in any minister's private affairs, but in the special circumstances, with Ivanov around, most counterespionage chiefs would have felt it incumbent on them to satisfy themselves with some inquiries.

Instead, three days after Ivanov was out of the country—on February 1, 1963—Hollis had issued this ruling: "Until further notice no approach should be made to anyone in the Ward *galère*, or to any other outside contact in respect of it. If we are approached we listen only."

This ruling astonished those of his officers who could see the dangers ahead for the government. Whatever Hollis's reasons for issuing it, this was the decision the Russians would have liked most—no further inquiries into Ivanov or any of his contacts. Even if people came forward to volunteer information, no action was to be taken on it.

Hollis's director of counterespionage was so concerned about the lack of action and its likely consequences that he put his view on record in a memorandum to the director general, dated February 4. It ran:

If a scandal results from Mr. Profumo's association with Christine Keeler, there is likely to be a considerable political rumpus. . . . If, in any subsequent inquiries, we were found to have been in possession of this information about Profumo and to have taken no action on it, we would, I am sure, be subject to much criticism for failing to bring it to light. I suggest that this information be passed to the prime minister and you might also like to consider whether or not, before doing so, we should interview Miss Keeler.

That was clearly a plea from a man who had both the interests of his service and of the government at heart, and Hollis was later to admit, with a rueful expression, that it was "filled with prophetic insight." Having read it and discussed it with his deputy, whom he always overbore, Hollis decided to ignore it. He argued that the whole affair was a political issue and, therefore, not MI5's concern. Thereupon, he issued another firm instruction against any further investigations.

He also continued with his policy of failing to inform Macmillan, who remained deprived of the facts for so long that the Labour opposition was eventually able to make a laughing stock of him in the House as the "didn't know prime minister."

When Hollis had been summoned by the home secretary, one of the things he told Brooke was about Ivanov's request to Ward for the delivery date of American atomic bombs to the Luftwaffe. This was the first time that this information had been given to *any* minister, though Hollis had known about it for more than a year and a half!

Another matter that Brooke raised with Hollis was the possibility of prosecuting Ward under the Official Secrets Act. After a few days' deliberation, Hollis advised against it, knowing that without Ivanov as a witness there was no chance of a conviction. The police pursued Ward on a charge of

living on immoral earnings, and while on bail, he died of a
drug overdose.

On May 29, by which time maximum damage had been
done to the government, the results of the police inquiries
reached the prime minister's private secretary. He immediately alerted Macmillan to the implications, and the prime
minister summoned Hollis to No. 10 Downing Street. For
the first time, he learned the full security aspects of the affair,
including the Ward-Keeler project for securing the atomic
bomb information from Profumo.

He recorded Hollis's visit in *At the End of the Day:* the
MI5 chief presented the project as though "atomic secrets" of
a technical nature had been involved. This was also the
impression conveyed to me when I discussed the matter with
Mr. Macmillan recently. This enabled Hollis to secure
Macmillan's agreement that the Ward-Keeler project was a
"ridiculous story" because Profumo had no "information concerning atomic secrets." In fact, of course, all Ivanov had
been after was a date, which Profumo could well have known.

Until that meeting with Hollis, all Macmillan had really
known was that Profumo had been involved in what he called
"a silly scrape over a woman" whom he had met at a "raffish
party" at Cliveden and that this woman was said to "share
her favors" with the Russian naval attaché. He had not
known even that until February 4, 1963, and the information
had come to his office from a newspaperman, not from MI5.

The chancellor of the day, the late Lord Dilhorne, who was
a close friend of mine, believed that Hollis was grossly at fault
for keeping the prime minister and the home secretary in
ignorance for so long but was averse to any public criticism of
him on that score because it would draw attention to MI5,
which ought to remain as secret as possible.

When the public interest in the affair was at its height, a
KGB officer, working in UN headquarters in New York, tried
to exacerbate it. This Russian, who had the code name
"Fedora," was working as a double agent, passing information
to the FBI, which Hoover rated so highly that he sent some
of it to the White House. "Fedora" claimed that after Ivanov
had left London, he had met him in Moscow and had a long
conversation with him. He alleged that Ivanov told him that
he had installed a microphone in Christine Keeler's bedroom

and that, by listening to her pillow talk, had obtained most valuable intelligence.

Hoover passed a copy of this report to President Kennedy with the suggestion that he might like to inform Harold Macmillan of its contents. Kennedy put it at the bottom of his pending tray, saying, "I reckon that Mr. Macmillan is in enough trouble already." "Fedora's" statement, which eventually reached MI5, was almost certainly false, though it is possible that Ivanov had been boasting in Moscow. Experts from MI5 had examined Keeler's bedroom closely and had decided that it was unbuggable.

Further evidence has since accrued that most of "Fedora's" material was deliberate KGB disinformation. He even fed in information, at one stage, that the Profumo scandal had been engineered by French intelligence, not the KGB. He also claimed that there was a Soviet spy inside the Atomic Weapons Establishment at Aldermaston in Berkshire, which turned out to be false and wasted much time.

Macmillan's sorry plight during the eventual debate on the Profumo Affair in Parliament on June 17 was described by George Wigg in his autobiography:

> The Prime Minister's defence contained some amazing admissions.... Three separate statements by Miss Keeler that she had been asked by Ward to obtain military information from Profumo had likewise never reached the Prime Minister—an admission that evoked the jibe "Nobody ever tells me anything!" That summed up the Prime Minister's case.

As a journalist involved in the Profumo inquiries at high level in Whitehall, I had known all the facts long before Macmillan did, and as I witnessed the prime minister's embarrassment from the press gallery, I spotted Sir Roger Hollis sitting not far away. I knew nothing then of the suspicion against him, which analysis of his behavior in the Profumo case was to fortify, but I wondered what was going on in his mind as he sat there, surveying the shambles, unknown to most people, expressionless and hunched in his seat.

It is inescapable that, for whatever reason, Hollis played the Profumo case long, thereby ensuring, whether deliberately or not, that maximum damage would accrue to the government. He did as little as possible as late as possible.

It was suggested to Lord Denning, as he recorded in his report,

> that Ivanov filled a new role in Russian technique. It was to divide the United Kingdom from the United States by these devious means. If Ministers or prominent people can be placed in compromising positions, or made the subject of damaging rumour, or the Security Service can be made to appear incompetent, it may weaken the confidence of the United States in our integrity and reliability.

With all respect to Lord Denning, this observation was stating the obvious because it had been an objective of the Soviet espionage and disinformation service since the start of the Cold War in the late 1940s, and even before. His conclusion, however, was beyond criticism. "If this was the object of Captain Ivanov, with Ward as his tool, he succeeded only too well."

There can be little doubt that this brilliantly successful exercise in Soviet subversion, taking maximum advantage of a sudden opportunity, was conducted by the Center in Moscow, with Ivanov taking day-to-day instructions. Horrific though it may seem, senior officers of MI5 were driven by the facts to suspect that the day-to-day moves of their chief, Sir Roger Hollis, had been similarly orchestrated.

It is clear from the Denning Report that Hollis made highly effective use of the guidelines laid down to govern the activities of MI5 when trying to explain his behavior, as he did later when interrogated about his strange actions during the Blunt case. He stressed that under a directive issued by a former home secretary in 1952, MI5's task was the defense of the realm as a whole and that no inquiry was to be carried out unless those directing MI5 were satisfied that an important public interest was at stake.

In retrospect, there can be no doubt that an important public interest *was* at stake and that it bore directly on the defense of the realm. So, at best, Hollis was guilty of a series of faulty judgments.

Though Hollis was not an impressive figure, Denning was

impressed by his arguments and made every excuse for him
in his report, as anyone who reads it must appreciate. The
phenomenal mystique attached to the post of director general
of MI5 automatically ensures that any incumbent will generate a considerable degree of awe, however disappointing his
exterior. Any hesitancy in answering a question tends to be
interpreted as laudable care in avoiding unnecessary disclosure, while a poor response, accompanied by a smile, tends
instinctively to be accepted as the best that can be expected
in view of the poor chap's terrible burden of state secrets.
Obviously, there are things he cannot possibly even hint at,
so we must give him the benefit of every possible doubt and
avoid embarrassing him by pressing him too hard.

There was an additional factor affecting the report, which
came to my notice only very recently. Shortly before he died,
Lord Dilhorne wrote to me, saying, "I suspect that I was the
only person who saw Tom Denning's report before he submitted
it. He made a number of alterations at my suggestion." These
may have been implied criticisms of the Security Service and
its director general, which, at the time, the Lord Chancellor
deplored "in the national interest."

Lord Dilhorne also claimed that, when writing his report,
Lord Denning had the benefit of a long document on the
affair that he, as the Lord Chancellor, had prepared at the
request of Macmillan before it was thought necessary to have
an independent report for public consumption. "You never
saw the report I made," Lord Dilhorne wrote in jest. "It was,
I think, only seen by Harold Macmillan, Harold Wilson, and
Tom Denning, who used so much of it that I could have
successfully sued him for breach of copyright!"

In that report, which has never been published, Lord
Dilhorne accused the MI5 chiefs of at least one bad error of
judgment in failing to alert the prime minister.

Though Sir Roger Hollis was not in the habit of expressing
his feelings and deplored any publicity about his department
so much that he vetoed even laudatory accounts of its wartime work by distinguished colleagues such as the late Sir
John Masterman, I am told that he was more than satisfied
with the Denning Report, though it revealed more about the
secret machinations of MI5 than had ever been told officially
before.

The MI5 officers, whose hands had been tied by one

negative directive after another, not only disagreed with the findings of the report but regarded the facts on which they had been based as a shameful indictment of their organization and of their leader in particular.

I shall be dealing shortly with the Blunt case in considerable detail, revealing why he confessed and all that he disclosed, including his leads to other suspects, such as the likely Fifth Man of the original Ring of Five. It is relevant, however, at this point to record Hollis's behavior with respect to the case.

As will be seen because of the nature of the unexpected event that led to the reopening of the interrogation of Blunt in 1964, Hollis had no option but to take some action. From that moment on, he seemed to do everything he could to help Blunt and frustrate those who were determined to extract every scrap of useful information from the self-confessed traitor.

As soon as Arthur Martin, the very experienced case officer handling Blunt, had induced him to accept immunity to prosecution in return for a full confession, he reported it to Hollis, who kept himself at a distance from the operation. Martin then wanted to interrogate Blunt without delay, but Hollis took the view that there was no need for hurry and the right course was to treat Blunt very gently. An argument ensued, and Hollis made it an excuse for suspending Martin from duty for two weeks. Martin insisted that, even if he had to stay away from headquarters for reasons he failed to understand, he should go ahead with the interrogation of Blunt, which was taking place in Blunt's flat, anyway. Hollis ordered him to leave Blunt alone.

As a result, Blunt was left free from questioning or surveillance for a fortnight. Nobody knows whether he consulted the Russians in that time and sought their advice about what he should admit when eventually interrogated. There is no doubt that he did mislead his interrogators later, especially over friends who were still in high places.

When Blunt gave leads to high-level suspects, whether knowingly or inadvertently, Hollis was most reluctant to give permission for them to be questioned. One, ruled out by Hollis as being "too close to retirement," turned out later to have been a major source of secret information for Guy

Burgess. When Martin complained again, Hollis took the almost unprecedented step of dismissing him from the organization. Martin assumed then that Hollis had realized that he suspected him and therefore wanted rid of him. That is still Martin's view. The view of Martin's former colleagues is that the dismissal of this outstandingly able counterintelligence officer was a major victory for the KGB.

Certainly, after Martin's departure, little progress could be made with any of the suspects indicated through Blunt, or through previous sources, until Hollis lost control of the situation with his retirement.

It is possible that, with regard to Blunt, Hollis was so appalled by the confirmation of the existence of a major spy in MI5 throughout the war that he wanted it played down in the interests of the department's reputation and of his own as director general. In that case, he would have to be judged at least derelict in his duty, for his senior officers were all most anxious to derive the maximum information from Blunt about the penetration of their organization.

Hollis's behavior in the Blunt case, as in the Profumo Affair, makes real sense only in the context that he was under regular KGB control himself. It was not in the Soviet interest for Blunt to be milked of all his knowledge, and if Hollis was guilty, there was always the danger that some remark, inadvertent or otherwise, might lead to him.

Though Blunt insisted that he had no idea whether Hollis was a fellow spy or not, because his controllers would never have hinted at it, he volunteered some information that increased suspicion against the director general. Blunt said that while his Russian controllers had urged him to secure information from many areas in MI5 while he had worked there, they had never suggested that he should try to discover anything from Directorate F, which was then being run by Hollis. Blunt admitted that this was peculiar and could suggest that the Russians already had a sufficient flow of information from that directorate that was obviously of prime importance to them.

The situation also suggested an explanation of why the KGB had allowed Blunt to quit MI5 as soon as the war ended. Blunt told his questioners that the KGB could easily have forced him to stay on and that, as he enjoyed the work, he would not have been "too unhappy" about remaining in

MI5 for a few more years. If Hollis had also been a spy, clearly earmarked for steady promotion, the KGB could afford to allow Blunt to leave.

With so much reference to so much supposition, I feel it necessary to state yet again that every allegation and suspicion that I record arose inside MI5 from loyal MI5 officers assisted by independent assessors from the Secret Service, all motivated purely by determination to solve the mystery of the stream of failures and root out any traitors responsible for them.

10
Interrogation Extraordinary

In retirement on a modest pension, Sir Roger Hollis went to live in a cottage in Catcott in Somerset. There he took part in the village life, becoming a rural district councilor, and is remembered by a near neighbor, Mr. F. M. Heywood, as "very pleasant, much liked in the village. He was quiet and never said a word about his old job, though we knew what it had been."

He played more golf, improving his game sufficiently to represent the county. He became captain of the Burnham-Berrow Club and president of the Somerset Golfing Union. None of this would seem to fit the character of a Soviet spy, but neither did Anthony Blunt's posts as director of the Courtauld Institute and surveyor of the Queen's pictures.

Hollis retained contact with a few old friends, who remember him with affection, but while it is customary for former chiefs of the security and intelligence services to meet in London on special social occasions, Sir Roger did not attend them. On one occasion, at a dinner for a retiring senior civil servant, all the former surviving intelligence and security chiefs were invited with one exception. "Of course, we didn't invite Hollis," the man who had organized the dinner explained. Nor did Hollis receive any of the appointments offered to men of distinction in their retirement, whereas Arthur Martin, the officer he had fired, was given a retirement post in the infrastructure of Parliament.

At the height of the suspicions against him, in 1966, he was awarded a KBE in the New Year Honours. I am told that those involved in recommending the Queen to give this routine award would not have been informed of the suspicions, and no attempt was made to stop the award. Nor was Anthony Blunt deprived of his knighthood when he confessed to having been a spy. That occurred only after his treachery became public knowledge.

Hollis became national news in February 1968 when he divorced his wife after thirty-one years of marriage. Lady Hollis, who died recently, named "the other woman" as Miss Edith "Val" Hammond, who had been Hollis's secretary in MI5 for eighteen years. Hollis was extremely secretive by nature, and if he did indulge in extramural clandestine activities, Miss Hammond knew nothing about them. Popular in the organization, she was promoted to officer rank after Hollis retired but left soon afterward to marry him in 1968. It seems unlikely that he ever told her that he was under suspicion or had been interrogated. He certainly never mentioned it to close friends whom I have questioned.

In 1970, Hollis was invited to MI5 headquarters in London and officially faced with the allegations about him. He was seen first by his successor, Sir Martin Furnival Jones, who said in a friendly way that the allegations just had to be cleared up. He was then transferred to a "safe house" nearby, which had been "taped and miked"—as he must have guessed—for a full interrogation that lasted two days. His interrogators, led by an ex-marine commando, John Day, were former colleagues, so the atmosphere must have been electric.

Hollis was taken through the whole of his early life and did not hold back on his friendship with Communists at Oxford or on his meetings with Agnes Smedley in Shanghai. But he was vague and misleading about his life after he returned to Britain. It was noted, for instance, that he said that he could not remember the address of the first house in which he had lived after his first marriage. Inquiries had shown that a former Oxford University friend, Archie Lyall, who had also been a companion of Burgess, had lived only four doors down. Lyall had worked in the Secret Service while Hollis was in MI5 in London, and, apart from the likelihood that they met professionally, they had used the same railway station.

Being a huge shambling man, fat, flamboyant, and irrepressibly amiable, Lyall would have been difficult to miss, yet Hollis denied that he ever knew that Lyall had been such a close neighbor. This was interpreted as a device to avoid admitting any connection with his former friend because anyone who had ever been involved with Burgess could be suspect, though, in fact, there was never any suspicion against Lyall.

Hollis could offer no satisfactory answer as to why he had been so doggedly determined to join MI5, agreeing that it was the prime target for any Briton recruited to Soviet intelligence. Weakly, he insisted that he just thought that the work would be interesting.

He claimed that he must just have forgotten to put a note about his friendship with Claud Cockburn in the office files. He denied ever having met Ursula Beurton in China, Switzerland, or Oxford. He explained that he had fired Arthur Martin because a "Gestapo," intent on investigating every failure, was forming inside MI5. (This may have been the origin of Sir Harold Wilson's later phrase about a small group of "fascists" among the officers in MI5.)

As befitted a professional, Hollis remained very composed throughout his interrogation, and whether guilty or not, was rated a "tough subject."

After an interval, for further inquiries, Hollis was brought back for a half day of interrogation, but he never broke. If guilty, he would have been aware of the strength of his position so long as he kept his nerve and declined to confess. As with Fuchs, Blake, Philby, and Blunt, the law was powerless to do anything without a confession, and having been "close to the horns" in those cases, and in others that had not become public, Hollis could feel totally secure either from prosecution or publicity.

The possibility of offering Hollis immunity was never seriously considered because it was realized that he must know that a prosecution would never be brought in any circumstances. Even if further evidence accrued, the government, whatever its complexion, would decide that a trial of a former director general of the Security Service would not be "in the public interest." Even if such a trial were held partly *in camera* its effects on relations with foreign intelligence services, particularly those of the United States, could be disastrous. The FBI and the CIA knew all the secret details of the Hollis case, but Congress and the American public did not. The sense of outrage that a trial would engender in the

United States could curtail the continuing interchange between Britain and America of intelligence and defense information.

The Hollis Affair might have been left buried within the vaults of MI5, but certain members of that service and of the Secret Service were so concerned about the Soviet penetrations which, in their opinion, had never been satisfactorily accounted for, that they agitated privately for an independent inquiry. They also wanted an independent method of electing the new directors general of MI5 and the Secret Service. In the past, this had been done by the prime minister, acting largely on the advice of the retiring chiefs, so that if a director general happened to be a Soviet agent—and Philby could have reached that position—he could recommend a successor of whom the Russians approved.

So, in the early summer of 1974, a spokesman for the Fluency Committee, Stephen de Mowbray, presented himself at No. 10 Downing Street and asked to see the prime minister concerning an urgent security issue. He did not see Harold Wilson, who had recently won the general election, but had a long session with the Cabinet secretary, Sir John Hunt, now Lord Hunt of Tanworth.

Hunt was already aware of the suspicions about Hollis. A few months before, during the premiership of Edward Heath, there had been discussions about the dangers of penetration of the security services by the KGB and particularly about the possibility that previous traitors, of whom Hollis might have been one, could have insinuated others at lower level, who might now be nearing the top. It had been decided then that some independent body, to which allegations of possible treachery might be referred, was desirable. For security reasons, it was also decided that the members of such a body should be senior privy councilors. When discussing possible names, the security problems seemed so severe that it was eventually decided to have just one privy councilor, an individual of long experience, of unquestionable integrity, who should be nonpolitical. The man eventually selected was Lord Trend, Hunt's predecessor as cabinet secretary, and he agreed to be the standing privy councilor to whom allegations concerning treachery in the security services could be referred.

After his session with de Mowbray, who seemed to be convinced that Hollis had been a spy and that there had been a serious cover-up by the security services, Hunt decided that the matter should be referred to Trend. He therefore suggested this to the prime minister, Harold Wilson, who agreed to the proposal in July 1974.

When Trend began his inquiry, he did not think it likely that he could take the matter any further than the internal investigations previously carried out by the Fluency Committee and on which assessments had been made by the chiefs of MI5 and the Secret Service. While some members of the Fluency Committee were convinced of Hollis's guilt and the rest took the line that the case was not proven either way, the chiefs had decided to consider Hollis innocent unless and until further evidence arrived to change their minds. This had enabled an embarrassing situation to be shelved— permanently, it had been hoped—and had spared the expenditure of further manpower and money on it.

As I have indicated, the security officers who continued to suspect Hollis, some of them being convinced of his guilt, believe that Lord Trend was impressed by the weight of evidence they had produced. I have been assured—and reassured—that Lord Trend told them so. Furthermore, those to whom I have spoken claim that they were never told anything to the contrary. They were left under the firm impression that the Hollis case was to remain in an unproven condition because no new evidence had become available to settle the issue either way. That was, therefore, my information when I wrote the first edition of this book.

In fact, Trend took almost a whole year before coming to a decision. After interviewing all the members of the Fluency Committee except one who was overseas, he spent two days a week over several months browsing among the relevant archives at MI5 headquarters in Curzon Street. He then consulted security and Intelligence chiefs, past and present, including Sir Dick White, the former head of MI5, who had recommended Hollis as his successor there. These men all advocated their past opinion that the evidence was not strong enough definitely to incriminate Hollis, though his innocence could not definitely be proved either. Trend then decided that before writing his report he should come to a judgment that would settle the case one way or the other because there was scant likelihood that any further evidence would ever accrue.

Before Mrs. Thatcher made her parliamentary statement

about this book, it was impossible to secure any official confirmation that the Trend Inquiry had ever taken place, much less obtain any information about its contents. Since then, I have been able to consult several people who have read it. They have all confirmed that no further evidence reached Trend during his year of deliberation. I have checked their information at several crucial points. Gouzenko, for instance, has assured me that no Intelligence officer has questioned him about Hollis since 1973.

So far as the facts were concerned Trend was in no better a position than the members of the Fluency Committee had been when they had completed their inquiries by interrogating Hollis.

The case really remained—and still remains—"unproven," but such a verdict, though long established in Scotland, does not exist in English law. Trend therefore took a value judgment and decided that while he could not be certain that Hollis had not been a spy, he should be given the benefit of the doubt. Unless further evidence arrived, the security departments should assume—which they did with relief—that Hollis had not been an agent of the KGB. Trend, however, was unable to offer any other explanation of the mass of evidence that had been stacked up against Hollis.

In his report to the prime minister, Trend also stated that there was no truth in Stephen de Mowbray's contention that there had been a "cover-up" of the Hollis Affair. In the Whitehall mind, a "cover-up" is a situation in which officials withhold embarrassing information from ministers. In the mind of most people, including myself, a "cover-up" is a situation in which both officials and ministers withhold embarrassing information from the public that employs them. In this latter and more general sense, there had been a total cover-up of the Hollis Affair and of most of the other security scandals disclosed in this book.

In 1975, Stephen de Mowbray was seen by Sir John Hunt and briefed on Trend's findings, though he was not shown the report. He declined to accept them, arguing that Trend had simply followed the convenient departmental line previously taken by the heads of MI5 and the Secret Service. The Cabinet secretary assumed that de Mowbray would inform the other members of the Fluency Committee that a verdict of "not guilty" had been entered against Hollis on the departmental books. He appears not to have done so, for as I have indicated, the other members continued to believe that the Hollis case had been left unproven.

The Trend Report was so secret that very few knew of its existence. Six years later, however, following the publication of this book, it gave Mrs. Thatcher the opportunity to give Parliament and the public the impression that Hollis had been "cleared" not only by Trend but previously by his colleagues, though she was at pains to point out that his innocence could not be proved. The *Times* put the situation more accurately. "Mrs. Thatcher has now officially revealed that there were serious professional suspicions about Sir Roger Hollis which do not seem to have been dispelled but merely disposed of, as it were, by majority verdict."

Mrs. Thatcher's statement was based on a brief supplied by the Cabinet Office in conjunction with MI5. There was an essential item in it that made no sense either to the security officers who had given evidence to Trend or to me. She said,

> The case for investigating Sir Roger Hollis was based on certain leads that suggested, but did not prove, that there had been a Russian intelligence service agent at a relatively high level in British counterintelligence in the last years of the war. None of these leads identified Sir Roger or pointed specifically or wholly in his direction. Each of them could also be taken as pointing to Philby or Blunt.

Blunt left MI5 in 1945 and had no further access to secret information. Philby left the Secret Service in 1951 and had no further access to secret information. Yet readers of this book will appreciate that several of the leads that made the Fluency Committee suspicious of Hollis occurred long after those dates. In fact, it was the singular lack of success in MI5 *after* 1951 that led to the setting up of the Fluency Committee. For some of the members of that committee, the "moment of truth" regarding Hollis centered on the suspicious circumstances of Philby's defection in 1963. Hollis's strange behavior over Mitchell and Blunt followed in that year and in 1964.

I have been assured by people who must know but are anxious not to be identified that Lord Trend did not limit himself to a consideration of the evidence relating to the war years but studied the whole of it up to and including the interrogation of Hollis in 1970. So either Mrs. Thatcher was misinformed in the brief provided for her by officials, or the statement prepared for her was selective in its references to the Trend Report to provide a political opportunity for an assertion that all the evidence was almost forty years old.

A letter from Lord Trend to me dated August 12, 1981 makes it clear that he declines to be associated with the suggestion that the leads could each be attributed either to Philby or Blunt.

James Callaghan, Margaret Thatcher's predecessor as prime minister seemed to be more straightforward when, during the Parliamentary debate on the Blunt case, he said,

> Blunt is merely one part of a highly complicated case that the Security Service has spent many years and many man-hours seeking to unravel to find the truth. . . . I do not think that the matter will ever be cleared up.

He had read the Trend Report but could not have been entirely satisfied by it.

I am convinced that there is no legal evidence admissible in a British court that could be brought against Hollis, were he still alive. But the mass of circumstantial evidence remains and is not really attributable to Blunt, Philby, or to anyone else who is known.

In a television interview, Sir Harold Wilson, who had reread the Trend Report a few days beforehand, confirmed that there had been serious leakages from MI5 and that some of them could have originated from Hollis.

The Hollis Affair remains of importance and interest to the United States, and for that reason, as well as others, this book was discussed by the U.S. Senate Intelligence Committee, chaired by Sen. Malcolm Wallop, within two days of its publication.

As many American readers will be aware, certain former members of the CIA, and James Angleton in particular, had cause to suspect that the CIA had been penetrated at a relatively high level by a KGB "mole." No such "mole" has ever been identified. So when I learned the full extent of the evidence against Hollis, circumstantial though it might be, I wrote to Angleton suggesting that the mole might never have been in the CIA but in MI5, which had access to much of the American information believed to have been leaked. He declined to comment, but I think the suggestion is worthy of serious analysis, for most of the important leakages seem to have occurred during the time that Hollis was in MI5 and to have ceased after 1965, when he retired. It may also be significant that the leakages from MI5 seem to have ended after that date.

Following the Trend Inquiry, improvements in the selection of the directors general and in the recruitment of new members to both MI5 and the Secret Service have been introduced. A Committee of Five, including the chief of the defense staff, now makes the recommendation to the prime minister for the appointment of new directors general. The prime minister, particularly so in the case of Mrs. Thatcher, is in regular touch with the heads of MI5 and the Secret Service. The days when a director general could studiously avoid contact with his political masters, as Hollis did, are over. Positive vetting of members of the security services is now more stringent and more regular. Internal checks against foreign penetration have been built into both services.

An effective test of whether high-level penetration of MI5 had ceased with the departure of Hollis was provided in the autumn of 1971 by the defection in London of a KGB officer, Oleg Lyalin. It was following this defection that the government, then headed by Edward Heath, expelled 105 Soviet intelligence agents, who had been posing as diplomats and trade officials, though this number was less than half the total known to be in Britain for subversive purposes.

What has not been known is that Lyalin had been recruited by British intelligence six months prior to his defection, which took place when it did only because he was stupidly involved in a drunken driving incident and was arrested by the police. Lyalin had been due to return to Russia, and the intelligence authorities had hoped that he would continue to supply information there, but following his drunken behavior, his expulsion from the KGB was almost certain.

Nevertheless, that the Russians had not learned that Lyalin was spying for Britain was excellent evidence that no high-level Soviet agents existed inside MI5. Sir Martin Furnival

Jones had insisted that only about ten people in MI5 who needed to know about Lyalin should be told, and nobody outside, in the Civil Service, Foreign Office, or government, was informed. There is no doubt that the Russians would quickly have withdrawn or liquidated Lyalin had they known of his treachery if only because he knew the names of so many other Soviet agents. Indeed, after his defection, he was regarded as such a likely target for assassination that his trial on the driving charge was quashed, and he underwent plastic surgery to change his appearance.

The success of the massive security and intelligence operation preceding the expulsions provided further evidence that both MI5 and the Secret Service were "clean," at least in the upper levels. The director general of MI5, Sir Martin Furnival Jones, expected that the Soviet ambassador would demand to know the reasons for at least some of the expulsions, and he had detailed evidence ready against every one of the 105. The Russian ambassador made no such demand, and it was clear that he and the KGB had been taken totally by surprise. It was the view inside MI5 that such a welcome situation would not have been possible a few years earlier.

In 1974, the British security services had a major triumph, which could never have been possible had there been a spy at the top in either of the organizations. They provided the lead resulting in the arrest of Guenter Guillaume, the personal assistant to Willi Brandt, then West German chancellor. It was proved that he was a Soviet bloc agent and former officer of the East German army, infiltrated into West Germany in the monstrously deceptive guise, so favored by the KGB, of a political refugee seeking asylum. Given every opportunity to make a new life, he insinuated himself into Brandt's entourage with such success that when the full extent of his treachery was appreciated, a senior British official at NATO military headquarters exclaimed, "My God, it's all gone!" Given the slightest whiff of suspicion against such a valuable agent, whose detection was eventually to end Brandt's political career, the Russians would have found some way of withdrawing him.

Not long after his final interrogation, Sir Roger Hollis suffered a stroke but virtually recovered from it. In 1973, however, he had a further stroke that killed him at the age of sixty-seven.

His brief obituary notice in the *Times* was composed by his old colleague, Sir Dick White, who, in line of duty, had been so deeply involved in the investigations into the Soviet penetration of MI5. However impressive the evidence may seem, the mind of the ordinary citizen boggles at the idea of a chief of the British Security Service sidling off at intervals to contact some Soviet controller and receive his next instructions. But that is exactly what Blunt and Philby did for many years without detection. And, as the next section will show, there were others in similar positions.

11
Professor of the Arts
—of Treachery

Anthony Blunt, the Communist traitor who eventually became surveyor of the Queen's pictures, was one of the most damaging spies ever to operate in Britain, contrary to the common belief that, compared with Philby or Maclean, he was in the second division.

His crimes against his country, dragged out of him during hundreds of hours of taped interrogations, are such an indictment of wartime security that every effort has been made to cover them from public knowledge. Before he gave his public interviews to the *Times* and on television, this man, who had given the Russians every official secret that came his way, had been advised to use the Official Secrets Act as a means of refusing to give answers that were no longer of any security value but would have pointed to the full extent of his treachery.

The information courageously given to Parliament by Mrs. Thatcher was carefully drafted from a brief supplied by MI5 to minimize the public outrage. Mrs. Thatcher was advised to say that the government did not know exactly what information Blunt had passed to the Russians. The catch, for which the prime minister was not responsible, was in the word "exactly." The details that the security authorities could have told the government from Blunt's confessions—as the reader will be able to judge for himself—were enough to have hanged him a hundred times over, had his treachery been discovered during the war.

After long and difficult research, I have been able to piece together the major parts of Blunt's confessions and the precise, and cowardly, reason why he made them. I shall deal with this reason at some length later but can satisfy the reader's curiosity at this point by outlining the crucial event.

Late in 1963, a middle-aged American, Michael Whitney Straight, belonging to the rich and famous family, was invited to undertake a task by the White House. Having a guilt complex about his secret past, he went to FBI headquarters in Washington to clear himself on security grounds after first deciding that he would not take the post. There he confessed that he had been a Communist while in England at Cambridge University, had been recruited to the Soviet interest, and had been in touch with a Soviet intelligence officer for several years. He named the man who had recruited him as Sir Anthony Blunt, whom he knew to have been an active Soviet spy. He said that he was prepared to give evidence in court against Blunt if necessary.

The FBI passed this information to MI5, and it was only when confronted by it in April 1964 that Blunt decided to confess, after first being assured that he would never face prosecution. Blunt has said publicly that he felt free to confess because something that happened in 1964 "freed him from loyalty to his friends." The sanctimonious hypocrite confessed because, for the first time in his treacherous life, he was frightened.

I have also been able to compile a list of those named by Blunt as fellow traitors and of others to whom he gave leads, sometimes unwittingly, together with the treasonable acts they are known to have committed or of which they are suspected. They include otherwise distinguished men and women, some now dead.

In the course of these inquiries, I have uncovered many intriguing new facts about Blunt's co-conspirators, Burgess, Maclean, Philby, and the probable Fifth Man of what the KGB called the Ring of Five. This man, discovered by an unwitting lead from Blunt, has not been heard of in the context of being a Soviet agent.

Here, then, is the true, unexpurgated story of the double life and the sordid times of Anthony Blunt, art expert, one-time knight, and long-term KGB spy.

The son of a London vicar, Anthony Blunt entered Trinity College, Cambridge, in 1926 at the age of eighteen to study

French and English and also to pursue his interest in the history of art. By the time he was twenty-five, he appeared to be so talented that he was made a fellow of his college and taken on the teaching staff. In the early 1930s, Marxism became the rage among Cambridge intellectuals, and Blunt was soon attracted by its deceptively logical answers to society's injustices and economic problems.

Blunt was also attracted to another Marxist and Communist, Guy Burgess, a former Etonian who arrived at Trinity in 1930. Both were homosexuals, and Blunt found Burgess a most entertaining companion intellectually. They were fellow members of the exclusive group known as The Apostles, whose major topic of conversation was communism and its merits.

Conversion to communism and active membership of the Communist party were being openly encouraged by certain dons, like Maurice Dobb. So the very promising situation was sized up by professional intelligence officers of the Soviet Union on the lookout for talented young men likely to achieve positions of trust, where they could eventually serve as valuable spies and agents of subversion. Burgess was among the earliest to be actively recruited to the cause of what is now called the KGB. He became the second member of what was to become the Ring of Five, having been recruited by Philby, who was the first. Burgess's immediate task was to recruit others, and among those he successfully hooked into the Russian cause was Blunt.

In the course of his interrogation, Blunt described just how Burgess had gone about the recruitment:

Anthony, we must do something to counter the horrors of Nazism. We can't just sit here and talk about it. The government is pacifying Hitler, so Marxism is the only solution. I am already committed to work secretly for peace. Are you prepared to help me?

Even in those days, the Communists had latched on to the word "peace" as a euphemism for subversion, and the work was always for the Comintern. Founded in 1919, the Comintern was supposed to be an international Communist organization for securing world revolution, but it had been quickly taken over by the Kremlin as an instrument for promoting Soviet expansionist policies.

Blunt, who had been trained to become a recruiter himself, then described how it was customary to point out that the work would be undercover and dangerous—a deliberately exciting appeal to young men and women. It was only later that the recruits found that they were committed to work for Russian intelligence, usually for life, and at any sacrifice to their careers and private lives.

As Alexander Foote, who was recruited when young, recorded,

> The loyalty of a Party member lies primarily with the Party and secondarily with his country. As a result he is prepared to take enormous risks, work long hours: for little pay, and live, if necessary die, for the ideals of the party, which means, in effect, for Moscow. It is from this overriding loyalty to Party rather than to patriotism that the Russian spy system derives its strength.

After agreeing to help, Blunt had been introduced without further delay to his controller, the Soviet agent who would meet him regularly, give him his instructions, receive any information he might secure, and ensure that he remained active in the Kremlin's interest. One of the controller's first acts was, almost invariably, to offer a small payment of money—"Just for your expenses, of course." Having signed a receipt, the recruit was then firmly hooked, especially as he was also required to pass over as much information as possible in his own handwriting.

Blunt was the third member of the Ring of Five, as Moscow called the five young Cambridge men recruited as spies and all known to each other as such. Burgess and Philby were the first two, and Maclean was the fourth. Blunt still insists that he never knew the identity of the Fifth Man, though, having eventually been confronted with MI5's candidate for that doubtful distinction, as I shall describe, he agreed that one of his former close friends at Cambridge fitted the bill.

When the Ring consisted only of Burgess and Philby, its controller had been a foreigner known to them only as

"Theo." He has since been identified as Theodore Maly, a tall, rather handsome Hungarian who had been a priest but had become an atheist and a Communist while serving as a chaplain in the First World War. He had joined the Soviet intelligence service and become a Soviet citizen.

"Theo" was an "illegal," meaning a Soviet secret agent with a false passport, who operated alone under some cover, rarely, if ever, contacting the Russian embassy, where spies posing as diplomats had diplomatic immunity and were therefore known in the KGB as "legals." This use of "illegals" as controllers dated from 1927 when a raid by Special Branch police on the offices of ARCOS, the All Russian Co-operative Society, in the City of London, proved that the Russians posing as trade officials were really spies and saboteurs.

Blunt never met "Theo" because by the time he had been recruited in 1935, "Theo" had been switched to Paris and been replaced by another man called "Otto," described by Blunt as being "short, with no neck and swept-back, straight hair." "Otto," a Czech who has never been satisfactorily identified, disappeared in 1938, and Blunt told his interrogators that, for some reason, all the "illegals" operating in Europe had been recalled to Russia on Stalin's orders and are believed to have been liquidated in the great purge, along with thousands of Red Army officers. It is certain that "Theo" met his death that way, returning to Moscow knowing that he would be shot. Another agent, Otto Katz—who could not have been "Otto"—was also murdered by his employers. A few who declined to return were eventually hunted down and assassinated.

Blunt confirmed what MI5 already believed, that neither Maurice Dobb nor any other Cambridge don was involved in actual recruitment to the KGB. Their role in the case histories of the Ring of Five, which was quickly swollen to a larger number, was to promote Soviet-style Communism among the undergraduates, creating a situation that the KGB could exploit.

Soon after Blunt had been recruited, Burgess told him that he himself had been ordered to appear to have turned against Communism and to get into the mainstream of life, where he might insinuate himself into an organization where he could be of best service to "the Comintern." As Blunt confirmed to MI5, a young high-grade recruit to Soviet intelligence was—

and may still be—urged to get himself on to the staff of MI5, the Secret Service, GCHQ, the *Times*, the BBC, the Foreign Office, or the Home Office in that order of priority. As will be seen, both Blunt and Burgess fulfilled the requirement admirably, but Burgess was angry at being ordered out of university life because he loved Cambridge and wished to remain there for postgraduate work, being academically exceptionally able.

Burgess explained that as orders would have to be obeyed, he would have to hand over his role as chief talent spotter to Blunt. Blunt was to fulfill the task ably, recruiting several important spies before he himself left Cambridge for London to take up an art appointment with the Warburg Institute.

By that time, Blunt knew that Philby was an active member of the Ring, and he was able to tell his interrogators how Maclean had been netted. Some time before the spring of 1935, Philby passed on Soviet orders to Burgess instructing him without delay to recruit Donald Maclean, an ardent and overt Communist. With some emotion, Blunt recalled how he had invited Maclean to stay with him to facilitate the operation by Burgess, a fellow guest. (In his statement to the *Times*, Blunt said that he did not learn that Philby and Maclean were spies until during the war. This was either a lie or a lapse of memory.)

At the outbreak of the war in 1939, Blunt took on the more prestigious post of deputy director of the Courtauld Institute of Art in Portman Square. He had a room there, of which he was to make interesting use, though he did not live in it.

He volunteered for war service and, prompted by his Russian controller, applied to attend a five-week military intelligence course at Minley Manor, Camberley, in Surrey, and was accepted. Almost immediately, the commandant, Brig. John Shearer, received information from the War Office revealing that Blunt had a Marxist past. He was therefore rejected, as Blunt recalled, "by the same post." It has been alleged that the evidence about Blunt's links with communism came from MI5, but I am informed that there was no such information on Blunt's file in MI5. Either some friend or fellow spy had eliminated the reference, or the War Office had a source that was better informed.

Whatever the truth, Blunt was recommended for a post inside MI5 itself, which, in 1940, was having to expand rapidly and was looking for likely officers. The normal mode of entry was through personal recommendation, and the person who suggested the appointment of Blunt was only a recent recruit himself, an art dealer called Tomas Harris—the spelling of his Christian name denoting his half Spanish origin. Blunt later confirmed that Harris had known of his Marxist views and former outspoken support for communism but insisted that Tomas had never been a Soviet agent, so far as he knew. Within five years of his recruitment, when he was a university teacher, seemingly destined for an academic life, Blunt had achieved the top target set for him by "Otto"— membership of the most secret British Security Service, MI5. From the moment of his entry to the London headquarters, his new Soviet controller took command of him and worked him relentlessly in the KGB's interest until the end of the war.

The most extraordinary aspect of the Russians' recruitment of young spies was their success in intruding them into positions where they achieved access to intelligence information of the highest value. They owed much to the talent spotters, who selected young people intellectually suited and socially equipped to gain entry to sensitive government departments.

The new controller, whom Blunt knew only as "Henry," has been positively identified as Anatoli Gorski, sometimes known as Gromov and, eventually, as "Professor" Nikitin of the Moscow Institute of History. After the liquidation of the "illegals," the Russians reverted to the use of "legals," and Gorski worked from the Soviet embassy in London from 1939 to 1944.

From the start, "Henry" found that he had a star performer in "Johnson," as he called Blunt in his secret dispatches to the Center in Moscow, though Blunt himself denies ever knowing this cryptonym, which is almost certainly the truth. One of Blunt's first jobs was in the Secretariat assisting the director general of MI5, then Sir David Petrie. Important documents therefore crossed his desk, and he never failed to report on their contents or even to take them out of the office so that the Russians could photocopy them.

One of the earliest documents Blunt saw resulted in the betrayal and death of one of the very few senior Russian officials ever to have been in a position to alert the British about the Kremlin's intentions.

Before the war, there was an officer in MI5, the late Harold "Gibby" Gibson, who had been brought up as a child in Russia and been at school there prior to the Revolution. Later, he met an old school friend, a Russian who had become totally disenchanted with communism and was working in the private office of Anastas Mikoyan, the long-surviving member of the Politburo. This Russian had also been working as an MI5 source-in-place for seven years, providing information of the greatest political value to the West. Blunt confessed that in 1940—well before Russia was in the war and was, in fact, assisting Hitler through a nonaggression pact and other means, including some interchange of intelligence—he handed a copy of one of the Russian's reports to "Henry." A few weeks later, "Henry" told him that the source had been eliminated. Certainly, no further reports were received from him.

Later, for many months, Blunt was the MI5 officer in charge of the "watchers," the men and women who carried out surveillance of hostile agents. Each week, he was responsible for allotting their various tasks to them, so he had to be told of every counterespionage operation in which they were involved and just where and how they would be working. He confessed that he regularly gave all this information to the Russians so that Soviet intelligence could operate against Britain in safety. It also enabled him and his fellow traitors to meet their own Soviet contacts without fear of being seen. With a thin smile, he recalled how the Russians had warned him against overdoing this particular service, as it could so easily arouse suspicion. In fact, on that issue, he never had been suspected.

Blunt also warned the Russians that the Communist party headquarters in London was being bugged by MI5 and how it had been done. The Russians warned the party, and a frantic search of its headquarters near Covent Garden was made by party officials. This led to an inquiry in MI5 to find out whether there had been a leak there, and Blunt, as one of the people who knew about the bugs, was interrogated. He lied with coolness and charm.

One of Blunt's most damaging services to the Russians was to keep them regularly informed about the personnel in MI5, where they were and what they were doing—what is referred to professionally as "the order of battle." As a result, the entire outfit was "blown" for the whole time that he was there.

In the registry of MI5, each file on its members is labeled: "Sovbloc Green," in the case of those believed to be unknown to the KGB; "Sovbloc Amber" for those who might be known; and "Sovbloc Red" for those definitely known. As a result of Blunt's activities alone, apart from those of other spies in the organization, every member was really "Sovbloc Red" for a period of five years. This may not have been so important once Russia had been forced into the war against Germany, but when Russia became the main adversary after the war, it greatly assisted the KGB in its anti-British operations, for many of the wartime members stayed on and reached top executive positions.

In similar ways, Blunt also prejudiced many American operations and endangered their personnel because he informed the Russians about the American intelligence organization, the Office of Strategic Services, whose members worked alongside MI5 in a joint endeavor from 1942 onward.

12
Agent "Orange"

One of the MI5 agents whom Blunt confessed to have "blown" early in his career in the Security Service could hardly be more surprising either to the public or to Parliament. It was Tom Driberg, at the time a journalist on the *Daily Express*, later an MP, chairman of the Labour party, and, finally, as Lord Bradwell, a Labour peer. The true facts about Driberg, who, in his autobiography *Ruling Passions*, confirmed his compulsive homosexuality but never mentioned his life as a spy, are a startling reminder that in the world of espionage nothing is ever what it seems.

Driberg was recruited for service in MI5 when he was still a schoolboy at Lancing College, an Anglo-Catholic foundation near Worthing in Sussex. He was drawn into espionage there by the late Maxwell Knight, well known for his BBC talks on natural history. Knight was employed by MI5 as what is called an "agent runner," a person who runs a group of agents and, to avoid suspicion, stays well away from headquarters, communicating the information that his agents produce by other means. His code name was "M."

On Knight's instructions, Driberg joined the Brighton branch of the Communist party, becoming wholehearted in his overt support. He continued this at Christ Church, Oxford, and later, when he joined the *Daily Express* in 1928. His mission was to infiltrate the party and report regularly on its activities and members to MI5. Through his considerable charm and intelligence, he achieved this, becoming a close friend of Harry Pollitt, the general secretary of the Communist party, and of Douglas Springhall, leader of the Young Communist League, who was eventually convicted of espionage for the Soviet Union in 1943.

In 1941, reports from an outside MI5 agent crossed the desk of Anthony Blunt, who knew the agent only by the code name "M8." As Blunt later confessed, he passed a copy of one of these reports to "Henry" because it concerned information about a secret airplane. Driberg, alias "M8," then writing for the *Daily Express* as "William Hickey," believed the information to have come from Lord Beaverbrook, the minister of aircraft production. His report also revealed that the Communist party knew about the machine and that this must surely be dangerous.

Blunt was asked by "Henry" to discover the identity of "M8," but after trying for six months, he failed. "Henry" then informed him that Soviet intelligence had discovered that "M8" was Driberg. With unusual clumsiness, the Russians immediately alerted Harry Pollitt, who summarily expelled "M8" from the party. In his autobiography, Driberg records how he was shattered when the news was conveyed to him, without any reason, by another Fleet Street comrade. As a good agent should, he continued to protest until he died that he never discovered why he had been thrown out, claiming that friends like Springhall were so embarrassed by the event that their lips were sealed.

Blunt told his MI5 interrogators in 1964 that the mode of Driberg's expulsion had infuriated him because it had touched off another internal inquiry in MI5, during which he was closely questioned, though he felt sure that he had managed to brazen his way through by lying persuasively. Blunt had told "Henry" that Pollitt should have been instructed to wait for a decent interval to elapse and then to have found some excuse for parting close company with Driberg. (Though Pollitt never knew it, there was another MI5 agent much closer to him in the form of a woman who had been recruited by Maxwell Knight as a school girl!)

Driberg's value to MI5 soared when he entered Parliament and was able to report, with steadily increasing penetration, on the activities of other members, both inside and outside the House of Commons. But the further exploits of this extraordinary character in the field of espionage form a story in themselves and, as they do not involve Blunt, will be reserved for chapter 21.

In Blunt's uninformative, and sometimes misleading, pub-

lic confession to the *Times*, he stressed the work that he did
for MI5 in running "a small subsection connected with
neutral diplomatic missions." The truth about his efforts there
will also surprise even those who have good reason to consider themselves knowledgeable about the Ring of Five.

The neutral countries, which continued to maintain embassies in London during the war, included not only genuine
neutrals, like Sweden and Switzerland, but pro-Nazi Spain
and Portugal as well as, during the early months, the pro-
British United States. Under wartime regulations MI5 had
access to their diplomatic bags and made full use of it,
devising ingenious ways of releasing the seals and refurbishing
them. Their diplomatic and intelligence radio traffic was also
carefully monitored. Blunt, who also dealt with signals intelligence (Sigint), had access to all the items of security and
intelligence interest relevant to his work. As he told his
interrogators repeatedly and without remorse, "You may assume that if I came across anything which could be remotely
of interest to the Russians, I passed it on." Among such
material were the names of neutral diplomats with character
weaknesses, or a liking for money, who might be recruited by
the Soviet Union as spies, as some of them were.

In his extremely valuable service to the Russians, Blunt
was assisted day by day by none other than the man who had
recruited him, Guy Burgess, whose main activities in this
field have been covered up with astonishing success, considering the reams that have been written about him.

It had been repeatedly stated that Blunt tried to get
Burgess into MI5 and failed. The truth is that Burgess joined
MI5 as a wartime supernumerary around about the same
time as Blunt did in 1940. Having renounced his overt
communism and behaved as though he was right wing, as
Philby had, he had been recruited in good faith through his
friendship with Sir Joseph Ball, a director of the Conservative
Research Department, who was an influential figure behind
the scenes in Whitehall. As luck always seemed to have it for
British traitors, Ball became temporarily involved with the
reorganization of the Security Service after the departure of
Sir Vernon Kell in the summer of 1940. Burgess used this
friendly contact to infiltrate his way into MI5.

Like Maxwell Knight, who had recruited Driberg and

several others, Burgess was an agent-runner with the code name "Orange," operating a string of sources outside and rarely visiting MI5 headquarters. So, though somewhat on the periphery, he had fulfilled the Russians' top-priority requirement, and his various wartime jobs in the BBC and the Foreign Office were largely cover for his work for MI5.

Whether by coincidence or clever design, the agents whom Burgess was required to run were mainly recruited from the embassies of the neutral countries represented in London. This meant that he had to pass the information he received from them to Blunt, who was the "head agent" inside MI5 headquarters for intelligence exercises penetrating the neutral embassies. This was reckoned to be a highly satisfactory arrangement by MI5 because the two were well known to be close friends and their regular meetings could arouse nobody's suspicions. And during their evening meetings at Blunt's room in the Courtauld Institute or elsewhere, Burgess could pass on his agents' reports to Blunt, who could take them to headquarters the following morning. As will be seen, it was an even more satisfactory arrangement for the KGB.

While intellectually scintillating, Guy Burgess was disheveled, riotous in his behavior, frequently drunk, and a pouncing homosexual, much given to shocking strangers, as well as friends, by his remarks. "I can never travel comfortably by train because I am always feeling that I ought to be having the engine driver" was the type of comment with which he sought to attract attention to himself. So how could such an outrageous character ever be a spy for anybody?

In fact, he was a highly successful spy both for MI5 and the KGB. Both regarded his behavior as excellent cover on the principle that anyone who talked and acted so recklessly could not possibly be a spy. Burgess could be discreet when it was essential to be so, as he had already shown by useful work as a freelance supplier of information about Nazi Germany to the Secret Service before the outbreak of war. He also had access to a remarkable range of influential and talkative contacts, including politicians.

Burgess recruited valuable agents for MI5 from the neutral embassies, the Swedish, Swiss, and Spanish in particular, and was not without success from the U.S. diplomatic missions.

While his prime loyalty was always to the KGB, he had no objection to also helping MI5 once Russia was in the war and it served the Kremlin's interests.

From the start, the KGB knew all about Burgess's work for MI5, but MI5 never got wind of his much *greater* effort for the KGB until he defected in 1951. There was no suspect file on Burgess in the records of MI5, only an account of his good work there. This, of course, was a major reason why the top management of MI5 was so determined to stop Burgess from ever returning to Britain. They did not want it known that he had been another Soviet spy inside the security and intelligence organizations.

As Blunt explained with some relish, his official MI5 partnership with Burgess suited them both perfectly for their really important assignments. Twice a week, Blunt would take out an attaché case of specially selected secret documents as "homework," which was permitted during the war when pressure of work was so great and transport difficulties were being created by the blitz. He took his spoils to his room at the Courtauld Institute, and there Burgess contributed voluminous reports on his own activities. One of them then handed over the suitcase to "Henry," or some other Soviet officer, at a prearranged point. They were taken to the Russian embassy in Kensington Palace Gardens, photographed, and returned in time for Blunt to take them back to the office next morning.

Blunt told his interrogators how he had been almost caught by a policeman who demanded to see inside his case while he was on the way to a meeting with "Henry." The police were making a search in connection with some criminal matter, but by giving a certain telephone number, Blunt managed to convince the constable that he worked for MI5. It had been a frightening experience, for he would have had difficulty, if reported to his employers, in explaining away some of the documents as "homework."

The Russians became so concerned about the enormous amount of documentary material that Blunt and Burgess were providing, particularly after the close brush with the police, that "Henry" provided them with special cameras so that they could photograph the documents in miniature and hand over only the cassettes. They did this for a while at the

Courtauld Institute until they found themselves so short of sleep that they rebelled and told the Russians that they were reverting to the old system.

Blunt could remember only one other occasion when Burgess had refused to obey Soviet orders. Though his Russian masters knew that Burgess was a homosexual, they were keen for him to marry a young woman who had high-level social political connections, but so peculiar were her sexual requirements that even Burgess found them "too wildly extravagant." To Burgess's amusement, the lady eventually became the wife of an eminent politician.

Burgess's notable work for MI5 against the Germans explains why he was never suspected as a spy, any more than Blunt was, until he defected. It also accounts for his close social connection with the then deputy director of MI5, Guy Liddell, and the freedom of their conversational exchanges. This has been held against Liddell by people who did not know that Burgess was an MI5 agent.

Referring to Liddell, Blunt recalled how he would occasionally remark to him, when dealing with an interesting document in the office, "What a pity we can't give this to the Russians." Then he would laugh inwardly because that was exactly what he would shortly be doing. When asked if he had ever experienced any pangs of conscience about being a traitor to his own country, all Blunt would admit was that he and Burgess "felt better about things" once the Russians were in the war.

As with Klaus Fuchs, the atomic spy, who thought it was unforgiveable that the Russians were not being told British-American atomic secrets, Blunt considered it irrelevant that the Russians declined to tell their allies anything at all. Alexander Foote, the Briton who did so much valuable espionage work for Russia as a member of the Swiss Lucy Ring and later defected back to Britain in 1947 when he found his Soviet masters to be so ungrateful, told MI5 that on strict orders from the Moscow Center, any information of no value to Russia was to be destroyed and on no account should be passed to any other ally.

This attitude was particularly heinous in view of what is almost certainly the truth about the Lucy Ring, though it has never been officially revealed. The Lucy Ring consisted of three main agents, which is why the Swiss knew it as "*Rote*

Drei" (Red Three). Foote was the radio operator, Alexander Rado, a Hungarian, was the nominal chief, and the main informant was Rudolf Roessler, a Bavarian exiled to Switzerland because of his anti-Nazi stance. Roessler's code name was "Lucy," and because his contribution was of such outstanding importance in the Red Army's defeat of Germany, the ring has been called after him. Roessler provided continuing details of the German battle order, troop movements, and tactical plans from before the Nazi attack on Russia in June 1941 until November 1943.

Roessler never revealed his source, though Foote, Rado, and others since were led to believe that it came from about ten dissident German officers in the high command structure. But it is inconceivable that such a group would have been prepared to see their own forces destroyed and their country invaded and demolished by Russia, however much they hated Hitler. Even more unlikely is the possibility that in securing and transmitting such a mass of information to Roessler over more than two years, they would not have been detected and caught. There is only one credible source of the information—the British code-breaking center at Bletchley Park in Buckinghamshire which, through the Counter-Intelligence operation code named "Ultra," was in continuous receipt of Germany's war plans and intentions. Recently, I have secured confirmation of this from secret intelligence sources.

It was in Britain's interests to help the Russians to defeat the German onslaught, but at the same time it was essential that the fact that Bletchley was breaking the German codes produced by an "unbreakable" cypher machine should never leak. An official channel was established whereby some of this information was relayed to Moscow after it had been doctored to look as though it had been obtained from spies and other more conventional means. With the war on the Russian front being waged on such a scale, so much information needed to be passed on almost daily that this could not be done without arousing Soviet suspicions of a massive code break, and there was the further problem that the Russians tended to disbelieve it, especially after one batch proved to be incorrect. With insight, it was argued that the Russians would be much more likely to accept the information and act on it if it came from their own trusted sources. My information is that most of it was therefore relayed to Roessler through intermediaries, probably located in the British diplomatic offices in Switzerland, and he gave the impression that he was receiving it directly from German sources, which were, in fact, mythical. The Russians may well have seen through the subterfuge because of the information being given to them surreptitiously from Bletchley by John Cairncross and possibly by other Soviet spies there, as I shall describe in chapter 16.

Under pressure from Germany, the Swiss were driven to break up the Lucy Ring in November 1943, but by that time the German defeat in Russia was assured. Roessler, who died in 1962, continued to refuse to reveal his sources, and when Foote was questioned by British intelligence in 1947, he told the story of the nest of German traitors in the high command, which he still believed.

It has been suggested that Foote was really a British agent working for the Russians as a double, but I can find no evidence for this. Throughout the war, he failed to pass any intelligence to Britain, including the fact that Ursula Beurton had been transferred to Oxford in 1940.

The fate of Alexander Rado, head of the Lucy Ring, illustrates very dramatically the totally selfish attitude of the Russians. He was later censured, among other "crimes," for passing to Britain information about Hitler's V2 rockets, which were being developed to destroy London. This information, which Rado had somehow obtained from the rocket station at Peenemunde, was of no value to Russia because of the short range of the V2, but the Kremlin disapproved of giving Britain any assistance that would help to lessen the bombardment of London.

After the Lucy Ring was shut down by the Swiss authorities, Rado found his way to Paris and approached the Russian embassy there for further work. He was flown to Cairo en route for Moscow, and fearing that he would be blamed for the closure of the ring rather than praised for its previous successes, he toyed with the idea of defecting to Britain. A British security officer in Cairo, Maurice Oldfield, later to become a most able head of the Secret Service, talked with him and telegraphed Secret Service headquarters in London to seek guidance. Once again, through the luck that seemed to favor the KGB, the telegram was handled by Philby, who, after taking instruction from his Soviet controller, instructed

Oldfield to ensure that Rado went on to Moscow. There he was awarded ten years' imprisonment for his magnificent efforts, after a secret "trial."

After serving his sentence, he moved to Budapest, where he became chairman of the Hungarian Geographical Society, cartography, in which he was genuinely expert, having been his cover in Switzerland. He wrote his memoirs but judiciously omitted mention of his experiences in the Soviet labor camp.

Blunt, Fuchs, and others like them were totally unmoved by the sacrifices made by British sailors and seamen in convoying war material to Russia, with great loss of ships and life. There is reason to believe that Blunt knew of the circumstances surrounding the loss of H.M.S. *Edinburgh*, a cruiser that had been crippled while on convoy duty in Russia. On the eve of May Day 1942, two powerful Russian destroyers, which had been part of the escort sent out from the Kola Inlet, returned to harbor pleading fuel shortage. Instead of returning, they remained in harbor over the May Day celebrations, during which time German destroyers found the *Edinburgh* and torpedoed her. I am told that Blunt was not prepared to be moved by any such events if they implied criticism of his beloved Russia.

Blunt had left MI5 before it received the details of the wartime KGB radio messages that American cypher experts were later able to decode. One of them, from the Center in Moscow, had been addressed to the Polish Communist underground movement, warning its members to lie low, as the Red Army had been instructed to halt its offensive on Warsaw to give the retreating Germans time to clean up the Jews and other undesirable Poles there. It is considered unlikely by those who interrogated Blunt that this message would have disconcerted him.

13
The "Klatt" Affair

Among the mass of information that Blunt gave to the Russians during the latter part of the war were details of the ultrasecret plans for "Fortitude," the code name for the operation to deceive the Germans into believing that the main Allied invasion would be in the Pas-de-Calais area, not in Normandy. This could have been extremely dangerous and could have cost thousands of lives, for at that stage in 1944, the Russians did not want the war to end quickly. Having the Germans on the run, they wanted to occupy as much of Europe as possible so that they could communize it. For some reason, the Russians chose not to inform the Germans of the British-American deception plans, or if they did, they were not believed.

Blunt managed to fool all his colleagues in MI5 by his imperturbable manner when seemingly in difficulties, and I have discovered only one self-incriminating remark prior to his confession. Col. T. A. Robertson recalled that when Blunt left the service in 1945 he said to him, "Well, it's given me great pleasure to pass on the names of every MI5 officer to the Russians." Robertson, who says that he knew that Blunt was a Communist and made no secret of it, passed on the information to those who should have taken note of it, but nothing was entered in Blunt's file.

It may well be asked why, when Blunt was in such a valuable position, the KGB permitted him to leave MI5 and return to the art-history world where his value would be minimal. The KGB does not let its agents off the hook out of gratitude, and it could easily have blackmailed Blunt into remaining in MI5 where there was a permanent position open to him with inevitable promotion. It is possible that the

Russians thought that there might be some value in having an agent closely connected with the royal household, for Blunt also became surveyor of the King's pictures for George VI on leaving MI5. But Blunt told his interrogators that he inclined to their opinion that the Russians felt he could be spared from MI5 because they had an alternative agent in place there.

Before I end my survey of Blunt's activities inside MI5, there is one incident, to which he confessed, that is worthy of record because it demonstrates the incredible lengths to which the Russians will go with deception and false information to achieve a long-term objective, whatever the cost in human life and suffering. Blunt confessed that soon after Russia was attacked in 1941, while he was dealing with signals intelligence in MI5, he betrayed a highly secret interception operation known by the code name "Klatt" because a Jewish intelligence agent called Klatt was believed to be involved in it.

The British radio-interception organization (now known as GCHQ, Government Communications Headquarters) had detected a regular stream of radio messages emanating from Sofia, the capital of Bulgaria, which had allied itself with Nazi Germany, and had managed to decipher them. It turned out to be information about Russia's forces and strategic plans for their use, which was being sent from Sofia, where Klatt was based, to the headquarters of the German Secret Service, the Abwehr, in Berlin. Furthermore, the British were able to pinpoint the Russian source of this information—a secret transmitter operating near Kuibyshev, on the Volga, where the KGB Intelligence Center had been evacuated when the fall of Moscow seemed imminent.

As the "Klatt" traffic continued to reach the Abwehr daily, the British could not understand why the KGB was failing to track down the transmitter and silence it. It transpired that an attempt by the Red Army General Timoshenko to retake the key town of Kharkov in May 1942 had been defeated by the Germans using "Klatt" information. The battle had cost the Russians 100,000 men and hundreds of tanks and guns.

As the "Klatt" traffic continued, MI5 reluctantly decided that it must be part of some gigantic double-cross system, which the Russians were using deliberately, staggering though the resulting losses had been. This view was still held when "Klatt" information led to the destruction by the Germans of a Russian convoy in the Black Sea. The only explanation MI5 could find was that "Klatt" was a double agent, ostensibly working for the German Abwehr but really operating in the interests of the Russians, who were providing what is known in the disinformation game as "chicken feed" for a greater purpose.

The riddle seems to have been solved near the end of the war by the Allied capture of a White Russian called General Turkhul, who had been a prewar agent of the British Secret Service in Paris. He admitted that after France fell in 1940, he had disappeared and worked for the Germans, becoming the head of a radio intelligence system with a branch in Sofia responsible for the "Klatt" traffic. The Germans believed that Turkhul, who had been a friend of Himmler before the war—hence his use by the British then—had Russian contacts through whom he was securing his marvelous information about Soviet battle dispositions and intentions. Turkhul told his Allied interrogators that indeed he had such contacts but only because he was, and always had been, primarily a Soviet agent. The Russians had deliberately been feeding him with information for onward transmission to Berlin. The Oriental reasoning behind this, Turkhul explained, centered on an army, said to total about a million troops, that had been recruited by another Russian General, Andrei Vlassov, who genuinely loathed the Stalin regime and was determined to help the Germans overthrow it.

Vlassov, one of the younger Red Army generals, had been captured by the Germans when the Soviet Shock Army, which he commanded, was defeated in its defense of Moscow. He volunteered to raise a Russian Army of Liberation from Red Army deserters and prisoners of war and, after some resistance from the Nazi leadership, was permitted to do so, operating from a base near Berlin. Until Hitler objected personally, there was a plan to set up a Russian government in exile, with Vlassov as a kind of de Gaulle.

His propaganda squads, operating near the front line, secured thousands of deserters, and the Germans equipped and trained the Army of Liberation for eventual use on the Russian front. Because of this army's size and success in securing deserters, Turkhul said that Stalin greatly feared the effect it might have if it appeared flying what would look like freedom's flag. Stalin was therefore pathologically determined to do anything, at any cost, to prevent its use and had instructed the KGB accordingly.

As the prime part of the deception, Turkhul had to convince Himmler and the German high command that Vlassov and his troops would suddenly change sides and fight with the Russians if ever they were taken to the Eastern front. He claimed to have information that Vlassov had been secretly in touch with the Kremlin to this effect.

The wonderfully accurate information that Turkhul continued to send to the Abwehr had been calculated to strengthen his credibility with Himmler and, through him, with Hitler. As Turkhul explained it, the deception, costly though it had been, had paid rich dividends. The Vlassov army was certainly never used on the Russian front proper, a portion of it, only, being deployed in the last-ditch fighting in Austria.

Previously, following false information sent over "Klatt" after the Russian defeat at Kharkov, the Germans were led to believe that the Red Army was finished, and they pushed on to Stalingrad, which, Hitler insisted, had to be taken. To capture the city, all the Germans had were two Rumanian armies, one Italian, one Hungarian, and their own Sixth Army. The Russians knew this from their own radio-intelligence network operating in Switzerland, the Lucy Ring. To combat the overstretched Nazi forces, the Russian high command had mustered thirteen Soviet armies.

In November, the Russians attacked at the junction of the German army and the Rumanians. The Rumanians were crushed, the Italians and Hungarians fled the field, and the German Sixth Army was encircled and destroyed. At that moment, the Vlassov army might conceivably have turned the scale for the Germans, Turkhul believed. It is certain that Hitler forbade its use on the Russian front, and while this may have been partly due to his racial prejudices, the disinformation he had received concerning its loyalty might well have been a potent factor.

Vlassov was eventually captured by the Russians and, along with the other Red Army generals who had joined him and were handed over to Stalin under the Yalta Agreement, was executed.

Blunt eventually provided independent proof that "Klatt"

had been a double-cross. He admitted that he had handed
the deciphered "Klatt" traffic to "Henry" for a few weeks but
had then been told not to bother with it any more because
Moscow knew all about it. From that date, Blunt himself had
assumed that the operation was a Soviet double-cross because
the "Klatt" traffic out of Sofia to Berlin continued until the
battle for Stalingrad.

Such sacrificial "chicken feed" for the long-term objective
is not unprecedented in Soviet intelligence. I have evidence
of an occasion when the KGB permitted the Germans to sink
a heavily laden Russian troopship to establish the credibility
of one valuable agent who had given them the necessary
information.

The KGB defines disinformation as the use of misinformation to confuse an adversary and, eventually, to make it do
the Kremlin's will. It was considered to have worked so
effectively during the war that its use was expanded afterward, a whole new Disinformation Department being created inside the KGB. The defector Golitsin revealed how
Alexsandr Shelepin, in particular, laid stress on it while he
was the KGB chairman between 1959 and 1961.

Golitsin said that in 1959 the Politburo had taken a consensus decision that because the risks of a nuclear exchange were
unacceptable, the Communist aims should be achieved by
other means if possible. Shelepin was asked to report on how
the KGB could assist and called a meeting of about two
thousand of his chief operators from all over the world. He
listened to their suggestions over several days, told them that
he would consider their ideas for six months, then formulate a
policy statement for the Politburo.

In his statement, Shelepin told the Politburo that while the
KGB was an elite force, it could be used more effectively if
disinformation and disruption were given prime priority. The
Politburo accepted his suggestions and ordered that the KGB
should concentrate on discrediting the Western nations by
spreading falsehoods, deceptions, and confusion, a campaign
in which the penetration and discrediting of Western intelligence services would be crucial. The media, fellow travelers,
and agents of influence of "liberal" bent were to be used to
the maximum extent to spread the false propaganda, which is
designed to undermine confidence in the Western nations'
own leadership and mode of government.

This policy has been so successful that, to quote James Angleton:

The myriad strategems, deceptions, artifices and all the other devices of disinformation, which the Soviet Bloc and its co-ordinated Intelligence services use to confuse and split the West have confronted our policy makers with an ever-fluid landscape, where fact and illusion merge—a kind of wilderness of mirrors, where honest statesmen are finding it increasingly difficult to separate the facts of Soviet actions from the illusion of Soviet rhetoric.

14
"The Most Ingenious
of Routes"

Athony Blunt had no further access to secret documents after he left MI5 in 1945 to become director of the Courtauld Institute and surveyor of the king's pictures. He did, however, remain in close touch with Guy Liddell, the deputy director of MI5, who, having no knowledge of his treachery, shared interesting MI5 gossip with him.

Blunt assured his interrogators that he had not given the Russians any information that may have come his way. His main controller, "Henry," had left London in 1944 to follow Donald Maclean to Washington so that he could mastermind his espionage effort in the British embassy and in the U.S. Atomic Energy Commission there. Working under the name of Anatoli Gromov and posing as a first secretary in the Soviet embassy in Washington, "Henry" controlled other KGB agents, including Elizabeth Bentley, an American who later defected to the FBI. Blunt insisted that "Henry's" successor, since identified as a KGB officer called Boris Krotov, left him alone after he departed from MI5.

Krotov, however, continued to run Burgess, with whom Blunt remained on the closest terms, though denying any homosexual relationship with him. So it is virtually certain that Blunt told Burgess anything concerning MI5 that he might have gathered and that it was duly reported to Krotov.

When he was exposed, Blunt denied publicly that he had done any spying after 1945, but much depends on the definition of that activity. Spies cannot function effectively in a foreign land without home-grown assistants to do routine work like finding safe houses, organizing dead drops, serving as paymasters, and so on. Such assistants are every bit as treacherous as the active spies, and under repeated cross-examination, Blunt eventually admitted to MI5 that he had continued to serve in this capacity.

He described, for instance, how he had emptied a dead-letter box under a tree on a common in the East End of London where Burgess had left information and where he found a pile of money left for Burgess by the KGB. He recalled how, when Burgess came back from Washington in 1951, having organized his return to Britain "in disgrace" so that he could convince Maclean that the net around him was almost closed, he met Guy off the *Queen Mary* at his request. Blunt agreed that Burgess's decision to travel by sea rather than by air suggested that at that stage there was no sense of urgency and that he and Philby must have known that Maclean was in no danger of immediate detention for inter-rogation.

Burgess then told him of the purpose of his return. Sitting at his Secret Service desk in the British embassy in Washington, Philby had been informed by secret telegram that Maclean was, with near certainty, the prime suspect concerning dangerous leakages of secret diplomatic information from that very embassy between 1944 and 1948. By that time, in 1951, Maclean was back in the Foreign Office in London, working as head of the American desk, but Philby had to be told because he was Britain's chief liaison man with the FBI and the CIA, which had a major interest in the case as the leakages involved messages between Churchill and President Truman.

Though Burgess was personally out of touch with any Soviet controller in London because he had been based in Washington, he knew exactly how to reestablish contact in order to secure final instructions for Maclean's flight to Russia if, as seemed certain, this became necessary.

The Russian intelligence officer in London who took command of the situation was Yuri Modin, a Soviet embassy official who for a time had controlled the Ring of Five under the code name "Peter." Modin was a highly experienced KGB man whom I have already mentioned as having organized the defection of Philby from Beirut in 1963.

Blunt described how he had remained in close touch with

Burgess during the crucial days before the sensational defection and how the surveyor of the King's pictures and professor of the history of art, as Blunt had become, had been given an arrangement for meeting Modin in case that proved to be necessary for his own safety.

According to Andrew Boyle in his book *The Climate of Treason*, Blunt played an essential role in the escape of Maclean—and of Burgess who fled with him—by warning them of the precise date on which MI5 planned to interrogate Maclean and break him. Blunt has publicly denied this and, according to my sources, he was then telling the truth. Blunt had no access to such extremely secret information, which would be tightly held, even by the imprudent Guy Liddell.

It is generally believed that the final warning, with the precise date fixed for the interrogation, also came from Philby, who heard of it in Washington and managed to get a message through to Burgess in London by telephone or by coded cable. In Mrs. Thatcher's statement to Parliament about the Blunt Affair in 1979, she said, "It was Philby who warned Burgess to tell Maclean that he was about to be interrogated." Previously, in *My Silent War*, Philby had told a story of how he had got a panic message through to Burgess in the form of a letter warning him that if he "did not act at once," he would have to send the car he had left behind in Washington to the scrap heap. This could well be KGB disinformation inserted into the book to support the fiction that Philby had been the source of the final warning. Clearly, it would have been simpler and more certain for the Soviet officer in London, Modin, who was in close touch with Burgess, to have given him any information originating from Philby in Washington. As will be seen, a letter would have been far too slow and uncertain.

There seems to be no firm evidence in the security services' records, or anywhere else, that Philby was ever told the precise date set for Maclean's interrogation. He certainly did not pass it on to the CIA or the FBI, where officers complained of being kept in the dark, and he would have been wise to have done so to appear to be about his proper business. As I have indicated, there was an alternative source nearer at hand—the Soviet penetration agent inside MI5, who could have warned his Soviet controller in London, who, in turn, could have told Burgess through Modin.

This is also the independent view of George Carver, a former senior officer of the CIA, as given to myself and to Dr. Christopher Andrew, of Corpus Christi College, Cambridge, who is conducting research into certain aspects of the British intelligence services. Referring to the events of May 25, 1951, Mr. Carver points out that at roughly ten A.M., British time, possibly a little earlier, there was a meeting at which Herbert Morrison, then foreign secretary, signed a paper authorizing MI5 to pick up Maclean for interrogation by Authur Martin, the case-officer. The evidence is strong that between ten and eleven A.M. Burgess received a telephone call or a visit that changed his whole pattern of activity. He had risen in his usually leisurely style, as witnessed by his flat mate Jack Hewitt, and was drinking his tea when Hewitt left for work shortly after nine A.M. Shortly before ten A.M., he was making normal social calls connected with a holiday he was hoping to take in Europe with another homosexual friend. It would seem certain that he would have read his morning mail by that time, so the information that alerted him had not come by letter. He started rushing around, securing a large sum in cash, buying a suitcase and clothes, and renting a car. That evening, he and Maclean left for France, hurriedly canceling engagements that they had clearly expected to keep in the following week. Carver contends that the timing does not allow for a cable about the coming interrogation to have been sent to Philby in Washington from the Foreign Office in London and for Philby to have then telephoned Burgess with the news, especially in view of the five-hour time difference between London and Washington. It would have been six A.M. in Washington when Burgess received his warning, and it is extremely unlikely that, if a message had been sent by the Foreign Office to Philby's office, he could have received it so early.

Carver also believes that it is most unlikely that if any notification of Maclean's impending interrogation was to be sent to Philby to pass on to the FBI and the CIA, it would have been dispatched before Morrison signed the necessary paper. Morrison might have decided to delay the issue, for there was argument between MI5 and the Foreign Office on the timing of the interrogation, and the Americans would then have been misinformed. Carver maintained "There just isn't time for a cable to go to Washington and action to be taken in the hour that elapsed between Morrison signing his name and Burgess getting the alert."

It seems to Carver, as it seems to me and to certain MI5 officers, that someone in the small circle in London who knew of the interrogation decision warned Burgess either directly or through the medium of a Soviet intelligence officer.

My thought has always been that the sequence of events on that day alone certainly raised the possibility that there was another person in the net who presumptively has not been discovered to this day, who occupied a very senior position, possibly in the Secret Service, but more likely in MI5.

The MI5 representative at the meeting with Morrison, whoever he was, could have been back at MI5 headquarters with the news within fifteen minutes. The headquarters in Curzon Street was only a few minutes' walk from Burgess's flat, where a note could have been delivered or a personal call made, the telephone being an unlikely and unsafe means. Of those in MI5 headquarters who had to be told of the outcome of the meeting, Hollis was certainly one.

A dramatic description, redolent of a spy thriller, of just how Burgess had imparted the final news to Maclean was given to MI5 by Blunt. Burgess was facing dismissal from the Foreign Office for his more than usually outrageous behavior in Washington, which he had contrived in part to engineer his expulsion to London. Nevertheless, though officially on leave, he reported to the Foreign Office in Whitehall from time to time and breezed into Maclean's office. Well-versed from experience in the tricks of the counterintelligence trade, he either guessed that the office had been bugged or had been told so. Without saying a word, he placed a written message in front of Maclean warning him of his peril and giving the time and place of a rendezvous. Maclean read it without even an expletive.

On his way out, Burgess noticed that two men were waiting in the corridor and one of them was foolish enough to

attempt to follow him. He realized that the man must be an
MI5 watcher, and this was the first observable evidence that
Maclean was under close surveillance, information that Burgess then passed on to his Foreign Office friend at the earliest
opportunity.

Stories that the MI5 watchers were so inexpert that Maclean
spotted them early and that their car even bumped into
Maclean's taxi are untrue. They were manufactured by the
KGB to denigrate MI5, being put on record in the book on
Guy Burgess that Tom Driberg wrote after visiting the former
spy in Moscow with KGB approval. The watchers are usually
superbly efficient, as witness the fact that while the security
authorities have often been required to enter accommodation
surreptitiously, they have never been caught in the act.

During his interrogation by MI5, Blunt resolved the mystery of why Burgess had defected, too, when it had been
intended that only Maclean should go. When Philby learned
that MI5 was almost convinced that the spy known in KGB
radio traffic as "Homer" was Maclean, he immediately alerted
his Soviet controller in Washington, with whom he was in
regular contact through meetings or dead drops. The KGB in
London was duly warned, but it faced a problem in contacting
Maclean. It knew, or could surmise, that Maclean would be
under close surveillance with the precise purpose of catching
him in contact with a Soviet intelligence officer, for that
would be evidence enough to warrant his immediate interrogation. The KGB might have been advised by its MI5 source
that Maclean was not under surveillance while at his home in
Surrey, but it could never be sure that such a restriction
would not be lifted as the case moved toward its climax.
Some intermediary with a reasonable excuse for contacting
Maclean was therefore necessary, and of those who knew of
Maclean's treachery, Burgess was best fitted because he had
access to him in the Foreign Office. The decision that Burgess should be used was not taken by Philby but by the KGB
officers concerned, who then told Philby what to do.

There was also an intractable problem for which Burgess's
services were regarded as essential, as eventually they proved
to be. Knowing the state of Maclean's mind after two years of
being aware that his cryptonym had been deciphered in the
KGB traffic and that his eventual exposure was likely, there
was grave doubt concerning his reaction to being ordered to

defect. His wife, on whom he felt dependent, was close to confinement. He had never been inside Russia, and the prospect of going there, friendless and unable to speak the language, could hardly be appealing. He also knew what had happened to "Otto," "Theo," and other loyal Soviet spies who had been called to Moscow in a hurry. They had been executed on Stalin's orders, and in 1951 Stalin was still in control.

The need for someone to explain at length to Maclean the absolute necessity for his defection was essential—in the interests of the Soviet cause as well as in his own. Burgess, the old friend who had recruited him, was the obvious choice. It has been said that Maclean and Burgess were never close friends, and it was true that in the later years they had not seen much of each other because they had been in different countries. But one of Burgess's former acquaintances, Eric Kessler, testified to MI5 that Burgess once told him, "I have such a friend in Donald Maclean that if I were ever in great difficulties, financial, for instance, he would go out of his way, forget his family even, to help me."

Blunt told MI5 that he believed that rather than defect Maclean could well have decided to be a martyr, bragging about his own exploits to show his contempt for the Establishment. While he would probably have tried to protect his friends, Blunt had little doubt that he could easily have been driven to confess all. This, Blunt believed, was also the view of Burgess and of Philby.

It has been suggested that the KGB behaved unprofessionally in sending Burgess to warn Maclean because it effectively ended Philby's career as a spy. But, in fact, the Soviet fears proved to be amply justified. Maclean was most reluctant to defect when Burgess talked to him. Acting on instructions, Burgess underlined the danger to all that they had striven for if he insisted on remaining to face interrogation. It is thought likely that Burgess was told to hint at the dangers of some violent action by the KGB if Maclean refused to obey orders and risked the destruction of an espionage and subversion apparatus built up over so many years.

Maclean's reaction was to blame Burgess for his terrible situation. "You got me into this mess, Guy, you damn well get me out of it." Eventually, he agreed to go to Moscow only if

Burgess would accompany him and remain there with him, at least until his wife was able to join him.

This prospect had as much appeal for Burgess as it had for Maclean. Burgess discussed it with Modin, who referred it back to the Center where the consequences were all too clear. The defection of Burgess would inevitably focus suspicion on both Philby and Blunt.

Some writers have even suggested that Philby, who was still in place and likely to be of continuing high value to the KGB, was deliberately sacrificed because, for reasons still unknown, it was essential to get Maclean away. It is much more likely that Philby was put at risk only because there was no alternative short of assassinating Maclean. Had Maclean broken under interrogation, he would have blown Philby, the other members of the Ring of Five, and possibly the suspected high-level "mole" in MI5, had he known his identity.

When Modin learned the date of the proposed interrogation, the Center realized that the escape plan had to be put into effect without delay, and to get Maclean away it was prepared to sacrifice both Burgess and Philby. Burgess himself could be spared because he was about to be fired from the Foreign Office and had no hope of reappointment to MI5 after his scandalous behavior in Washington. Philby was still most valuable and had every prospect of becoming more so, but as he was considered to be highly professional, there was every chance that he might bluff his way through any inquiry into his involvement in the defections.

Following Burgess's reports on his meetings with Maclean, the KGB realized that it would have been a mistake for Maclean to have undertaken the defection journey on his own even had he been willing to do so. He would have been far more likely to have been picked up drunk in Paris by the French police than to have ended up safely behind the Iron Curtain. This was therefore an additional reason why Burgess should be ordered by Modin to accompany him. If the two old friends were seen traveling to the continent for the weekend by some mutual acquaintance, it should occasion no suspicion, while it could be dangerous for Maclean alone to be seen in the company of some Russian courier, who might be recognized as such.

It is possible that KGB fooled Burgess into believing that as soon as he had seen Maclean safely on to some airplane or boat bound for Soviet bloc territory, he could return home. That would account for the details of his departure that strongly suggested that he believed he would be returning within a day or two. In the result, he was required to travel all the way to Moscow and to remain there. The KGB was wise to do this in the view of MI5 officers who studied the many facets of the case. Burgess had not only been drinking to wild excess but had also been taking drugs, and his general behavior was thought to be symptomatic of such a deterioration that he, too, might easily crack under interrogation.

There can be little doubt that Burgess remained behind the Iron Curtain with extreme reluctance. His loathing of Russia as a place to live and his longing for London may well have accounted for his eventual fallout with Maclean in Moscow, as reported by a friend, the late John Mossman. It was Maclean's fault that he was there. Had Maclean been man enough to flee on his own, he and Philby might have remained unsuspected for many more years.

Burgess's yearning for the home country he betrayed so systematically expressed itself pathetically. A former friend, the late Whitney Straight, elder brother of Michael Straight, who looked him up while visiting Moscow, reported, "Burgess was wearing his Old Etonian tie and I found him very patriotic. Whatever he has done, I think he has retained his fundamental interest in England and he loves the old country. . . ."

As Blunt recalled, when questioned about Burgess, the renegade Old Etonian had led such a lush life that MI5 should have queried the source of his income. For years he had run what amounted to a private dining club at the Dorchester Hotel, with influential politicans, diplomats, and businessmen attending and talking freely as they enjoyed the good food and wine for which the Russians paid. Despite Burgess's scruffiness and reputation for deliberately shocking conduct, there were many distinguished people who could not resist his company, including several who must have known that he was a Russian spy because he had tried to recruit them. When his treachery became apparent by his defection, they still kept his secret until interrogated themselves after the unmasking of Anthony Blunt.

Recourse to old MI5 records during the debriefing of Blunt

recalled that suspicion had been slightly aroused when Burgess had arranged a meeting between Lord Inverchapel (formerly Sir Archibald Clerk Kerr) and Anatoli Gorski, the Soviet spymaster who was later found to have controlled Blunt and others under the code name "Henry." Inverchapel, who was then on leave in London, was the British ambassador in Moscow and on such close terms with Stalin that the Russian dictator allowed him to take his Russian valet with him when he left the Soviet Union. The meeting had been arranged by Burgess at the request of another man who turned out to be a KGB agent, an Austrian journalist working under the name Peter Smollett but whose real name was Peter Smolka.

Blunt confirmed, as had long been suspected, that Smollett, who worked in the Russian Department of the Ministry of Information during the war, was a professional KGB agent. MI5 had been disinclined to question Inverchapel, who could easily have fabricated an excuse for meeting a Russian "diplomat" in line of duty while on leave. They expected that he would put in a report about the meeting to the Foreign Office, but he never did so. Burgess, when questioned, had shrugged off the conversation as being of no consequence, and MI5 never discovered what had transpired. Many doubts have since been raised about Inverchapel, who had once worked in China, where he had been associated with the KGB recruiter, Agnes Smedley.

Mr. Gordon W. Creighton, who was first secretary under Inverchapel in Chungking, has told me how Guenther Stein, a member of the Soviet spy ring run by Richard Sorge, had secured British nationality and journalistic cover jobs through Inverchapel's influence.

Immediately after the disappearance of Burgess and Maclean, Blunt received an urgent message to meet Modin, which he duly did in London. Modin warned him that because of his known friendship with Burgess and their professional relationship in MI5, he was bound to come under deep suspicion himself. In the inevitable interrogation, likely to be hostile, it was felt in Moscow that he also might talk too freely and give leads to other British-born agents still active for the Soviets. Modin told him that the KGB Center had decided that the safest way out of the situation was for Blunt to defect as well. It was a clear order, and Modin stressed that he had the

escape arrangements all prepared and that there was little
time for argument.

Nevertheless, Blunt insisted that he did need time to
think, particularly in view of his royal appointment. Sitting in
the comfortable splendor of the beautifully appointed director's flat in the Courtauld Institute, surrounded by his valuable art collection—including the big Poussin oil painting that
he had picked up for £80 in Paris and, currently worth a
fortune, was tastefully framed above his mantelpiece—he
decided that he could not bear to leave the country he had
consistently betrayed for the grimness of a meager apartment
in Moscow.

To Modin's surprise, Blunt told him that he intended to
remain because he was confident that he could handle the
situation. He was sure that MI5 had never entertained
serious suspicion of him before and therefore could have no
hard evidence against him. As for being able to lie his way
through any interrogation, however harsh, he reminded Modin
that he had applied the KGB advice successfully before—
admit nothing, deny everything, but keep on talking to
discover how much your interrogators know.

Furthermore, Blunt argued, whatever MI5 might eventually discover, the government would not sanction any prosecution against a personal servant of the monarch. Presumably,
when balancing the pros and cons of the defection, the KGB
Center had taken into account the extra damage to Anglo-
American relations through the additional publicity that the
involvement of a royally appointed knight would occasion. So
Modin must have been concerned for his own position following his failure to induce Blunt to obey orders. His success in
getting Maclean and Burgess away must have stood him in
sufficiently good stead for him to have been given responsibility
twelve years later for the Philby defection.

Soon after it was established that Maclean and Burgess had
been spirited out by the Russians, the security authorities
became confident that they knew the identities of the three
KGB spies referred to in the Moscow-London radio traffic as
"Hicks," "Stanley," and "Johnson." They knew that Burgess
was "Hicks" and felt sure that "Stanley" was Philby. Believing
that "Johnson" was Blunt, they subjected him to the interrogation that Modin and the Center had feared.

When Mrs. Thatcher made her statement on Blunt to

Parliament in 1979, she said that he had originally been questioned after a witness had belatedly reported that he had heard Burgess remark, back in 1937, that he was a secret Comintern agent. That was true, but the prime reason for Blunt's quick interrogation after the disappearance of Burgess was their previous association inside MI5.

Much has been made of the fact that Blunt was interrogated eleven times between 1951 and 1964, when he eventually confessed. Those grillings, carried out by Helenus Milmo, the barrister, and Jim Skardon, who had broken Fuchs, were tough, but as Blunt has confirmed, most of the interrogation sessions were "comfortable conversations" simply because the interrogators had no hard information with which to confront him. They were relying on admissions he might make, and as Blunt had predicted so confidently to Yuri Modin, he was able to handle the situation by consistent lying.

Most of the sessions were held in the months following the double defection, and just how comfortable they were can be judged from the following extraordinary episode. As one of the first moves in the investigation of Burgess's disappearance, MI5 needed to search his flat in New Bond Street. Blunt was found to have a set of keys to it, so he opened it up, entered it with a team of MI5 men, and offered to help in the search. Though he was under suspicion himself, his help was accepted.

In the untidy three-room flat, there were stacks of letters from friends, some of them homosexuals, who were furious when they were eventually interviewed by the security authorities. Most of the letters were in shoe boxes, which Burgess also used for storing the hundreds of bank notes he received at intervals from his Russian controller.

None of the letters read by the MI5 men over the ensuing days produced any definite lead about the escape, but there had, in fact, been one letter in the flat containing a vital clue to the Ring of Five, and after his confession thirteen years later, Blunt revealed with some amusement how he had managed to remove it.

Burgess was a great reader, and the flat was full of books, each of which had to be shaken for possible hidden documents. Only one document was found, and it chanced to be in the section of the shelves being searched by Blunt. It was a letter to Burgess from Philby, and it told him that if ever he

were in desperate straits, there was a certain woman living in
London to whom he could go for help, as this woman knew
about Philby's secret life. It was, in fact, Flora Solomon,
whose evidence finally enabled the security authorities to
induce Philby to admit that he was a spy, in 1963. Had they
seen it then, in 1951, they would certainly have interviewed
Mrs. Solomon and she might have given them the evidence
they needed. Unfortunately for MI5 but in line with the
usual luck of the Ring of Five, Blunt realized the importance
of the letter when he glanced at it and put it, unnoticed, in
his pocket.

When eventually recounting this story to MI5, Blunt showed
no remorse at having enabled Philby to escape. Apart from
the fact that in 1951 he was still an ardent Communist,
prepared to help the KGB, if asked, he feared that the lead in
the letter might loop back on himself. Furthermore, he
retained great admiration for Philby: "Ah, Kim was a real
professional. Kim never faltered; never had doubts."

Blunt also described how he and Philby used to meet
frequently after the 1951 crisis, when Philby had been forced
to resign from the Secret Service because of deep suspicion
against him in the CIA and in MI5, and how they would
discuss their chances of continuing to survive exposure.

He revealed that he had paid a visit to the Middle East in
1961 and had seen Philby in Beirut, meeting him in the
British embassy where he should have been *persona non
grata*. Philby was then working as a journalist for the *Observer* and *Economist*, but as nobody in the Secret Service
thought he was anything but loyal, he had been taken back
on the payroll as an agent-runner. Blunt had gone around to
Philby's flat in Beirut where his host had said, "I have been
asked by our friends to make contact with you, Anthony, but
I told them that you are not in a position to do anything
useful." Blunt said that he had answered, "That is so, Kim."

This admission is proof enough that though Blunt claims
that he greatly regrets what he did to his country, he had firm
evidence that Philby was still an active KGB agent in 1961
and kept quiet about it.

When exposing Blunt in Parliament, Mrs. Thatcher revealed
that on one occasion between 1951 and 1956 Blunt helped
Philby to recontact Russian intelligence. Blunt's detailed

account of this episode is even more like spy fiction, though unquestionably true.

In 1954, Blunt was delivering a public lecture on the history of art, and when it ended, a group of enthusiasts clustered around him to ask questions. Among the upturned faces, he was astonished to see that of his old controller "Peter"—Yuri Modin, the man who organized the defection of Burgess and Maclean and instructed him to go, too. Modin handed him a picture postcard of a painting and asked his opinion. Written in a semicircle, in what Blunt recognized as Guy Burgess's handwriting, was the message "Meet me at 8-o'clock tomorrow night, Angel, Caledonian Road."

This instruction referred to a standard rendezvous of the past, but when Blunt attended it, there was no Burgess, only Modin, who asked him to set up a clandestine meeting with Philby. Presumably, Modin had induced Burgess to write the message in Moscow in the belief that Blunt would be unable to resist going to meet him, while he might decline a straightforward contact with Russian intelligence.

Blunt accomplished Modin's modest request by writing to Philby, who was then in England, and he believes that this was the occasion to which Philby referred in his book, *My Silent War,* in the passage describing how "through the most ingenious of routes" he had received a message from his Soviet friends "conjuring him to be of good cheer."

Blunt may be mistaken and the "route" may have been very different, as I shall describe in a later chapter. Nevertheless, a backtrack of MI5 showed that Modin had returned specially to Britain by surreptitious means because he was not supposed to be in the country for any official purpose.

Recently I have been able to establish why the KGB resumed contact with Philby after severing it in 1951. Peter Smolka who, by that time, was running a toy factory in Austria, was an old friend of Philby, having shared a journalistic enterprise with him before the war. The KGB feared that Philby might have been "turned" by British Intelligence after his dismissal from the Secret Service so Smolka, whose loyalty to the Russians was never in doubt, was closely questioned about him for several days. He convinced the KGB that Philby would never work against the Soviet Union. Philby was therefore reactivated for future use.

15
An Unlikely Informer

Throughout the years after the defection of Maclean and Burgess in 1951, Blunt, for all his bland composure, must have been haunted by the fear that some Communist defector might expose him. As I have outlined, this is exactly what happened in 1964, though by an individual who was probably not on Blunt's list as a likely informer.

The prime minister chose not to disclose the details during her exposure of Blunt. I appreciate her reasons, but I can describe the incident and its consequences in sufficient detail to demonstrate the truth of them.

Among several overseas students talent spotted and cultivated by the Ring of Five at Cambridge and then recruited by Soviet intelligence was Michael Whitney Straight, a young American who was exceptionally talented and politically minded. He was an open Communist and had visited Russia. A contemporary, T. E. B. Howarth, has described him as "the most glamorous figure of the Cambridge far left. With the prestige of a double first in economics to add to his reputation as Cambridge's leading socialite, Straight was a very potent influence on his generation."

Straight has described to me how Blunt, then a young tutor at Cambridge, had recruited him to work secretly for the Comintern in 1937:

While I was at Cambridge, my best friend, John Cornford, was killed fighting in the Spanish Civil War against the Franco forces. Blunt said that it was up to me to make a similar sacrifice by going underground to provide information for the "International."

144

Straight was a member of a student Marxist circle centered on The Apostles, and Blunt had seized his opportunity while he was in an emotionally charged state, ideal for recruitment. My informants say that Blunt then introduced him to the mysterious Soviet controller called "Otto," but Straight tells me that he cannot recall him. He does remember, however, being taken by Blunt out of London to a roadhouse on the Great West Road to be introduced to one of his "friends" in June 1937 and suggests that this might have been "Otto."

Because of his family's banking background, Straight was asked to provide financial and commercial assessments for "the party," and it all seemed harmless enough. Once he was in the net, Blunt told him that the Russians wanted him to return to the United States and join the J. P. Morgan Company where his father, Willard Straight, had been a partner. Straight says that he refused and asked to be left alone. Blunt, who appeared to be sympathetic, told him that his plea would be "carefully considered."

When Straight returned to Washington, he became a speech writer for President Roosevelt and his Cabinet in the Interior Department and later worked briefly in the state department. He was soon approached by a Soviet controller who called himself Michael Green. This Russian approached Straight about a dozen times over the subsequent eighteen months. Straight recalls:

> Some of these occasions were social, such as the one on which I had dinner with him and his Kansas-born wife in a restaurant in New York. On six to eight occasions I gave him written appraisals of my own opinions concerning the issues facing America. I remember only one of these, in which I argued that the Nazi-Soviet Pact, which I abhorred, should not be extended from a military pact to a political alliance. I have great remorse about it, but I don't think it either served the Russians or damaged the United States.

There is no doubt that Straight underwent a change of heart and decided to distance himself from the KGB and communism in general. He resigned from the government service early in 1941 to write articles for the *New Republic* and to help organize an interventionist movement called

Fight for Freedom. "Green" occasionally telephoned him but with no result, and Straight says that the Russian made no attempt to threaten him when he told him that he was leaving government service. He saw "Green" for the last time in 1942, after which he volunteered for military duty, joining the army air corps and training as a bomber pilot.

In 1948, Straight returned to England to attend the annual dinner of The Apostles, the exclusive Cambridge club, and found that Burgess was presiding and that Blunt was also there. Straight had a row with another Communist member, and Blunt and Burgess demanded to see him the following morning, when they accused him of deserting the cause. Straight says that for the first time he learned that Blunt had been in MI5 during the war and that Burgess had joined the Foreign Office. There was a stormy session, and Straight says that he threatened to report Burgess to the security authorities unless he left government service. Burgess obviated this by assuring him that he was about to leave and return to the BBC, anyway. As Blunt had left MI5 and was full time in the art world, Straight decided that no action was necessary in his case.

Late in 1963, President Kennedy, shortly before he was assassinated, asked Straight to be chairman of the National Council for the Arts. "This brought the issue of my past to the surface of my mind," Straight told me. "It was hardly a classified post, and my record would not, I think, have turned up in a security check." Straight decided against taking the job, but went to see Robert Kennedy, the president's brother, then attorney general, who called in the deputy chief of the FBI.

Among the admissions he made was a statement that he had been recruited to the KGB cause by Anthony Blunt, whom he knew to have been a Soviet agent. He said that he would be prepared to give evidence against Blunt in court if necessary. This was MI5's first hard evidence against the traitor who, on the accession of Queen Elizabeth in 1952, had become surveyor of the Queen's pictures. It has been widely assumed that the incident in 1964, which, according to Blunt, "freed him from loyalty to his friends," was the death of Tomas Harris, his art-dealer friend who had managed to get him into MI5 in 1940. Harris did die in 1964 under suspicious circumstances, but the incident that brought about Blunt's confession was the one I have described.

After receiving the information, the MI5 chiefs, then led by Sir Roger Hollis, who was close to retirement, discussed the situation for several weeks before taking any action. It was decided that, even with the new evidence, there was little chance of prosecuting Blunt successfully if he continued to deny everything, as he probably would.

There was also the embarrassing difficulty of the royal connection over so many years and the general objection to another public scandal that might have adverse effects on the interchange of intelligence secrets with the United States. The CIA and the FBI knew about Blunt, but Congress and the American people did not.

It was agreed inside MI5 that the main purpose of confronting Blunt with the evidence was to induce him to talk in the hope that he would give a lead to the still unknown Fifth Man, to others he and his friends might have recruited, and to the identities and methods of the Soviet intelligence officers who had been involved.

Arthur Martin, the case officer who was to handle Blunt and who had unsuccessfully interrogated him before, suggested that the only way to secure his cooperation was to offer him immunity from prosecution, if this could be legally obtained. Hollis was diffident about the idea but later concurred when he realized that the immunity could be offered in such a way as to ensure that there should never be any publicity, adverse to MI5, about Blunt's treachery.

The attorney general, the late Sir John Hobson, was then approached, and after careful consideration of the delicate royal connection, he agreed that Blunt could be offered immunity from prosecution, if he agreed to confess and to continue to assist the security authorities in their further investigations. Because the recent offer of immunity to Philby had been followed by his swift defection, the possibility that Blunt might react in the same way was briefly discussed but rejected on the grounds that fifty-six-year-old Sir Anthony, as he then was, had too much to lose.

After further reflection inside MI5, a meeting was arranged in April 1964 at the Home Office, which is responsible for MI5. Present were the Home Office permanent secretary, Sir Charles Cunningham, Sir Roger Hollis, and Sir Michael Adeane (now Lord), the Queen's private secretary.

Adeane was informed that Blunt was suspected of having been an agent for Russian intelligence but was to be offered immunity. He asked what action the authorities would like the Queen to take regarding Blunt's royal appointment if Blunt agreed to confess. He was told that it would be advisable for the Queen to take no action whatsoever because, otherwise, traitors to whom Blunt might point could take evasive action. The security authorities would also be deprived of the element of surprise in approaching these people.

As Blunt had no access whatever to any information of interest to Russia as a result of his work for the royal household, Adeane raised no objections. He then alerted the Queen to the distasteful circumstances and related MI5's plan for using Blunt as a counteragent if he made a genuine confession. In the interest of national security, the Queen agreed to take the official advice, and this was made known to the security authorities. The attitude that should be adopted toward Blunt if he failed to confess was left in abeyance.

On April 23, Blunt was interviewed by a case officer who was not Jim Skardon, as has been suggested, but the more senior and very experienced head of an MI5 counterespionage section, Arthur Martin, selected because he was then the top specialist in inducing difficult subjects to talk. Blunt, who was interviewed in his flat, was first told of the American's statement to the FBI, which he completely denied, as had been expected. He was then given to understand that this lead had been successfully followed up so that there was further evidence available.

While Blunt was wondering whether this was a bluff—which it was—the case officer told him of the attorney general's offer of immunity from prosecution. As had previously been agreed with Hollis, this was phrased in such a way that it was clear to Blunt that the offer also meant that there would be no publicity and that he would be able to continue with his royal appointment, retain his knighthood, and pursue his life and career normally.

Blunt then poured himself a stiff gin—he was a heavy gin drinker—sipped it for a few minutes while appreciating his situation, and then confessed that he had indeed been a long-serving agent of the KGB. Blunt never made a written confession. He was interrogated at intervals until 1972, the total adding up to more than two hundred hours of close questioning, which was tape-recorded.

Martin prepared a brief of the statement Blunt had made on April 23, which constituted his confession, for the queen's private secretary, who received it in June.

Normally, writers do not really know what the Queen does or says, but because of a fluke circumstance I *know* that the Queen was properly alerted to the Blunt situation by Adeane as soon as he had received the brief of the confession. She merely asked what the official advice was and, on being told, agreed to accept it in the national interest. Presumably, the Queen experienced some distaste, but she rarely had occasion to meet Blunt. This was perhaps as well, considering that the regime to which he had been dedicated had murdered her relatives and detested monarchs on principle.

The brief that had been passed to Adeane contained none of the details disclosed in this book as they were considered unnecessary for the purpose. The Queen is on record as having expressed no interest in the sordid details of such matters. In his *Diaries*, Richard Crossman recorded how, while staying with the Queen in 1967, he had started to discuss the Philby story, then running in the Sunday newspapers. The Queen dismissed the subject by saying that she did not read "that sort of thing."

I have already described the extraordinary behavior of the MI5 director general, Sir Roger Hollis, in suspending Blunt's case officer from duty almost immediately after he had secured the confession. This gave Blunt a completely free run for a fortnight, allowing him to recover his composure and possibly consult with the Soviet embassy, destroy any documentary evidence, and make any other dispositions.

Later, due attention was also focused on the fact that, once again, Hollis had chosen to keep his prime minister in ignorance of a most sensitive matter of great potential political embarrassment. Just as he had failed to alert Harold Macmillan personally about the dangers surrounding the Profumo Affair, so he failed to alert Sir Alec Douglas Home about the immunity granted to Blunt, though he did tell the home secretary, Henry Brooke.

When the case officer was permitted to begin the interrogations, to which Blunt was required to submit as part of the immunity deal, they were carried out mainly in Blunt's flat at the Courtauld Institute. In spite of the spy's increasing requirement of gin, his memory proved to be excellent except when asked for information that implicated possible fellow agents still holding eminent positions in the civil service and elsewhere. It was noticed that he had an eye twitch, and this became more acute when the discussion turned to any of his friends who were suspect.

Among the first questions posed to him was "What did the Russians tell you to do if you were ever interrogated?" The answer came out pat. "Deny everything, volunteer nothing, but keep on talking because then you will find out what they know."

By and large, the talks were "comfortable," but in the hope of breaking him concerning the missing member of the Ring of Five, it was decided to mount a hostile attack. "You realize that people have died and been tortured as a result of what you have done?" he was told with sudden sternness. "Now come on, who else is there?" For a moment, Blunt appeared to lose his composure, then smiled as he realized that his interrogators had no new information. "There was nobody else," he said quietly.

This was almost certainly a lie, as an incident staged in Brown's Hotel, in Dover Street near Piccadilly, and described in chapter 17, demonstrates.

At no time did Blunt express remorse or repentance about the men he had betrayed.

At one point Michael Straight visited London and agreed to a confrontation. The two met cordially, and Blunt did not appear to be angry about the way he had been "shopped." Perhaps, having been freed from the nagging fear that some defector might suddenly expose him, he had reason to be grateful to his old friend. Straight remains haunted by the fact that he waited so long in going to the FBI because, had he done so before the war, Blunt would have been caught before he did so much damage, as might Burgess. He says that he thought of exposing Blunt after the war but could not face the prospect of a confrontation with Senator McCarthy in Washington or with Blunt in an English court.

In 1972, with Blunt producing less and less, it was decided to end his interrogations unless something specific turned up from a defector or some other source. This followed an analysis by an independent officer, a woman, who concluded that Blunt had told about most of the people who had been Communists and about some who had been spies but would not deliberately point a finger at any of his former friends, who might still be in important positions. He was prepared to talk only about those who, through age or retirement, were no longer vulnerable.

It was concluded that during his interrogations he had lied and misled MI5 over some of his dealings with the Russians. It was suspected that he had met with his Russian friends on more occasions after the war than he had admitted. Furthermore, he had not changed ideologically and was proud of what he had done. Nevertheless, if some of the highly productive leads he had given had been unwitting, the MI5 men congratulated themselves on having bluffed such a tough and unrepentant Communist into confessing anything at all.

Nothing further concerning Blunt transpired until later in 1972 when he was rushed to hospital for a major operation for cancer, which it was thought he was unlikely to survive. There has been much conjecture as to why, at that stage, the attorney general, then Sir Peter Rawlinson (now Lord), and the prime minister, then Edward Heath, should have been informed of the truth concerning Blunt. I can clarify the situation.

The security authorities, who never trusted Blunt after his halfhearted confession, feared that he might leave a statement with his solicitor for posthumous publication, either detailing his full activities or continuing to serve the Soviet interest with a mass of misinformation, possibly drafted by the KGB. Sudden publication of either statement by a newspaper could have been damaging to a government not informed of the truth in advance.

In addition, there were fears that a former friend of Blunt and Burgess, the late Goronwy Rees, a professional writer, was poised to reveal Blunt's treachery as soon as the traitor was safely dead. Rees, who had known that Burgess was a spy for many years before he defected, was hoping to salve his social conscience for failing to warn the security authorities concerning his suspicions about Blunt, though he had made a belated statement about Burgess, much against Blunt's advice.

Alerted by MI5, the prime minister and his advisers considered what action they should take to forestall such a predicament, and to this end they had to be given all the details so that a counterdocument could be prepared. This document, which was prepared by the Home Office and bore the title "If Blunt dies...", also gave some information about the other members of the Ring of Five. It also contained two lists of names—those of people found to have been Soviet agents or believed to have been, following the interrogation of Blunt, and those of people still under investigation.

A copy of the counterdocument was passed to Sir Michael Adeane, who was in his last year as private secretary to the Queen. It is not known whether he showed it to the Queen or not. Knowing Lord Adeane, as he now is, I suspect that he would have spared her the details, especially as none of the people in the lists had any connection with the royal household, save for the various honors they had received. In the result, Blunt proved to be as tough physically as mentally, and he survived his ordeal, so that the detailed document has still never been published.

The hundreds of hours of tape recordings covering the Blunt interrogations had been transcribed and then summarized. As I have recorded, the tapes and transcripts were destroyed on Hollis's orders before he left MI5 in 1965, so the document had to be compiled from the summaries.

I have already described most of the information that Blunt revealed as the payoff for the immunity. I now propose to deal, as openly as libel laws permit, with the identities of those Britons whom he named as agents or for whom he gave productive leads either deliberately or when off his guard. Several of the most important are still alive, their reputations and honors intact.

16
The Truth
about John Cairncross

When Guy Burgess's flat was searched in 1951, security men found a bundle of handwritten notes confirming affairs inside the Treasury. There were also pen portraits of various officials written as though by a talent scout giving information about character weaknesses and other features that might be exploited. The notes dated from the early 1940s, and their continued existence was evidence of the carelessness and slovenliness in Burgess's character, so atypical of a highly successful spy, as he undoubtedly was. The papers were not signed, and their author might never have been traced but for a fluke occurrence. An MI5 case officer, who had acquired a new secretary from Whitehall, sent for the file in which the papers happened to have been placed. She recognized the handwriting as that of her previous superior, a young civil servant called John Cairncross, who had been on the Treasury staff in Whitehall in 1940.

As it already seemed certain that Burgess had been a Soviet recruiter and active spy, it seemed likely that the Treasury information, which could have been of value to the Russians, had been provided as an espionage service.

It was known that Cairncross had been a scholarship boy from a poorly off home in Glasgow who had gone to Cambridge, where he had done brilliantly in modern languages. It was soon discovered that he had been an overt Communist in 1935 when, though intending to pursue an academic career, he had suddenly changed course to enter the Foreign Office.

When confronted with the notes early in 1952 by MI5's Arthur Martin, Cairncross denied being a spy or any kind of Soviet agent. He admitted having supplied the notes at Burgess's request but said that he had no knowledge that Burgess was a Soviet agent and did not believe it could possibly be true.

As Cairncross had to concede that he had written the notes and that they contained some classified information, which could have been of value to a foreign power, and particularly to the Russians in their political negotiations with the Germans in 1940, he offered to resign. His resignation was accepted, and he obtained a post with the UN Food and Agriculture Organization in Rome.

The public heard nothing of this until after Blunt's exposure in 1979, when Cairncross openly acknowledged his former communism and his unfortunate association with Burgess and Blunt. When questioned by journalists in Rome, he admitted that he had given Burgess the offending notes and had resigned as a consequence without a pension but, understandably, volunteered nothing further. He has, therefore, since been dismissed from the haul of known Soviet agents as "small fry."

The truth is very different. As an active spy throughout the war, in highly sensitive positions, Cairncross was a "big fish" and did great damage to his country.

While Blunt always attempted to cover his close friends during his interrogations, he was open about Cairncross, whom he seemed to dislike. He admitted having talent-spotted him as a potential spy while teaching him at Cambridge and having alerted Burgess to this effect, though the actual recruitment had been achieved by an even more sinister Communist agent, James Klugman.

An MI5 officer therefore traveled to Rome to interrogate Cairncross, who, knowing that he was outside the jurisdiction of the British Official Secrets Act, made a complete and contrite confession of his treachery.

He admitted what the MI5 men already knew about his recruitment to the service of the KGB, explaining that he had experienced poverty and had concluded that Soviet-style communism was the only way of securing social justice, though he claimed that he had since realized he had been hopelessly misled in this respect by other Marxists.

He disclosed that Klugman had introduced him to the ubiquitous "Otto" on a special visit to Regent's Park, where they were unlikely to be seen. In accordance with the usual practice, "Otto," who was also running Burgess, Maclean, Philby, and Blunt, had instructed him to reject his open communism, go "underground," and get himself into the Foreign Office instead of pursuing an academic career, as he would have preferred. Cairncross officially quit the Communist party in late 1936.

Cairncross recalled how his Glaswegian accent was of some concern to "Otto," who felt that he needed to improve his diction if he was ever to get into the top echelons of Whitehall. "Otto" also advised him against marrying a "bourgeois" wife because he had already lost a very promising agent, whom he had recruited at Cambridge, through marriage to a woman too "bourgeois" to condone his spying for Russia. (MI5 is confident that it knows the identity of this short-time agent, who is now a life peer.)

Acting on "Otto's" instructions, Cairncross competed for entry to the Foreign Office, passed top of his list, and began work there in the German department, where Donald Maclean was also then located. Cairncross remained in the Foreign Office for two years, and he admitted that after "Otto" had been recalled to Moscow in September 1938, he handed his documentary material to Burgess, who passed it to Litzi Philby, Kim Philby's estranged Austrian wife, who was then working in London as a full-time Soviet agent.

Litzi had been a militant Communist, divorced and living with her parents in Vienna, where Philby had married her in 1934. He brought her to London soon afterward, and so superficial was the checking of entrants into the Secret Service that nobody in authority knew that Philby was married to a Russian spy until 1946, when he needed a divorce. Even then, no effective notice was taken of it.

In 1938, at the suggestion of his Soviet controllers, Cairncross applied for transfer to the Treasury. This is believed to have been preferred by the Russians because Maclean was already covering for them in the Foreign Office.

Cairncross admitted that in his early days he had been given money by the Russians but only in small amounts as expenses. This included the purchase price of a cheap motorcar to facilitate contacts with Soviet controllers outside London.

In 1942, after he had given Burgess the notes that ten years later were to betray him to a minor extent, he managed, because of his fluency in German, to get himself on to the staff of the most secret establishment involved in the war effort. This was the so-called Government Code and Cypher School at Bletchley Park, Buckinghamshire, famous for its cracking of the German enigma-machine codes by the superbly ingenious processes known by the code name "Ultra."

He worked there as an "editor" dealing with air intelligence. He described how he used to visit London weekends and pass "Ultra" secret documents to his Soviet controller, who, at that stage, was "Henry"—Anatoli Gorski. One batch, which he remembered with some pride, concerned details of the strength and dispositions of the Luftwaffe before the Battle of Kursk, an important turning point for the Russians. Cairncross received a commendation from Moscow for that effort, while "Henry" was eventually awarded two Orders of Lenin for his espionage efforts in Britain. Later, a "man of military bearing" took him over.

Cairncross also told his interrogators how, on another occasion, he had supplied information from Ultra sources that enabled the Russians to destroy hundreds of German aircraft on the ground. Sir Winston Churchill called the people at Bletchley "the geese who laid the golden eggs and never cackled." In fact, Cairncross cackled all the time—directly to the Russians.

With some force, Cairncross argued that he had only been assisting an ally and had therefore indirectly helped to defeat the common enemy, but, in fact, his behavior was reprehensible in the extreme. The Russians were being given relevant information they needed by an official London-Moscow route, as I have described, but only after it had been dressed up to make it look as though it had been obtained from some other more conventional source.

The need to hide the truth that Bletchley Park was cracking the German codes day by day was paramount for the success of the eventual Allied invasion of Europe. Cairncross's treachery meant that the Russians knew the true source, and had this leaked to the Germans, he could have been the most damaging spy of the war. There were German spies in Russia who might have got hold of it, and it has been established that the KGB was in close touch with senior German intelligence and security officers who were taking out personal insurance against the possibility of a Nazi defeat. The defector, Goleniewski, revealed how one of these was Heinrich Muller, a notorious Gestapo chief. So it was not impossible that, at some stage, the Russians might have leaked the "Ultra" secret deliberately to hold up the British-American advance while they overran more of Europe.

In 1944, Cairncross moved from Bletchley, then part of the Secret Service, to Secret Service Headquarters in London. The KGB did not object because they probably had other sources there, as records of deciphered Russian radio traffic suggest. I have talked to several of his former colleagues who remember him well. At first, he worked in German counter-intelligence, then switched to Yugoslav affairs, one of his field officers being Klugman, who was then based at Bari in Italy. Cairncross admitted that he continued to spy there so that the Russians secured a direct reading of the Allied plans concerning the future of Yugoslavia, a matter of great political significance to Moscow.

Cairncross remained in the Secret Service until the end of the war and then returned to the Treasury, where, colleagues recall, he was known as "Butch" in spite of his slight build, or because of it. He never rose to eminence there but had excellent access to high policy documents and assessments of the U.K. economy, which, he admitted, he continued to hand over to the Russians.

In September 1945, with the war at an end, Cairncross, who until then had been meeting with his Soviet controller twice a week, was reduced to meeting once a month—as were Blunt and Burgess—because he did not have so much material to transmit. He remained in touch with the KGB and at the time of the Maclean and Burgess defection in 1951 was called to an emergency meeting with his controller in a wood in Surrey. It was decided that he was unlikely to become suspect and continued to spy actively from inside the Treasury until early in 1952, when he was challenged about the papers found in Burgess's abandoned flat.

When he admitted the authorship of the papers but strenuously denied he had been any kind of agent, he was allowed to resign and move to Rome because that was all that MI5 knew about him then. He took care not to return to England because of his fear that more information about him may have come to light. Though the war was over, what he had done during it had been a capital offense, as was later pointed out to him by his interrogators. Cairncross said that the KGB had lost interest in him once he had left London, and that is believed to be true.

Cairncross was not granted immunity either from prosecution or publicity. On the contrary, he was told that if ever he came under British jurisdiction, he would be prosecuted, which was a sure way of preventing his return to Britain. Offenses against the Official Secrets Act are not extraditable.

His information about the part played in his recruitment to espionage by James Klugman, then a senior official of the British Communist party, was the first hard evidence of Klugman's treachery. So MI5 decided to use Cairncross to try to break Klugman into making a confession, which might uncover other spies. Cairncross was told that he could return for a limited visit to England without fear of prosecution if he agreed to help.

Acting on MI5 instructions, Cairncross saw Klugman and, with some courage, threatened to expose him, pointing out the damage it would do to the Communist party. He promised to keep quiet if Klugman would cooperate with MI5, but Klugman refused to do anything of the kind, and the attempt came to nothing. Klugman, who was a committed Stalinist, did all he could to undermine his own country and promote the Soviet Union until his timely death in 1977.

In the course of his long interrogations, both in Rome and in London, Cairncross identified several other Britons who had served the KGB. These included a senior civil servant who had also been recruited at Cambridge. He refused to be interviewed by security men but was nevertheless removed from access to secret information. This did not prevent his further promotion in the civil service or the award of an important honor. At the time of writing, he still has an influential political position.

Another Cambridge Communist, who, according to Cairncross, had operated inside the Treasury and in the Cabinet Office, also refused to be interviewed. He, too, was later promoted in the Civil Service and is currently a director of a famous company.

Cairncross's espionage activities for the Russians covered fifteen years, much of this time from positions providing access to highly secret intelligence. He must, therefore, be rated as an extremely damaging spy, far removed from the "small fry" status previously awarded to him. But was he the Fifth Man of the Ring of Five? He had all the obvious attributes—recruited at Cambridge, a friend of Burgess and Blunt with early knowledge that Philby and Maclean were also Soviet agents. He was controlled by "Otto" and then by "Henry," who were both assigned to the Ring of Five. Like the other four, he was an eminently successful and damaging spy.

Evidence provided by defectors has, however, indicated that while the Fifth Man of the original ring became a civil servant, he was also a scientist, which would rule Cairncross out. Furthermore, the security authorities do not think that Blunt would have been so forthcoming about the real Fifth Man as he was about Cairncross. Instead, he tried to shield the scientist who is believed to have been a member of the Ring of Five, as I shall now record.

17
The Real Fifth Man?

The person believed by the security authorities to have been the Fifth Man of the Ring of Five and who, being still alive, can shelter behind the libel laws, was traced by an inadvertent lead given by Blunt. After he had categorically denied knowing the identity of any other members of the ring beyond his close friends, Maclean, Burgess, and Philby, Blunt had remarked, "If you are looking for other people who might have been recruited by Burgess, then pay attention to those he praised lavishly, because he always tried to recruit them."

The interrogators took Blunt at his word and compiled a list of people whom, according to the recollections of friends, Burgess had praised. One of them proved to be a defense scientist in a most sensitive position in the government service. This person is not Dr. Basil Mann, the atomic scientist living in the United States and recently named as the Fifth Man, and against whom I am assured there is no evidence. The man in question has no connection with atomic science.

So long as Hollis remained head of MI5, he refused to allow the Blunt case officers to interview the scientist. Soon after he had retired, in 1965, however, inquiries involving telephone tapping and surveillance revealed that the scientist and his family—though associated with Blunt and Burgess, he was not a homosexual—were still secret Communists. It was also discovered that MI5 had been warned about the man ten years previously, but nothing had been done.

As the man was about to be given special clearance to visit secret American installations, he had to be pulled in sooner than the authorities would have liked, for an interrogation that lasted six weeks.

He admitted that he was still a committed Communist and had breached the civil service security rules by failing to admit it on his positive vetting form. He admitted meeting "Otto," the early Russian controller of the Ring of Five, while he himself had been at Cambridge. He agreed that he had ceased to be an overt Communist and had made a pretense of seeming to be right wing in order to secure a post in a government defense establishment.

The scientist insisted that he had never given any secret information to the Russians, but when confronted with evidence, he admitted that he did occasionally meet Russians from the Soviet embassy and appreciated that they might be intelligence officers. Again, he admitted that he had breached security regulations in failing to report such contacts even if they had been innocent.

He was then shown a spread of photographs of Soviet bloc intelligence officers and picked out pictures of two whom he had met. One was Yuri Modin, Blunt's controller for a time and the man who had supervised the defection of Burgess and Maclean. The other was Sergei Kondrashev, a senior KGB officer who had served in Britain. It seemed unlikely that he would have met two such active spy masters on purely social terms, and what followed made it even more improbable.

Four years previously, in 1962, the important KGB defector, Anatoli Golitsin, had reported on Kondrashev, saying that he had been specially trained to control two very important spies in Britain. One proved to be George Blake, the spy inside the Secret Service (see chapter 19), while the other, who had not then been detected, was known to be in defense work. Golitsin had recalled how this Communist scientist had quarreled with Kondrashev, whom he considered to be "too bourgeois" for a Russian Communist.

When the suspect Fifth Man saw Kondrashev's photograph, he exclaimed, "I hated the man. He was so bourgeois. You know—he wore blazers and had a pet poodle!" Such are the chance remarks that can mean so much to an alert counterespionage interrogator who has done his "homework."

As a last-ditch effort to induce the suspect to talk, there was a confrontation between him and Blunt in Brown's Hotel.

The interrogators provided plenty of drinks—gin for Blunt, sherry for the suspect, and watered whiskey for themselves. During the long session, which lasted until after midnight, they talked about the Russian intelligence officer Yuri Modin, and among the slips the suspect made was to call him by his code name "Peter," which he would be unlikely to have known unless professionally involved with him.

The suspect was the first to leave, whereupon Blunt, who had polished off a whole bottle of gin, remarked, "You have convinced me that he was one of us." He then recalled that after the 1951 "crisis," when Philby had been very toughly interrogated by Helenus Milmo, Philby had told him, "They didn't seem to know about my return to Cambridge after I got back from Austria. Thank God they didn't!" Blunt then suggested that Philby might well have been referring to the recruitment of the Fifth Man. Burgess had accomplished that recruitment, but Philby had been involved in it in some way. What was known about the suspect's life and activities at Cambridge fitted the date of Philby's return.

As the suspect had been positively vetted three times, at intervals, and each time had failed to admit that he had been a Communist, he knew that his career was blighted. He also knew that he would be barred from further access to secrets and was not allowed to visit the American installation, the CIA being given the reason.

To induce him to confess, he was offered the chance of immunity from prosecution if he would cooperate, but he ignored the proposal as though he had not heard it, perhaps reserving it in his mind in case he might, one day, be faced with harder evidence.

The MI5 chiefs, then headed by Sir Martin Furnival Jones, met with civil service representatives to decide what other action should be taken against the suspect. As he was quite close to retirement—and perhaps to cover up the suspicion that could have serious consequences for the Anglo-American exchange of defense secrets—he was transfered to non-secret work and later retired on full pension.

18
A Haul of Suspects

Another prominent Englishman, knighted for various services, was followed up after Blunt's advice that Burgess tried to recruit anyone he had praised highly. He admitted that Burgess had told him that he was a Comintern agent and had tried to recruit him but claimed that not only had he declined but had tried to talk his friend out of his dangerous treachery.

The man admitted that he knew that his plea had failed and that he had never reported on Burgess even when he himself had achieved an important position in the Foreign Office after the war. He had no reasonable explanation of this dereliction of duty, and MI5 still list him as a possible former agent.

As a result of another lead given by Anthony Blunt, MI5 became highly suspicious of Bernard Floud, then Labour MP for Acton and previously labor relations adviser to the independent television companies. Nothing could be done about him because soon after Harold Wilson became prime minister in October 1964, he introduced new rules making all MPs and peers immune to investigation by the security authorities without his special permission.

It has long been standard practice that when a new prime minister takes office, the Security Service is asked for the names of any MPs of his party about whom he might have need to be concerned. While no reasons are given with the list, Wilson apparently thought that some of the names given to him were so unlikely that MI5 had been overdoing its inquiries or might do so in the future. Senior MI5 officers also believed that Wilson was partly motivated by complaints he had received from some of his MPs who believed that they were under surveillance—as some of them were.

163

Whatever his reasons, he decreed that members of Parliament—MPs and peers—were to be immune from surveillance of any kind, such as telephone tapping, the opening of letters, the examination of bank accounts, or shadowing. Exceptions would be made only with his personal permission, and MI5 was told that this was unlikely to be given on the evidence of defectors alone.

Whether Blunt counted as a "defector" was a moot point, and there was the additional problem that Wilson had not been told about Blunt, who was still under active interrogation. So no move was made against Floud.

In 1967, however, Wilson wanted to make Floud a junior minister. It is also standard practice that if a prime minister wishes to give office to an MP who is on his list of MI5 suspects and might require access to secret information in the prospective post, he must specifically ask MI5 if it has anything to tell him to that MP's detriment.

It was known that Floud, who had been an open Communist at Oxford University, had been recruited to the Soviet cause there by James Klugman, who operated there as well as at Cambridge. Floud, who retained his ideological sympathies with communism while serving in the Intelligence Corps during World War II, had in turn recruited others, including a woman who later managed to insinuate herself into a highly sensitive position in the Home Office. This woman had been interrogated and had named Floud as her recruiter.

Wilson was therefore told that there were serious suspicions against Floud involving Communism—as a member of Parliament he had kept his Communism secret from the Acton Labour party—and possible espionage. He then gave permission for Floud to be interviewed so that the security authorities could judge whether his activities had been no more than youthful folly.

Floud was interrogated closely for two weeks, during which he denied all knowledge of any connection with the KGB. Then, on being shown evidence, he claimed that he could not recollect it. The MI5 men suspected that he was still in touch with Soviet intelligence but told him that if he confessed his past activities and could convince them that he was no longer involved, they would not object to his appointment.

Floud did not react to the offer even after prolonged thought, so he was interviewed again. This produced nothing further, and while MI5 could not give him clearance, they intended to persist with their questions and inquiries for a little longer. After an unproductive session in October 1967, Floud, who had already been suffering from depression exacerbated by his wife's death earlier in the year, went home, wrapped himself in a blanket with a gas poker, turned on the tap, and killed himself.

There is a widespread belief among responsible MPs, including, for example, Enoch Powell, that the civil service staff of the Home Office has been heavily penetrated by extreme left-wingers. Leads provided by Blunt and others have satisfied the security authorities that not only is the charge true but that some of the extremists have been active agents of the Soviet Union. The woman whom Floud had recruited was one of these.

This woman, who is still alive, admitted that having been willingly recruited into the service of the "Comintern," she had been instructed to forswear her open communism and to get herself on to the staff of the Home Office. Being bright and well connected, she managed to do so. Whether by fluke or by design, she soon found herself in the department handling the official written requests from MI5 for the home secretary's permission to tap the telephones of suspects and to open their letters. As a result, she knew who was under suspicion and saw the warrants granted by the home secretary.

When interviewed, she claimed that she had not only given up spying before she became involved with the warrants but had abandoned her Communist beliefs because she had become totally disenchanted by the behavior of the Soviet regime both inside and outside Russia. The security men were unconvinced.

An even more extraordinary situation involving the Home Office arose as a result of another disclosure by Blunt. This concerned a woman colleague at the Courtauld Institute, Phoebe Pool, with whom he had collaborated on a book about Picasso. Blunt said that she had acted as a courier for Soviet agents, including the woman at the Home Office, whom I have mentioned. When Blunt tried to jog her memory, she recalled meeting "a sinister little Russian in Kew Gardens" to whom she passed on messages. She also named two men and said that they should be contacted urgently and warned that

MI5 would soon be after them. One of these was a former senior diplomat, Sir Andrew Cohen, a former member of The Apostles Club and close friend of Blunt, now dead. The other was a senior civil servant in the Home Office. Fortunately, the prime minister of the day was told of his background, which included close friendship with members of the Ring of Five.

Sadly, Phoebe Pool herself could not be questioned by the security men. Soon after Blunt had spoken of her, she threw herself under a train. Her suicide may have been expedited by fear of being confronted by MI5, but one of her contemporaries at the Courtauld Institute told me that the prime cause may have been her progressive deafness.

The woman who had been involved with handling the surveillance warrants named another high-level civil servant, stating that she knew he had been a Communist. He was known to have been a friend of Blunt, who was questioned about him. "He was never 'in the game,'" Blunt had assured his questioners, but because the man had held such sensitive positions, including a spell in the Cabinet Office, it was decided that he should be interviewed.

Having retired from the public service, he had moved abroad, where he was outside the jurisdiction of the Official Secrets Act, so it was hoped that he might talk freely. He did so, up to a point. He admitted that he had always been a Marxist and had remained a close friend of Guy Burgess. He insisted that Burgess had never tried to recruit him to the Soviet cause, but later, when mellowed by a few drinks, he added, "He didn't need to recruit me. I had no secrets from him."

When this information was given to Blunt, he smiled and said, "I can tell you now that he was the best source Guy ever had for the Russians."

There was good reason to believe that the man had taken fright just at the time when Maclean had been warned that evidence of his treachery had come to light through the decoding of the KGB radio traffic. It is thought that he was warned that his own activities might also be revealed in the same way. Though questioned again, he declined to commit himself, and nothing further was done because he was safely abroad. He is still alive at the time of writing, with a knighthood and other honors.

Several others named by Blunt, but without much detail, were approached, and some agreed to be interviewed. One of them, who had lived with the promiscuous Litzi Philby, went on to become an ambassador.

Blunt was more forthcoming about a man he had recruited himself in the 1930s, volunteering his name and some details of what he had done. This man held a position that gave him access to valuable secrets during the war but now works for a commercial company. When faced with Blunt's evidence and following a personal encounter with him, he admitted to having been a spy but managed to convince MI5 that he had ceased to help the Russians when he had married, realizing the danger to his family. No action was taken against him.

Another senior civil servant, who was still in Whitehall when Blunt gave a lead to him, turned out to have been an active Communist who had acted as a courier for other Soviet agents as well as supplying information himself. He was completely uncooperative, so that all the security authorities could do was to ensure that he received no further promotion. It was only because of their action that he was denied a knighthood.

Blunt also pointed the finger at another Cambridge acquaintance whom he knew as a Communist and who might have been recruited as a spy. This was the late Paddy Costello, a New Zealander who became professor of Russian at Manchester University. He had come under special suspicion in 1961 when it was discovered that while serving in the New Zealand consulate in Paris, he had signed New Zealand passports for Peter and Helen Kroger, the spies in the Navy Spy Ring. It was on these false passports that they had entered Britain for, in fact, their true name was Cohen, and they were American citizens.

Costello was known, too, to have provided an accommodation address in London for the wife of a Swedish diplomat spying for Russia. He was also observed meeting with a Soviet agent only shortly before his death in 1964.

Among the foreign students who were recruited by the KGB, according to Blunt, was a Canadian called Herbert Norman. He joined the Canadian diplomatic service, and while he was ambassador in Cairo, he was recalled to Ottawa to discuss his Communist past, which had come to light following inquiries in the United States. Just prior to his departure, a CIA man in Cairo was imprudent enough to try to encourage Norman to talk to him about his links with the Russians. Later, the CIA man quoted the Canadian as having said to him, "I can't go back to Ottawa because, if I did, I would have to betray more than a hundred people"— probably meaning people who had secret links with the Communist party rather than known Soviet agents. That night, he jumped from the roof of an apartment block, where he had a flat.

When questioned about Norman for corroborative evidence, Blunt said "Herb was one of us." There is no doubt that by this remark Blunt meant that Norman had been a recruit to Soviet intelligence. He was not referring to homosexuality, as apologists for Norman have suggested.

Several of the men whose names were volunteered by Blunt were beyond interrogation because they were already dead. One of these was a homosexual friend of Burgess called Tom Wylie. During the war, Wylie had been a high-level duty officer in the War Office in Whitehall, and he had a flat there. Blunt said he had been a most valuable source because Burgess used to drop in there for a drink in the evenings and browse through the papers in the "in trays." There was no evidence that Wylie was a deliberate spy, and just as he was to be questioned about his relationship with Burgess, he died of a heart attack.

The same fate overtook Sir Andrew Cohen, one of Blunt's close friends at Cambridge, who became a diplomat and was about to be questioned after statements made by Phoebe Pool.

The particular friend of Blunt, whom MI5 would dearly have liked to interrogate was already dead when Blunt was induced to confess. This was Tomas Harris, the former art dealer who had managed to give Blunt his great opportunity for big-scale treason by getting him into MI5.

Harris, son of a Spanish mother and an English father, had been a successful art dealer, mainly in Spanish paintings. Tommy, as he was known, was a talented artist who then turned to art dealing himself and became wealthy in his own right. At the outbreak of war, as a contribution to the fight against Hitler, he and his wife served as rather grand housekeeper-cooks to a defense establishment near Hertford for teaching the techniques of sabotage.

Harris was introduced there by his old friend Burgess, who had managed to insinuate himself on to the staff. From there, Harris secured a transfer as an officer to the section of MI5 that ran the double-cross system, whereby German agents were "turned" to work for the British either because they volunteered or as an alternative to execution or imprisonment for life.

He had an outstanding qualification for the work because of his knowledge of Spain and Portugal and became head of MI5's Iberian section. He proved to be a most ingenious exponent of deception techniques, mainly designed to mislead the Germans about Allied invasion plans. The particular agent he ran, code named "Garbo," was the most effective of the war.

After the hostilities, Harris gave up art dealing and devoted himself to painting and collecting, spending more and more time in Spain and Majorca. He was, therefore, not available for interview by his old MI5 colleagues when he naturally came under suspicion following the defection of his friends, Maclean and Burgess.

Most of his colleagues whom I have consulted do not believe that he was an active Soviet spy or even a Communist. But he was named as having served as a courier during the Spanish Civil War for Philby, who, while reporting from the Franco side, needed to get information to the Russians. The person who named him was Flora Solomon, whose other accusations eventually led to the exposure of Philby as a spy.

It is also believed that Harris may have assisted in the escape of Melinda Maclean from Switzerland to join her husband in Moscow in 1953, but there was nothing illegal in that, and he may have been doing it to help an old friend. That is the view, for instance, of such a balanced former colleague as Col. T. A. Robertson. Others are also prepared to believe that any financial assistance Harris may have given to Philby was no more than his natural generosity, though it remains possible that he was serving as a paymaster for the Russians.

Harris was killed in January 1964 in a car crash in Majorca. The police could find nothing wrong with the car, which hit a tree, but Harris's wife, who survived the crash, could not explain why the vehicle had gone into a sudden slide. It is considered possible, albeit remotely, that the KGB might have wanted to silence Harris before he could talk to the British security authorities, as he was an expansive personality, when in the mood, and was outside British jurisdiction. The information, about which MI5 wanted to question him and would be approaching him in Majorca, could have leaked to the KGB from its source inside MI5. Flora Solomon's allegation against Harris was in the same MI5 document as her accusation of Philby, and there is little doubt that the latter leaked to the KGB, as I have described.

Even if Harris was a Soviet spy, he was definitely not the Fifth Man of the Ring of Five. Nor, as I have already established, was his death the reason why Blunt was prepared to confess.

Not all the inquiries that followed Blunt's leads were on such a somber note—and some had humorous touches. One currently well-known academic, who was interviewed because his Communist affiliations at Cambridge had come to light, admitted to having induced his girl friend—now a prominent Labour politician—to smuggle a letter to Paris addressed to the Soviet agent, James Klugman. On his express advice, she had taken it in sewn in her knickers!

The interrogation of Blunt led to the detection of at least one further treacherous member of the Secret Service who cannot yet be named for legal reasons as he was allowed to "retire" prematurely to prevent open scandal. This man had held several important foreign assignments. When confronted with evidence of his duplicity by Sir Maurice Oldfield, he scoffed at the organization's inability to take any action against him so long as he refused to confess. Incredibly, this man attended Oldfield's memorial service at the chapel of the Royal Naval College at Greenwich in 1981, where the officer who had been instrumental in exposing him was appalled at his brass nerve.

The evidence against other possible Soviet agents accruing from Blunt's confession and MI5's reaction to it admirably demonstrate the difference between counterespionage operations and police work. The MI5 investigators almost invariably have to work on evidence that is not only slender but inadmissible in a British court of law. Their main initial source, defectors, can never be introduced as evidence, first, because the identity of the defectors themselves cannot normally be revealed at the time and, secondly, because as traitors to their own countries, their credibility could so easily be undermined by a clever defense counsel in open court. Evidence obtained by surreptitious methods like telephone tapping, on which counterespionage operations heavily depend, is inadmissible, as it can be held to be faked.

Having no powers of arrest or legal authority of its own, MI5 cannot require suspects to undergo interrogation. They can only be invited to do so, and if they refuse, as several of the suspects named by Blunt did, little or nothing can be done.

The offer of immunity to traitors like Blunt and Philby is as distasteful to the loyal members of MI5 as it is to the public, but all too often it is their only means of securing information from someone who will, otherwise, remain free, anyway.

These limitations are rightly regarded as a greatly preferable alternative to the knock-in-the-night powers enjoyed by the KGB and other secret police—properly so-called because they have powers of arrest. But in the view of MI5 itself and of many others knowledgeable in the field of espionage, they have been overdone with respect to members of Parliament. There is no conceivable justification for making any section of the community immune to investigation by the proper authority, which MI5 is, when reasonable suspicion exists. The rules laid down by Wilson, and which limited MI5's inquiries in the Floud case, are still in force unless recently changed by Mrs. Thatcher. Once such privileges are accorded to Parliament, they tend to be "set in concrete."

I have more, later, to disclose about the penetration of Parliament. At this point, I can state with certainty that the security authorities were convinced that it was in the national interest that certain Labour MPs, including junior ministers, should be investigated because of known contact with Russians listed as KGB officers. They were not allowed to do so because of the standing restrictions and, in one glaring instance, where formal request for permission to investigate and, if necessary, interrogate was made to the prime minister of the day it was refused.

The mixed-bag results of Blunt's interrogations raise a further question. Was it really necessary to keep him on as surveyor of the queen's pictures until his normal retirement in 1972 and then to continue his prestigious connection by appointing him adviser for the queen's pictures and drawings, a post he held until 1978?

The theory that his removal from his royal post, even after a decent interval, might alert the Russians to the fact that he had confessed never made much sense. If Blunt was still in regular touch with Soviet agents in 1964, they would soon realize that something had happened when he stopped seeing them if they had not already been warned during the fortnight when Blunt was "on the loose." It was odds on that any such Russians would be members of the Soviet embassy, with diplomatic privilege, so that MI5 would be powerless to do anything about them.

As regards those civil servants and others likely to be named by Blunt or for whom he might give leads, it seems improbable that they would have taken fright if he had quietly left the royal service. The danger that they would defect in any event was minimal.

The sensible explanation, which is supported by my confidential sources, is that continuation in royal employment was an integral part of the immunity package deal offered to Blunt and that he would not have accepted it without the ongoing privilege. This likely requirement by Blunt must have been made clear to Sir Michael Adeane and, through him, to the Queen. Nevertheless, as the official advice was that everything possible should be done to ensure Blunt's cooperation, Her Majesty accepted it.

When the Blunt Affair became a public scandal in 1979, it was widely assumed that the Queen was both embarrassed and angry at being shown to have been used as cover for an intelligence exercise. Because of the fluke circumstance, to which I have already referred, I can state with confidence that the Queen was quite unflustered and was in no doubt that the advice she had been given had been correct, as she herself had been in accepting it.

While the Queen's reactions to the Blunt Affair caused much public discussion in the autumn of 1979, the private concern in the security and intelligence world centered on the unprecedented official exposure of Blunt by the prime minister, Mrs. Thatcher, in Parliament. I asked Sir Harold Wilson whether he would have been so forthcoming, and he replied that not only would he have declined to reveal such details, but he believed that all other prime ministers he had known would also have declined.

I suspect that Sir Harold was right concerning the likely reaction of Clement Attlee, Sir Winston Churchill, Sir Anthony Eden, Harold Macmillan, Sir Alec Douglas Home, and, perhaps, Edward Heath. But he was wrong about his successor, James Callaghan.

In 1978, Merlyn Rees, while home secretary during the Callaghan administration, realized that the Blunt story was bound to break one day—probably through the book being prepared by Andrew Boyle—so he decided that a full statement should be prepared in readiness for publication if necessary.

Because of the royal connection, the Queen was approached then for her view concerning the consequent publicity. The Queen replied that she would take whatever advice was offered on the issue.

The document that had been prepared in 1972 for possible use in the event of Blunt's death, outlining his main acts of treachery, was brought up to date by the Cabinet Office at the request of Merlyn Rees. With the agreement of Sam Silkin, the attorney general, James Callaghan was advised that if Blunt was exposed, then a full and accurate statement should be given to Parliament and that there was no way of avoiding it. Callaghan agreed "with distaste," and a draft statement was prepared. Though this statement was no doubt reexamined by the Tory administration, it formed the basis of the announcement that Mrs. Thatcher eventually made to Parliament.

While MI5 had been required to cooperate with the Cabinet Office in the preparation of the statement, there was strong feeling among senior officers of that organization and in the Secret Service that the government was reneging on the package deal made with Blunt. The immunity had clearly included immunity from official exposure in the eyes of both Blunt and the MI5 case officer who had negotiated the arrangement. While there was no sympathy for Blunt, as such, there was fear that other traitors would be far less inclined to cooperate in return for immunity in future and would still escape prosecution simply by refusing to be interviewed.

The facts that I have presented show that Mrs. Thatcher

herself had little option in the matter, as the main decisions
had already been taken, including consultation with the
Queen. Her statement was regarded as being remarkably full,
but from information I have received, I doubt that either she
or Mr. Callaghan were given the details of Blunt's activities
that I have described.

There are some Conservative MPs, including one junior
minister very close to her, who believe that Mrs. Thatcher's
statement was designed to trigger off a major inquiry into the
state of the security and intelligence services and that she was
"within a hair's breadth" of announcing one. If that was so,
there had been a change of heart by the time the issue of
such an inquiry was debated in Parliament.

It is not my purpose in this book to urge that such an
inquiry should be made. The conviction that "a flue brush"
should be put through the two organizations—held by MPs
on both sides of the House—would assuredly have merited
support in the fairly recent past, but the information at my
disposal suggests that both are now "clean." The only residual
doubt lies in the possibility that traitors who are now dead or
gone managed to insinuate young successors who may still be
there.

One aspect of the prime ministerial statement on Blunt
with which I and most of my informants take issue is the
insistence that "the director general of the Security Service
followed scrupulously the procedures that had been laid
down." The director general was Sir Roger Hollis, and all that he
did scrupulously was to make sure that he did not lay himself
open to censure by failing to obey the laid-down rules when
it suited him to obey them. His general handling of the case
can hardly be described as scrupulous, while his suspension
of the case officer for the crucial fortnight after Blunt's
confession was unprecedented. I suspect that Mrs. Thatcher
was not informed of that event, and I have established that
the attorney general, Sir Michael Havers, had not been told
about it before he made his statement in the Blunt debate.

The same apologia for Hollis was made in the official report
on the Profumo case by Lord Denning, when his behavior
had been so patently inept as to appall his own colleagues. I
have no doubt that Lord Denning was motivated by sympathy for a man doing what is perhaps the most difficult job in
the entire apparatus of government, but in the result the

presentation of Hollis as a man of scrupulous integrity, always working within the laid-down procedures, was not justified by his actions. Had the Denning Report criticized Hollis's handling of the Profumo case, as I and others believe it should have, then the consequent parliamentary debate might have concentrated some of its fire on a more justifiable target instead of directing it all on to Harold Macmillan, who was already the injured party.

19
Spies in
the Secret Service

Ever since MI5 and the Secret Service (MI6) were established consequent on the reorganization of military intelligence in 1905, there has been jealousy and rivalry between them. The Secret Service, which could claim to date back to the reign of Elizabeth I, considered itself both senior and superior. "Empire building" by both organizations led to wide overlapping of duties in the counterespionage field, exacerbating competition and rivalry, which have been detrimental to both services and to national security as a whole.

Both have tended to hoard their information instead of sharing it. For many years, MI5 was barred from access to Secret Service files and had to request information in writing. Quite recently there was a case in which MI5 had hard evidence that a member of the Secret Service had a Communist past, which he had not declared, but failed to notify its sister service of the fact.

This antipathy expressed itself as burning resentment in the late 1960s after the Secret Service had been castigated so severely in public for harboring two Russian spies, in the shape of Philby and George Blake. With the proof of Blunt's treachery inside MI5 and the immunity deal whereby it was to be concealed forever, it was felt in the Secret Service that MI5 was "getting away with it." This childish reaction was greatly intensified as the suspicion against MI5's director general, Sir Roger Hollis, gathered momentum. The Secret Service knew all about it because it had members on the investigating committee.

There was no reasonable basis for the Secret Service pressure that there should be some public exposure of the evidence that the Soviet penetration had been every bit as severe inside MI5. If Philby had accepted immunity to prosecution, the public would not have been told of his guilt and would have presumed him innocent. Nevertheless, this pressure was one of the driving forces that eventually led to the Trend Inquiry into the accusations against Hollis and Mitchell.

The crusading attitude of those Secret Service officers who applied the pressure was even less justifiable because there were still hidden skeletons in their own cupboard. I have already mentioned John Cairncross and other former members of the Secret Service whose treachery was discovered following leads from Blunt. In addition there was one major self-confessed spy whose existence has been entirely concealed from the public. During the MI5 investigation into his activities, which amounted to treason in war, he was known by the code name "Emerton." I shall reveal his identity and his acts later in this chapter, but first it is convenient to discuss certain aspects of the Blake case and that of the Russian defector Oleg Penkovsky.

I have mentioned how the first clue to the existence of the Navy Spy Ring run by Gordon Lonsdale came from a Polish intelligence officer who sent information to the CIA under the code name "Sniper." The CIA did not know his identity or his nationality until he eventually defected to the United States via Berlin on Christmas Day 1960, taking with him files on intelligence agents of the industrial, scientific, and technical bureau of the Polish Intelligence Service, together with a mass of other information concerning Red Army plans and operations, all of extreme interest to Britain and other NATO countries as well as to America. He turned out to be Col. Michal Goleniewski, aged fifty-eight, an important member of the UB, the Polish equivalent of the KGB, with which it had close links.

Before he defected he had disclosed, in 1959 in his written reports, that the Russians had been regularly receiving copies of British Secret Service documents. This information was immediately passed to the Secret Service by the CIA. The Secret Service chiefs knew that an unknown number of their secret documents had been stolen from a safe in Brussels, and they conveniently assumed that "Sniper" must be referring to them.

Before defecting, "Sniper" (later known in the United Kingdom as "Lavinia") also warned the Secret Service that there was an active KGB spy operating inside it known in the KGB as "Diamond." He said that the information that "Diamond" had been supplying was of the greatest value to the Russians. Whatever the Secret Service did, or did not do, it failed to find "Diamond."

Goleniewski would have continued "in place" in Warsaw for longer but was driven to defect because he found out that someone in the West had warned the KGB that there was a spy in the Polish UB acting for the CIA. He was regarded so highly by Soviet bloc intelligence that he was asked to seek out the American spy. "We have evidence that there is a 'pig' in your organization," a KGB liaison officer had told him, using the KGB expression for a traitor. Realizing that the suspicion must soon fall on himself, "Sniper" decided that it was time to escape, and he reached the United States in January 1961, accompanied by Howard Roman of the CIA and taking with him his German mistress rather than his wife.

The CIA had reason to believe that the leak to the KGB about the "pig" inside the UB came from someone at a high level in the Secret Service or in MI5 who had seen the material forwarded to them from Washington.

A CIA officer visiting London to discuss "Sniper's" information with MI5 had suggested that the evidence pointed to his being a senior officer in the First Department of the UB, as indeed he proved to be, being the head of the technical and scientific department.

With the agreement of the CIA, a Secret Service man was sent to the United States to interrogate Goleniewski, who had already been told that the British had failed to find "Diamond." The defector was terrified that the interrogator might be "Diamond," himself, who had been sent to kill him on KGB orders. As Goleniewski knew, the KGB has a sophisticated spray, disguisable as a pen or cigarette lighter, which can simulate the fatal symptoms of a heart attack. So he declined any face to face encounter. Instead, he insisted in being in one room with the interrogator in another and an interpreter running between them.

The defector ridiculed the idea that the Secret Service documents he had seen were those filched from any safe and was contemptuous of the failure to find "Diamond" and deal with him, as he assured his interrogator the KGB would have done.

He was able to describe the highly secret documents he had seen. These even included the "watch list" supplied by Secret Service headquarters in London to its agents in Poland, listing individuals they needed to keep under surveillance.

When the interrogator returned to London, where Goleniewski always refused to venture, the Secret Service chiefs were quickly convinced that "Diamond" undoubtedly existed and was still inside the organization. When a list was examined of those who had had access to the documents the defector had described, an officer called George Blake stood out beyond all others, especialy as Goleniewski had said that he had worked in Berlin, but it was decided that he had too many successes to his credit to be a spy. They ignored the fact that all espionage organizations, and the KGB in particular, allow their agents to notch up a few successes to maintain their credibility with their employers.

It soon became obvious, however, that the hemorrhage of secrets to Russia had suddenly ceased when Blake had been posted in 1960 to attend a course in Arabic at the school, jointly run by the Secret Service and the Foreign Office, at Shemlan near Beirut. For example, Goleniewski had seen an extremely secret report by the Requirements Division of the Secret Service for 1959, but nothing had arrived from the London source for 1960.

The Secret Service station chief in Beirut, Nicholas Elliott, was given the job of inducing Blake to return to London without arousing his suspicions. He succeeded brilliantly. Blake returned to discuss "a new job involving promotion," but Elliott had sat up all night wondering if he would defect.

It may be significant that the Secret Service did not inform MI5 of the impending arrest of Blake and that information did not leak to the KGB, as happened in the case of Philby. Incidentally, Philby, who was close by, in Beirut, had no knowledge that Blake was a KGB agent. Nor, it seems, did Blake have any certain knowledge concerning Philby's KGB role, as it is routine practice for any well-run espionage agency to keep its spies in separate compartments so that, if caught, they cannot betray others.

Blake was questioned by an ace interrogator, Terence Lecky. I give his name because he has left the service and his outstanding success has been publicly attributed to someone else. The spy denied everything repeatedly, while encouraging his questioner to talk and so reveal how much he knew. Lecky's menacing glances at an imposing pile of files, allegedly full of evidence, that he had ostentatiously loaded on to his desk knowing how thin his case was, produced not a flicker of response.

If Blake had continued to hold out, no case could have been brought against him. But, literally, at the interrogator's last throw, he broke down and confessed to a horrifying string of treacherous acts on behalf of the KGB.

He described how he had been present at the original planning of Operation Gold, a 1,500-foot-long tunnel to be driven under the East-West demarcation boundary in Berlin to tap Red Army cables carrying coded signals and scrambled telephone conversations. The tunnel, which was equipped with the most sophisticated recording equipment, originated in the basement of a building that appeared to be a warehouse modified as a radar-listening station. Blake confessed that he had given away the secret to the Russians early in 1954, before even a spit of the tunnel had been dug. This Anglo-American enterprise cost at least $25 million to build and operate for the year that the Allies thought that they were tapping Soviet military secrets. Instead, they were listening to a mass of coded misinformation, larded with occasional accurate material to serve as "chicken feed." The effort in decoding the bogus information was so stupendous that Operation Gold should be renamed Operation Dross.

The Russians allowed the operation, including the construction, to continue for two years before moving in, partly, perhaps, to protect its informant, Blake. They then took maximum propaganda advantage of this "imperial duplicity," opening the tunnel for inspection by journalists. It was but one of many examples of the patience of the KGB in playing disinformation games.

Much of the know-how for building the Berlin tunnel had come from a previous all-British enterprise called Operation Silver. This was a much shorter—sixty-foot long—tunnel built from under a private house on the outskirts of Vienna to link with cables originating in the headquarters of the Russian occupation forces in the city. British engineers had been able to tap the cables for several years with useful results concerning Soviet intentions. Blake was not then in a position to know of the operation and to betray it.

Blake confessed that while working at headquarters in London, he had betrayed everything he could about the Secret Service, including the "battle order"—the personnel and how and where they were deployed. This was to have serious repercussions later.

While working in West Berlin, he had met KGB agents freely in the Eastern sector, contacting them regularly in a big department store and handing over a mass of information and copies of documents he had photographed. This had aroused no suspicion because he had been given permission to contact Russians in pursuit of his undercover duties. He also handed over information that enabled the KGB to kidnap prominent East Germans who had defected to the West and to abduct them back behind the Iron Curtain.

Blake's description of how he had operated in his West Berlin headquarters was a terrible indictment of the security there. At lunchtime, when all offices containing secret papers had to be locked, he hid behind his desk to give the security guard the impression that the room was empty. He then had at least an hour and a half to photograph documents without fear of interruption. It has been believed that Blake, whose original name was Behar, was converted to communism while in a prison camp, following his capture during the Korean War when he was operating out of the British embassy in Seoul. It is now thought that he was probably already a Communist when he joined the Secret Service in 1948, after undertaking wartime intelligence work for the navy. He could have been talent-spotted or even recruited while attending a Russian language course at Downing College, Cambridge, in 1947. One of the people there is now known to have been a recruiter for the KGB and, later, an active agent. There is no evidence whatever that he was recruited by Burgess, as has been suggested.

Why did Blake confess? The answer probably lies in the undoubted resentment that he felt at the way he believed he had been treated by other officers in the Secret Service. Because he was half Jewish and spoke English with an accent, being Dutch on his mother's side, he was convinced that they looked down on him. So, perhaps, it gave him satisfaction to show his superiors just how cleverly and to what an incredible extent he had fooled them.

Steps bordering on the ridiculous were taken by the Foreign Office, acting on behalf of the Secret Service, to cover up the scandal of Blake's activities. The secretary of the D-Notice Committee requested the media to suppress any information that they might discover. This was followed by a D-Notice urging the withholding from the public of the fact that Blake had ever worked for the Secret Service or betrayed any state secrets. There were dark hints that the lives of other agents were still in danger, though those who could be withdrawn already had been. The concern in Whitehall was understandable, but it had nothing to do with security, only with embarrassment. The greatest embarrassment the authorities could have suffered would have been Blake's retraction of his confession in court. Lord Dilhorne, who, as Sir Reginald Manningham Buller, had been attorney general at the time, told me that though Blake had signed his confession statement, a prosecution could still have failed had he claimed that it had been secured under duress and was, in fact, false. There was anxiety right up to the time that he pleaded guilty. This also enabled the authorities to blanket many of the details of his crimes, which became known only because George Brown (now Lord), who had been told of them by the prime minister, Macmillan, leaked them to me because he was convinced that the cover-up was pure face saving by Whitehall.

The KGB must have been astonished when Blake confessed because, presumably, they would have known that there was no legal evidence against him. But any distress at losing such a valuable agent was amply compensated for by the disruptive effect of his activities on Anglo-American intelligence relations when these became public. Much of the effort made by Macmillan and his government to blanket the horrific details of Blake's treachery was to conceal from the British public the inefficiency, which had allowed such a spy to operate for so long inside the Secret Service. The main objective, however, was to conceal the facts from the U.S. Congress after the Fuchs and Maclean cases had already done so much damage to the reputation of Britain as a safe ally with whom to share secrets.

Blake was staggered by the unprecedented sentence of forty-two years, which, as it happened, amounted to about one year for every British agent he had betrayed, many to their death. In retrospect, however, the security authorities believe the severity to have been counterproductive, for it must have deterred others from confessing. In any event, the sentence proved to be academic because Blake escaped from Wormwood Scrubs in 1966 after serving only six years and, with KGB assistance, reached refuge in Moscow.

The Blake case is evidence of the depth to which the Secret Service has been penetrated by Soviet spies. It was also a further instance of the total failure of the parent organization or of MI5 to suspect a spy's existence until given the information "on a plate" by a chance defector.

In the minds of many former members of the Secret Service and of some still there, the greatest triumph for British Intelligence since the war was the defection of the Russian intelligence officer Colonel Oleg Penkovsky in April 1961. In the minds of many members of MI5, however, Penkovsky was a Soviet "plant," the key figure in a Soviet disinformation exercise of the highest political consequence.

Whatever the truth, an analysis of the facts as they are now known raises grave suspicions. Penkovsky, a senior member of the Chief Intelligence Directorate of the Soviet General Staff, was in his early forties when he first approached the West in order to defect. He walked quite openly into the American embassy in Moscow, a building that, as he must have known, was under constant surveillance by the KGB. The Americans rejected him as an obvious plant—what the CIA calls a "provocation agent."

He received the same treatment from the Canadians when he openly approached one of their officers in a Moscow hotel. As a third resort, Penkovsky approached the British Secret Service through a British businessman who had need to visit Moscow and other Iron Curtain capitals and had been given some intelligence training. His name was Greville Wynne.

Once the British became convinced of Penkovsky's *bona fides*, as they quickly did, the American CIA decided that it might as well take an interest, and the running of Penkovsky became a joint Anglo-American operation from its effective start. On April 20, 1961, Penkovsky had his first debriefing session in London, which he was visiting as a member of a Soviet delegation, ostensibly to further Anglo-Soviet trade in the field of machinery and electronics. Two British Secret Service men and two CIA officials asked the questions. Officers of MI5 were involved only in organizing the interrogation arrangements and countersurveillance in the Mount Royal Hotel, where the delegation was staying.

Penkovsky brought with him some Red Army rocket training manuals, which gave detailed information about missiles already in use, along with copies of some rocket training lectures. His most startling news was his statement that missiles of the type described in the manual were shortly to be established in Cuba, only two hundred miles off the American shore, where they would be capable of threatening many cities.

His information convinced the U.S. National Security Council that it had been mistaken in believing that the Russians were so far ahead of the Americans in rocket development that there was a dangerous "missile gap." This belief had been responsible for crash programs in speeding the production of American missiles to close the gap, one of them, called Thor, being already installed on the east coast of England.

There is no doubt that Penkovsky's information not only provided President John F. Kennedy with advance information about the Cuban missiles but gave him confidence in taking a tough stand with the Kremlin by blockading Cuba and insisting that the missiles be withdrawn. In the result Khrushchev withdrew the missiles, an apparent climb down that has always been hailed as a victory for Kennedy and for the West.

Penkovsky also gave the names of hundreds of Soviet intelligence officers, including that of Eugene Ivanov, the Soviet naval attaché in London who was to be a central figure in the Profumo Affair—though Penkovsky could not have foreseen that. He gave other information believed, at the time, to be of great importance. So why should there be any doubts about him?

The first doubt was raised by his original behavior, which had been incredibly imprudent for a professional intelligence officer. His blatant walk-in to the Americans and Canadians had been suspicious in itself. Then, after one of the interrogation sessions in the Mount Royal Hotel, he had demanded an immediate payment of £1,000 in notes.

When it was suggested that it would be unwise to be seen spending so much money in London shops, which was his purpose in asking for it, Penkovsky lost his temper and cried, "Whose neck will get it, yours or mine? The stuff I gave you tonight is worth more than £1000!"

He got the money and spent it all, mainly on presents for senior officials and their wives back in Moscow. It is not known whether he was observed by the KGB handing so much cash across counters, though it would be normal practice for an eye to be kept on such a Russian visiting Britain. According to Greville Wynne, in his book *The Man from Moscow*, it would have been of little consequence, anyway. When Penkovsky had to buy a large extra suitcase to hold all the loot, Wynne asked him how he would get it through the Moscow customs. "Oh, General Serov will see to that," he replied. Serov was the reigning head of the KGB.

Penkovsky returned to London in July for a trade exhibition, to which he escorted Madame Serov. At that time, he was interrogated at great length, as he was again during a visit to Paris in September. He had been equipped to take photographs of secret documents, but as Wynne's trips behind the Iron Curtain were infrequent, some more regular courier had to be found. The courageous wife of Rory Chisholm, the chief Secret Service man in Moscow, posing as a diplomat there, agreed to take on the task. On fourteen occasions, Penkovsky strolled in parks and other places where Mrs. Chisholm "happened" to be with her children and handed over films while pretending to talk with them and give the youngsters sweets.

When George Blake was further interrogated in prison after his conviction, he said that he had betrayed Rory Chisholm to the KGB before the officer had ever left London for Moscow. He had picked out the Chisholms, husband and wife, from photographs shown to him by a Russian intelligence officer. It would seem most likely, therefore, that Penkovsky's meetings with Mrs. Chisholm were probably watched by the KGB from their start. It is certain that they were being monitored by early 1962 and that Penkovsky was aware of it.

After Greville Wynne had been arrested on behalf of the

KGB while visiting Budapest in November 1962, he was taken to the Lubyanka Prison in Moscow and grilled for weeks. During one session, they played him a tape recording of one of his conversations with Penkovsky. He recognized it as one of their earlier talks in a room in the Ukraine Hotel. This was firm proof that they had been under surveillance from an early stage. So either Penkovsky had been quickly "blown" or had been a fake from the beginning.

A reexamination by MI5 of the information brought in by Penkovsky showed that almost all of it could be classed as "chicken feed"—genuine information provided to establish confidence in Penkovsky so that his major objective could succeed.

The technical information about the rockets was several years old. Many of the GRU Intelligence officers he identified were already known as such in the West. He did not provide a single lead to the identification of any Russian spies actually operating in the West, which was most unusual for a defector of his potentiality. Penkovsky was deputy head of a combined operation between the GRU and the KGB to collect and collate scientific intelligence, yet he declined to give any information of consequence in that field. He produced very little about intercontinental missiles or Soviet reconnaissance satellites, on which he should have been knowledgeable because of his position.

Some of the "facts" he did provide turned out to be misleading—perhaps deliberately so. For example, he said that Soviet scientists had developed a nerve gas that was doubly as effective as anything available to the West. The Americans spent a huge sum trying to make something similar without success, and it is now believed that the information was false.

But what about the true and immensely valuable information about the proposed location of Russian missiles in Cuba? When the defector Golitsin was debriefed in 1962, he told the CIA that, three years previously, when he had completed his current task in the KGB, he was looking around for a move to a more interesting department. Knowing a senior officer in the Disinformation Department, which had been given heightened status, he approached him. The officer had agreed to take on Golitsin but explained that he would be unable to arrange a transfer for another year because a traitor had been discovered inside the GRU. Until the ramifications of his activities, which affected the KGB, had been thoroughly explored and rectified, it would not be possible to proceed with a major disinformation exercise against the West, in which there could be a role for Golitsin.

The traitor was a certain Col. Peter Popov, who had been recruited by the CIA in 1953. He had given the code names of nearly four hundred "illegal" agents operating for the GRU, many of them being eventually identified, and had done other damage to the Soviet intelligence machine. He had been betrayed eventually to his death probably by George Blake, who confessed that he had known all about Popov. With the good fortune that so often smiled on British traitors, Blake had by chance been sitting in an intelligence post in West Berlin when Popov had breezed in while trying to contact the CIA.

Golitsin now believes that the major disinformation exercise that his colleague had forecast was the Penkovsky Affair and that it succeeded. So do some senior officers of the British security and intelligence services.

Their view is that Khrushchev's purpose was essentially to force President Kennedy into a commitment not to invade Cuba, which was, and still is, far more important to the Kremlin as a center for the spread of communism in the Caribbean and South America than as a base for missiles.

Any medium-range rockets on Cuba were soon to be outdated by intercontinental missiles based on Soviet soil. Moreover, Khrushchev could have been in little doubt that no American president could really countenance the presence of Russian nuclear rockets so near to the United States. In fact, if installed, they would have given the United States an excellent excuse, in the eyes of the world, for invading Cuba and unseating Fidel Castro and his regime.

Though Khrushchev appeared to climb down by withdrawing the missiles, Kennedy agreed in return not to invade Cuba. The result at the time of writing, eighteen years later, is that Castro and the Communist regime are still in power and *all* American cities are threatened by Soviet missiles.

Independent evidence that this could have been Khruschev's objective was provided by the Czech defector, Maj. Gen. Jan Sejna, in his debriefing by the CIA, Sejna testified that when defending his handling of the Cuban missile crisis, Khrushchev pointed out that the main purpose had been achieved—the procurement of an American agreement not to interfere in Cuba. Cuba had been "saved for communism."

The American U2 spy plane had been shot down over Russia and its pilot, Francis Gary Powers, captured in May 1960. Eisenhower, then president, had forbidden any further flights over the U.S.S.R. There were no Western spies on the ground in Russia, so the United States remained blind to Soviet missile developments until the first spy-in-the-sky satellite was launched at the end of 1962. This situation, which may not have been accidental, meant that the West lacked any means of checking Penkovsky's claim that there was no "missile gap." So it could have been disinformation.

Penkovsky was tried along with Greville Wynne in Moscow in a propaganda show trial aimed at discrediting the British and Americans as a gang of war-mongering spies, using methods to which the Russian peace-loving government would never stoop. There had previously been a rehearsal, and a claque had been selected to laugh and jeer at the required moments.

The precise timing of the trial was unusually interesting. After the Soviet spy in the Admiralty, William Vassall, had been convicted, a public inquiry into certain political reper-cussions of the case was held under the name of the Vassall Tribunal, opening its proceedings in January 1963. This generated worldwide coverage of the ruthless way in which Vassall had been recruited by KGB homosexual blackmail. Shortly after the tribunal's report was published, it was announced in Parliament that there would be a debate on it. On the afternoon of that announcement the counselor at the Soviet embassy, Romanov, was sitting in the public gallery, as was his frequent custom. The next day, the Kremlin an-nounced that the public trial of Wynne and Penkovsky would open in Moscow on the same date.

The Moscow show trial received worldwide publicity. The KGB also used it to expel eight British "diplomats" and five Americans, whom they knew to be intelligence agents. There was a substantial reorganization of the GRU with postings and retirements, but if the Penkovsky Affair had been a disin-formation exercise, that would have been a necessary re-quirement.

After the trial, it was announced that Penkovsky had been

summarily executed by firing squad, but that sounded most unlikely. The KGB's practice is to interrogate a traitor over a very long period before silencing him. Wynne believes that Penkovsky committed suicide while in prison, but there are others who believe that he may still be alive in Russia under a different name. He did not have close ties with his family, as his behavior with women, while in London and Paris, indicated.

What is certain is that the *Penkovsky Papers*, a book published in 1965 and alleged to be compiled from diaries and other documents secretly penned by Penkovsky and smuggled out of Moscow, was a CIA concoction. I was officially told this in advance when offered the British serial rights on the book during a visit to New York. Penkovsky left no diaries. The concoction was compiled from tapes of the long interrogation sessions during his visits to London and Paris.

There are many who cannot bring themselves to believe that Penkovsky was a fake, if only because, having accepted him as the greatest Soviet defector ever, their professional reputations are bound up with his integrity. Some of those, however, do not deny that he was "blown" soon after contact with the West was made. One of these, James Angleton, suspects that the KGB source of this act of treachery was British and could well have been a high-level officer of MI5.

The number of people in any security organization who are given the name of a defector who is still "in place" is strictly limited, for obvious reasons. But, though MI5 was only marginally involved in the Penkovsky operation, Sir Roger Hollis had taken the unusual step of asking for the defector's name and had been given it.

The major public disaster for the Secret Service was, of course, the scandal of Kim Philby, culminating in well-deserved, worldwide publicity following his defection to Moscow in 1963. It was apparent that until the unexpected evidence of his treachery arrived from Flora Solomon in 1962, he had duped almost all his former Secret Service colleagues with the exception of the director general, Sir Dick White, who had moved over from MI5 already convinced of Philby's guilt.

To what extent his colleagues were motivated by loyalty to a friend or determination to protect the good name of the service, which was of the highest repute throughout the world, may never be known. But both they and certain members of MI5 were culpable in failing to take note of events that should have aroused deep suspicion. The Volkov Affair, which I have described, was one of these.

In the first place, Philby had twice been cleared for entry by MI5, when he managed to insinuate himself with Burgess's assistance into a side branch of the Secret Service in 1940 and then into the Secret Service headquarters in the following year. His Communist past had been so well known in Cambridge that an alert security organization should have discovered it, especially at a time when Russia was not an ally but tied to Nazi Germany by a nonaggression pact.

What is more unpardonable, both on the part of MI5 and the Secret Service, was their failure to find out that Philby was married to a Communist, so ardent as to be an active agent for the Soviet Union. Philby's first wife was a Viennese Jewess called Litzi, who continued to live in London and keep in touch with Philby even though he was already cohabiting with the woman who became his second wife. The latter was to have three children by him and was about to give birth to a fourth when he finally married her.

Philby told Blunt that he delayed a divorce from Litzi for so long because he feared that there would be an inquiry into why he had concealed the fact that he was married to an ardent Communist and that her activities could not withstand investigation. In fact, when he did raise the matter with his superiors, MI5 told them that Litzi, who was by then living in East Berlin, was known to be a Soviet agent. Nothing whatever was done about it so far as Philby was concerned. All that transpired—after Philby had defected—was that one of his Secret Service colleagues was fired after it was discovered that he had lived for a while with Litzi in London and, knowing her Communist and pro-Russian connections, had failed to report the fact.

It was a friend inside MI5, Tomas Harris, the deception expert, who suggested the move that enabled Philby to burrow deep into the center of things in the Secret Service. Harris knew that the section involved with Spain and Portugal, on which he himself was a specialist in MI5, was under-manned and that Philby had experience of the Spanish Civil War. It was friends in MI5 who helped Philby to conspire against his chief and to replace him as head of the Iberian section. They also assisted him to take over the new Russian section when the Secret Service set this up in 1944.

Philby was in regular contact with Soviet controllers in London and never seems to have taken any important decision without consulting them. While there was no known reason to keep him under surveillance, the controllers themselves were subject to it, or should have been. There is also evidence that, like Burgess, Philby was living beyond his means, yet this seemed to cause no wonder or concern.

In view of all this and more, it seems possible that friends in MI5 might have been doing more than turning a blind eye to suspicious circumstances.

There was evidence, too, of blind eyes inside the Secret Service. When the allegation of the existence of a Russian spy, code-named "Elli," inside MI5 was first made in 1945 by the Soviet defector, Igor Gouzenko, secret telegrams to this effect were sent to MI5 and to the Secret Service. As Philby was by that time in charge of the Russian section of the Secret Service, one of the telegrams came to him. Examination of the "Elli" files after Philby's defection showed what he had done with the telegram. Normally, it would have been filed flat, but the "Elli" telegram handled by Philby had been folded in four. Clearly, he had taken it outside the office to show to somebody who, in all probability, was his Soviet controller.

Several other officers must have seen that file, but none of them seems to have wondered why the telegram was creased, or if they did, nobody appears to have questioned Philby about it.

Though Philby was not then very senior, the freedom of action allowed him was remarkable. After the "Elli" telegram had arrived, the director general of the Secret Service, then Sir Stewart Menzies, suggested to Philby that he should go to Ottawa and interrogate Gouzenko. Philby asked for a day "to think about it," meaning to give himself time to consult his Soviet controller. He then suggested that his MI5 counter-part, Roger Hollis, should go instead, and Menzies agreed.

The reason why Philby decided against leaving London at that time, probably on Soviet advice, only became apparent during the backtrack inquiries after his defection.

The Volkov case, which he believed could have brought about his downfall as well as that of other British spies, began in late August, and Philby had not resolved it to his advantage until early September. He was back from his fruitful journey to Istanbul when Gouzenko defected on September 5, and if Menzies had ordered him to go to Ottawa instead of requesting him, he would have been on his way on September 7. With the possibility that the collapse of the Volkov defection might lead to inquiries as to its cause, it was to Philby's advantage to remain at headquarters where he might be able to cope with any discrepencies with his persuasive brand of glib excuses. As usual, he got his way.

What the security authorities would like to know—purely for the historical records—is whether Philby's Soviet controller suggested that he should recommend Hollis as his replacement for the Gouzenko interrogation. As I have recorded, Hollis did not send back much information and played down the "Elli" allegation.

The existence of another Secret Service spy, believed to have operated for Britain's enemies, perhaps for thirty years, was uncovered in 1965. The event has been so carefully concealed for political purposes, as well as for reasons of embarrassment, that many of his former colleagues will be astounded by what I have to tell. For this man was held in the highest regard by most senior officials in Britain and America and—as it transpired—in some rather unexpected countries, too.

The spy's name was Charles Howard Ellis, known to his friends as "Dick." He was a career intelligence officer best known for his wartime service as second in command to Sir William Stephenson, the "Man called Intrepid." In that position, he had access to the most secret operations of British Security Co-ordination, the Anglo-U.S. Intelligence organization set up in New York under Stephenson at Winston Churchill's request.

Ellis was an Australian, born in Sydney before the turn of the century, in 1895. He joined the British army, serving with missions on the Russian border immediately after World War I and becoming fluent in the Russian language. Eventually, he left the army to complete linguistic studies, including German, at Oxford and the Sorbonne.

For a short time, he served as a Foreign Office diplomat in various posts; then, in 1924, he joined the Secret Intelligence Service. As he had married into a White Russian emigré family, the Zilenskis, who were domiciled in Paris, he was posted there with a journalistic job as cover to operate in the large White Russian community, which was known to be heavily penetrated by Soviet military intelligence.

Among the agents Ellis recruited in Paris to work for Britain was his brother-in-law Alexander Zilenski, who was a valuable source because he had access to a man called Waldemar von Petrov. Paris was then the center of White Russian hopes of overthrowing the Soviet regime and one of the White Russian leaders was a certain General Turkhul, with whom von Petrov was friendly. The advantage of this gossip chain to British intelligence in the thirties lay in the fact that Turkhul—the same general to whom I have already referred in connection with the "Klatt" Affair—had ingratiated himself with Heinrich Himmler and Alfred Rosenberg, who were both close to Hitler.

Such a complex chain is typical of the sources on which secret services depend for "raw" intelligence, which then has to be cross-checked at other points. As World War II drew near, Ellis used the chain to send back a mass of confidential information about Nazi affairs to his headquarters in London.

Unfortunately, much of this intelligence turned out to be faked, and though Ellis managed to blame his sources, he fell out of favor with his Secret Service chiefs. Gradually, he rehabilitated himself and was forgiven. In 1940, in the uniform of a colonel, he was posted to serve on "Intrepid's" staff in New York. There he worked with such apparent effect that he was eventually awarded the U.S. Legion of Merit, to add to his CMG, CBE, and OBE.

In 1944, he returned to Secret Service headquarters in London on promotion to become the controller dealing with Southeast Asia and the Far East and was soon also made controller of North and South American affairs. This meant that, effectively, he became No. 3 in the entire Secret Service hierarchy, controlling its activities in about half the world.

Soon after Maclean and Burgess defected in 1951, MI5 began looking for evidence against Philby, believing that he must have been the Third Man. Among the documents they examined was the record of information provided by a prewar Soviet defector called Walter Krivitsky.

It is apposite, at this point, to consider briefly the career of this extraordinary Russian because, had proper notice been taken of his revelations, many, if not most, of the spies mentioned in this book might have been detected long before they inflicted so much damage.

Krivitsky was one of six young men from a small town who became pioneer members of the Soviet espionage machine. After giving valuable service, at considerable sacrifice, they all died violent deaths, being murdered on Stalin's orders or committing suicide to escape assassination. By 1936, Krivitsky was chief of the Soviet military intelligence for Western Europe, deeply involved in the exchange of military intelligence between Russia and Germany. The following year, when hundreds of agents were ordered back to Moscow to be liquidated in Stalin's insane purge of suspected traitors "plotting" against him, Krivitsky defected to the West in Paris.

There he gave French intelligence so much information concerning the entire Soviet network in Europe, including Britain, that it filled eighty large volumes. The French presumably used the information of value to themselves but passed none of it to anybody else. The eighty volumes were stored in an old barge on the Seine and left there for so long that the bottom of the vessel fell away and all the material was lost. That, at all events, is the official French version of what happened, but there are those who suspect that pro-Soviet agents inside French counterintelligence made sure that Krivitsky's revelations were suppressed.

In the hope of escaping assassination, Krivitsky moved to the United States where he was debriefed again, though not so thoroughly as in France. In 1939, allegations that he had made about Soviet penetration of British government departments were passed to MI5. One of these led to the detection and prosecution of a cypher clerk called King in the Foreign Office. Another referred to a diplomat in the Foreign Office, who could have been Donald Maclean. A third described a man who had been a journalist used by the KGB while working for a British newspaper as a correspondent in the Spanish Civil War. This could well have been Philby.

Krivitsky was therefore invited to London in 1940 for special debriefing by MI5, which was carried out by the woman officer, Jane Sissmore. Among the many statements he made was an allegation that a White Russian, von Petrov, known to have been working for the British Secret Service, had really been a Soviet agent working for the Red Army network, the GRU. Von Petrov had been particularly valuable because he had an important espionage source in the British Secret Service who fed him highly sensitive information.

While discussing his own position, Krivitsky told Miss Sissmore how he lived under daily fear of assassination by Russian revenge killers. "If ever you hear that I have committed suicide, don't believe it. I will have been murdered." He returned to the United States, and in February 1941 his body was found in a Washington hotel bedroom with a fatal head wound inflicted by a soft-nosed bullet. A verdict of suicide was recorded because he left farewell notes. Some friends who read their contents were in little doubt that Krivitsky had killed himself, but I have spoken to a Mrs. Beryl Edwards, who was with Krivitsky's wife, Tania, in Montreal when she received news of her husband's death. Mrs. Krivitsky was convinced that her husband had been murdered by Stalin's assassins, and when the note to her arrived, she remarked, "The writing is Walter's, but the words are not," meaning that he had written it with a pistol at his head. There is evidence that a KGB "hit man," who was also an expert locksmith, was in the United States at the time.

Mrs. Edwards said that there had been three apparent attempts to kill Krivitsky while he was sheltering in Montreal, in spite of protection by the Canadian authorities. She told me that Krivitsky, whom she described as "small, very dynamic and highly intelligent," had been very depressed after visiting MI5 in Britain. He had said, "They just didn't want to listen," she recalled.

Ten years later, when the MI5 team investigating Philby was examining the Krivitsky material, it recovered the thick file on von Petrov from the old records. This file showed that, according to the testimony of an officer of the German Secret Service, the Abwehr, interrogated after the Nazi collapse, von Petrov had also been working for him. The officer had stated that von Petrov had assured him that he had an excellent source of high-grade intelligence inside the British Secret Service and that the Abwehr had no doubt that he was telling the truth because he consistently produced information of the utmost value. The German had also recalled that the secrets from this British source had not reached von Petrov directly but through an intermediary called Zilenski, who was also working for the Abwehr.

Following up this lead, MI5 found that another captured German officer of the Abwehr had confirmed the information and had been able to name Zilenski's British source as a certain Captain Ellis. Furthermore, he had known that Ellis was an Australian and had a Russian wife.

The Abwehr officer who had dealt personally with the material brought in by von Petrov reported that Ellis had supplied documents showing the detailed organization of the British Secret Service and information about secret operations. Among the latter was the fact that, almost up to the outbreak of the war, British intelligence had been tapping a special diplomatic telephone link that Ribbentrop, the German ambassador in London, used when speaking directly to Hitler.

Senior Secret Service officers were asked by MI5 to consult their records of this operation. They reported back that the Germans had suddenly abandoned the telephone link for no known reason. They agreed that the Germans might well have been warned by somebody that the British had been eavesdropping. But they denied that Ellis had ever been involved in the operation and insisted that there was no way he could possibly have known about it.

Meanwhile, the MI5 investigators had discovered further evidence about a sensational international event, the "Venlo Incident," which might incriminate Ellis. In the early days of the war, when Holland was still neutral, two British intelligence officers from the Secret Service, Maj. H. R. Stevens and Capt. S. Payne Best, based at The Hague, were lured across the border at Venlo into Germany. There they were captured by the Gestapo, grilled and held prisoner, finally ending up in a concentration camp.

When they returned to Britain, they reported that it was evident from the questions they were asked that German intelligence had detailed knowledge of the organization of the British Secret Service and of the personalities running it. This was confirmed by another captured German officer, who volunteered the information that a source inside British intelligence had told them how to get hold of Stevens and Best and how best to question them.

There was no proof that the source was Ellis, but he had been in the right position in the Secret Service to have provided the information. Furthermore, there has been no trace of any other spy working for the Germans at that time.

To pursue this lead—in the 1950s—MI5 needed access to the Secret Service files, but this was denied to them. The Secret Service chiefs were already hotly denying the MI5 allegations that Philby was a spy and were not prepared to believe that Ellis had been one, too. They dismissed the evidence of the captured German officers as faked.

The MI5 men were particularly anxious to grill Ellis, not simply to clear up the wartime German evidence but because they had reason to suspect that he had been later recruited by the Russians. The Secret Service chiefs would not permit it. The Secret Service has always insisted on being responsible for its own security and conducting its own counterespionage investigations, so the attempted intrusion by MI5 was deeply resented, as it had been over the Philby case.

Not until ten years later, when Philby defected in 1963 and MI5 could prove that its suspicions about him had been justified, was the Ellis case reopened as part of the general inquiry into the penetration of both services by the Russians.

When the investigators were at last allowed to examine the Secret Service files, they discovered the original report by the Abwehr officer naming Ellis. By the usual ill chance, it had landed on the desk of Kim Philby, who had scrawled across it, "Who is this man Ellis? NFA." NFA meant no further action, and none had ever been taken. At that time, Ellis, by then a colonel, was sitting in an office a few doors down from Philby's in Secret Service headquarters in Broadway, Victoria.

This action by Philby strengthened the suspicions that Ellis had been recruited by the Russians, possibly through von Petrov or perhaps because they had found out about his past activities with the Germans and had been able to blackmail him.

The investigators decided to concentrate on the lead concerning Ellis's involvement in the betrayal of the British tapping of the Ribbentrop-Hitler telephone calls. The operation had been carried out by the security section of the post office, so a search was made of its archives. The official records of the operation were found, and attached to them was a list of six Secret Service officers, proficient in German, who had been fully briefed so that they could act as translators of the conversations. At the top of the list was the name C. H. Ellis.

Satisfied that Ellis had been a spy for Germany, at least until the British were driven out of Europe in 1940, MI5 decided to investigate the possibility that he had continued to spy for the Nazis afterward or had been recruited by the Russians.

Ellis had been with the "Intrepid" organization from 1940 to 1944, and it was already known, from captured German documents and the interrogation of German prisoners, that there had been more than one spy inside it. The Germans had known, for instance, that Leslie Howard, the film actor, had been carrying out secret war missions for Sir William Stephenson. They had been told that he would be on a certain airplane and had been able to shoot it down over the Bay of Biscay.

Had Ellis been one of these spies? Not much could be learned about his activities in New York or in the posts he held soon after the war in the Far East and Southeast Asia. So the inquiries were concentrated on his behavior after he had returned to London.

It was found that just when MI5's investigations into Philby's complicity in the Maclean-Burgess Affair had been gathering momentum, Ellis, then in his late fifties, had suddenly decided to retire and return to Australia because of heart trouble. It had not seemed unusual at the time, but his later behavior strongly suggested that his "heart trouble" was an excuse for getting himself abroad, where, even in a British dominion, he could not have been extradited for offenses under the Official Secrets Act.

To keep the inquiries as secret as possible, the investigators always referred to Ellis as "Emerton" in documents and in conversations. But, as Philby's old colleagues were still refusing to believe that he was a spy and were still in touch with him, one of them who was in the know might have gossiped to him about the suspicion surrounding Ellis. Philby might then have alerted Ellis, for they were friends, and within a short time, Ellis was to do a similar service for Philby.

After the customary farewell parties, Ellis emigrated back to Australia in late 1953. There, though he was supposed to be too ill to do further intelligence work, he quickly signed a two-year contract to work for the Australian Secret Intelligence Service, the counterpart of the British organization from which he had just retired.

Shortly after doing that, and in line of duty, he called on Sir Charles Spry, the director general of the Australian Security Intelligence Organization, the counterpart of MI5. Spry told him, in good faith, that his agency was in touch with an important KGB officer based in the Russian embassy in Canberra and that there were high hopes that he would defect. The man's name was Vladimir Petrov.

This Petrov, who was no relation to the von Petrov whom Ellis had known earlier in Europe, was head of the Soviet espionage apparatus in Australia, and as it was discovered later, his wife was also a career KGB officer. So it was expected that he would bring with him documents and information about other KGB agents operating in Australia and, perhaps, elsewhere in the world.

If Ellis was a Russian spy at that time, his consternation on hearing this can be imagined. After emigrating all the way from Britain to escape possible arrest there, he would find himself faced with possible betrayal in Australia. While neither country would be safe, it would be easier to defect from Britain than from Australia, which was as distant as it could be from any Communist haven.

Ellis's immediate behavior suggested that he was in a state of panic. He resigned his two-year contract only *nine days* after signing it, claiming that he had to return to Britain to marry a woman he had met there shortly before leaving.

Believing his story, the Australian security authorities asked him to serve as a courier so that the British Secret Service and MI5 could be brought up to date, in total secrecy, about the precise situation concerning Petrov. He did this after arriving back in Britain—along with the motorcar he had so recently bought in Australia in March 1954.

Though some of his old Secret Service colleagues may have

known about MI5's previous suspicions concerning Ellis, he was nevertheless briefed, in return for his news about Petrov, on the state of the investigations into Philby, about whom there was still no firm evidence. He was specifically told not to see Philby or talk to him. His response was to leave a note for Philby at his club, the Athenaeum, asking him to lunch.

Philby, who was under telephone surveillance, rang Ellis and fixed a lunch appointment. It is not known what they discussed, but that same afternoon, Philby telephoned his current girl friend to say "the clouds are parting." In his book *My Silent War*, there is a chapter called "The Clouds Part" in which he relates how, after being ignored by the KGB for two years (save for the probable payment of money), he received "through the most ingenious of routes" a message from his Soviet friends conjuring him to be of good cheer.

It is possible that Ellis was that "route," though as I have already described, it could have been via Anthony Blunt. Philby avoided making reference in his book to Ellis, admitting only that Maclean and Burgess had been fellow traitors.

Under interrogation, Blunt has since confirmed that Philby, who was supposed to be remote from any secret information, knew about the impending defection of Petrov in Canberra some weeks before it took place, as it eventually did with sensational publicity in April 1954. Further confirmation has since come from Sir William McMahon, a former prime minister of Australia, who reiterated in the Australian Parliament that he knew that the Russians had been "tipped off" about Petrov's pending defection, though he had no knowledge of the source.

It may therefore be asked why, if Ellis, Philby, and Blunt knew about the defection, it was not prevented, as Volkov's had been. There is evidence that the KGB did know and mistimed Petrov's defection by only a few hours. Two tough diplomatic couriers sent to Canberra from Moscow were later involved in the attempted removal of Mrs. Petrov, who accepted a last-minute offer to defect herself when the plane, bound for Russia, stopped to refuel at Darwin. The later defector, Anatoli Golitsin, provided evidence that the two officers sent from Moscow to bring back both the Petrovs were severely disciplined for failing to do so.

As I have pointed out, the MI5 investigators did not have

the opportunity fo reopen the case against Ellis until after Philby had defected, early in 1963. Such inquiries not only take time but can be expensive. The case officers had taken the trouble, for instance, to show photographs of Ellis, who was short and slim with fair hair that had turned white, to several people living abroad who might have known him to be a Soviet agent. One of these was the widow of Richard Sorge, who thought she recalled his face, though her memory was not good. Another, the widow of Ignace Reiss, a highly successful Soviet spy of Ellis's vintage who had been murdered by the KGB's "Smersh" assassination squad, thought she recognized him but could not be sure.

It was 1965 before the case officers decided that they could get no further without direct action. It was therefore agreed that the time had come for a full interrogation of Ellis, hostile if necessary, to be conducted jointly by officers from the Secret Service and from MI5. As the recently appointed head of counterespionage in the Secret Service was cooperative, Ellis, by that time fully retired and on the pension list in England, was asked to attend for interview.

He was told bluntly that there was serious evidence impugning his loyalty and was confronted with the report of the German officer who named him as a spy. His response was that it must be a forgery. He insisted that he had never heard of the secret telephone link between Ribbentrop and Hitler. Though severely shaken when shown his name at the top of the post office list, he said that he could not recall any involvement. The interrogators then threatened to bring over the German officer and confront him with his evidence. They ended the session by giving him twenty-four hours to think about that.

The following day, Ellis, who was kept under surveillance against his possible defection, arrived with a document that was an abject confession of his guilt in spying for Germany up to 1940.

He complained that the Secret Service had sent him into the field in Europe with inadequate training, which was probably true. He said that it was his unfortunate recruitment of his brother-in-law, Alexander Zilenski, that had turned him into a spy for the Nazis. While Zilenski had produced some useful information for Britain, he was also selling any secrets he could get both to the Germans and to the Russians, being in the game purely for money. Ellis explained that he had run into debt because his British pay was too low and had borrowed from Zilenski, who then started pressurizing him for information to sell to the Germans and Russians.

He claimed that, at first, the information he handed over was trivial, but Zilenski, urged on by his Soviet contact, then threatened to expose him to his Secret Service chiefs unless he provided more valuable material. Ellis excused his action by pointing out that his wife had been ill and that he needed money for her treatment. So he had taken the easy way out, becoming more and more deeply compromised.

Under further questioning, he admitted handing over detailed charts of the organization of British intelligence before the war, knowing that they would go both to Germany and Russia. This had been the source of much of the information that the Abwehr used during its interrogations following the Venlo kidnappings.

He confessed that he had betrayed the British intelligence achievement in tapping the Hitler-Ribbentrop telephone link, knowing that the information was going to Germany. He also admitted making use after the war began of a brother Secret Service officer to deliver secrets, unwittingly, in an envelope delivered to an agent, whom he knew to be working for the Germans, and to bring back a package containing money.

Ellis denied having continued to spy while in the "Intrepid" mission in the United States, being aware that his interrogators had no evidence in that regard. Nevertheless, his confession constituted unquestionably the worst case of British espionage to the Germans both before and during the war.

When told that he had committed treason in war, and could have justifiably been hanged, he broke down and pleaded physical frailty against any further cross-examination, but the interrogators were determined to continue their probing on the following day.

He continued to deny any secret dealings with the Russians and insisted that it had not been the Petrov Affair that had caused him to return so precipitately from Australia. He said that he had returned to marry a girl and, under pressure, gave her name. Inquiries soon showed that she had already been happily married at the time and, though she had met Ellis, had never had any intention of marrying him. Ellis then pleaded that his memory must have been at fault and gave the name of another girl. This, too, proved to be a false trail.

He denied that he had met Philby on his return from Australia, which was known to be a lie, or that the Secret Service had warned him not to contact his former colleague.

Fearful that he might collapse under the strain of further grilling, it was decided that, as a last throw, Ellis should be offered immunity, after the attorney general had been consulted, if he would confess his treacherous activities with Russia and name his contacts. He refused to believe that immunity would really be granted and held to his position regarding any Russian espionage after 1940.

The interrogators' consensus, as entered in the case records, was that Ellis had spied for Russia after the war, not for ideological motives but because he would be under heavy blackmail pressure from the KGB. Through Zilenski, the Center in Moscow knew that Ellis had supplied secrets for money, and it was considered inconceivable that it could resist applying pressure when he was in such a sensitive post, both in New York and later when he returned to the Secret Service proper. It was concluded that it would never be possible to make a detailed assessment of the damage he had done, but if, as seemed likely, his treachery had covered something like thirty years, it would have put Philby's in the shade.

To illustrate the extraordinary relationship existing over so many years between the Secret Service and MI5, I have purposely reserved an item of Ellis's career, which occurred after his unexpected return from Australia in such a hurry. Incredibly, in spite of the peculiar circumstances and the known suspicions of MI5, Ellis was taken back, part time, into Secret Service headquarters in London. There he assisted in the "weeding" of Secret Service files—the extraction of material considered, by an expert such as himself, to be of no further value so that it could safely be consigned to the shredding machine.

If he was still an active spy or keen to cover up past evidence of his own operations and those of his pro-Soviet colleagues, the damage he may have caused in destroying leads to KGB activities is incalculable. Fortunately, there were documents concerning himself and Philby that did not come his way.

I have recently received further independent confirmation of Ellis's treachery from former colleagues of his and from an international authority on intelligence and defense affairs who prefers not to be named. This authority had been involved in the setting up of "Interdoc," the International Documentary Center, an organization involving intelligence affairs. Interdoc needed a London representative, and Ellis had taken on the appointment. In early 1970s, a representative from the Secret Service called on my informant to ask if he had been responsible for recommending Ellis because Ellis was known to have been a spy for Germany and was suspected of having been a Soviet agent, too.

The disquiet among those senior Secret Service men who had not been able to bring themselves to believe that Dick Ellis could possibly have been a spy was intense. After their recent failure to smother Philby's treachery because he had defected rather than accept immunity, they decided that "in the interests of the Service" the Ellis case should be completely suppressed. It has been until the original publication of this book. Considering how many Secret Service officers eventually learned about Ellis's treachery, it is astonishing that it never leaked before. The secret was so closely held that Ellis's relatives and intimate friends never heard of it and still find it hard to believe. Ellis's daughter wrote to Mrs. Thatcher asking her to deny my disclosure, but the prime minister had to decline because she was aware of the truth of it.

In 1962, when Montgomery Hyde published his biography of Sir William Stephenson under the title *The Quiet Canadian,* a foreword was contributed by that outstanding American ambassador to Britain, the late David Bruce. In it, Bruce referred to Ellis as "that remarkable, unpublicized individual." It was a fair description. Little was known of him outside the security services.

Ellis also had another prerequisite of the successful undercover agent—brass nerve. When the more extensive and less accurate book *A Man called Intrepid* was published in 1976, a special historical note was inserted by the publisher. It had been written by Col. Charles Howard Ellis, when an old man living, apparently, in honorable retirement in Eastbourne in Sussex. It contained the paragraph "From New York, while the United States was at peace and at war, Britain ran the most intricate integrated intelligence and secret operations

organization in history. Could such activity be kept secret?"
Ellis, who died in 1975, almost certainly knew the answer.

With Ellis, Philby, Cairncross, and others who appear to
have been less important, the Secret Service was heavily
penetrated before and during World War II and for some
years afterward. What is the position today?

As with MI5, there have been improvements in the regular
vetting of existing officers and agents of the service and the
recruitment of new ones. Documentary films, some of them
records of actual operations taken clandestinely, others made
for the purpose, are used to demonstrate how members of the
security services can be suborned by the KGB. Control of
documents, which was lax in the past to a near-criminal
extent, has been tightened with the involvement of electronic
and other technological devices to help prevent unauthorized
removal. Surveillance of known Soviet bloc agents has been
intensified, where resources permit.

Much, of course, depends on the leadership of the organization, and this has been patchy, to say the least. Sir Dick
White made important changes when he took command after
moving from MI5 in 1956. He banned any resort to violence
by members of the organization, an action that explains why
monsters like Idi Amin are not assassinated before they kill so
many others. Nobody in the Secret Service is licensed to kill
anymore. Even the internal traitor Philby was allowed to
escape to continue to serve an organization that would have
liquidated him without compunction in comparable circumstances.

Even in the past, such assassinations were rare, though
they did occur on occasion. In the operation to oust Mossadeq
and restore the Shah of Iran in 1953, the Secret Service had
successfully organized the murder of an Iranian police chief
in an exercise code-named "Boot."

As the crisis over the unilateral takeover of the Suez Canal
by Egypt's President Nasser deepened in 1956, it became
clear in Whitehall that there was only one solution to the
problem—the toppling of Nasser, by assassination if necessary. To this end, the Secret Service, in collaboration with
leaders of the Special Air Service (SAS), put forward a
detailed plan of an operation to kill Nasser, along with his

bodyguards and anyone else who might be in the way. Plans of a building where, it was known, Nasser was likely to be on a certain night showed that it should be possible to introduce canisters of a poison gas, which would be quickly fatal. It was strenuously argued that this could save both British and Egyptian lives, but Anthony Eden, then prime minister, vetoed the scheme. He did so partly because of the objection to the use of gas but mainly because he demurred at the assassination of a head of state, though the Special Air Service gave an assurance that any evidence of their involvement would be removed so smartly as to be deniable.

Eden turned a blind eye, however, to an alternative Secret Service operation. This was to be controlled by an officer posing under the name of "Colonel Yarrow," in which the killing was to be accomplished by Egyptian officers using a cache of weapons hidden in the sand. This remained part of the Suez Operation but was bungled by the Egyptian officers, who paid for their failure with their lives.

Such misfortunes seemed constantly to dog the Secret Service's attempts to help resolve Britain's international problems. On another occasion, a large cache of arms was concealed behind a false wall, specially built on to the front of a house, in a Middle East country. Regrettably, a lorry ran into the wall, and machine guns, rifles, and other weaponry tumbled out on to the street. The owner of the house, who had moved into it since the cache had been stored and knew nothing of it, subsequently had a hard time at the hands of the local secret police.

In the past, the Secret Service has had no qualms about handing over a captive to a third party intent on killing him. One former officer has described to me how a certain Mikal Trinsky, who had taken money from Polish Jews to help them to escape and had then betrayed them to the Nazis, was kidnapped by the Secret Service and handed over to the Jews concerned. Trinsky's head was eventually used as a football.

Sir Dick White ended such robust measures so completely that during the reign of one of his successors, Sir Maurice Oldfield, a policy statement was circulated through Secret Service headquarters assuring the staff that no violence of any kind would be involved in the espionage and intelligence operations conducted by the organization. This followed a claim by criminals that the Secret Service had supplied them with weapons and explosives to carry out intelligence work against the IRA.

Sir Maurice, who was a personal friend of the author, was profoundly religious, as well as most merciful, and his experiences highlighted the difficulties facing any intelligence chief who believes in the sanctity of human life. While he was deputy director general of the Secret Service in the late 1960s, the KGB captured one of his overseas agents, who was not known to him personally. The KGB knew that the agent had a great deal of useful information and was determined to use any means, including physical torture, to elicit it. It was made known to Sir Maurice through ingenious means that the agent would be prepared to take a lethal pill if this could be supplied to him. As Sir Maurice had to make the decision as to whether to provide the means of enabling a human being to take his own life, he suffered agonies of doubt before putting duty before his religious code of conduct. The pill was smuggled to the imprisoned agent and duly swallowed.

As I have mentioned, in connection with MI5, the new director general for the Secret Service is now recommended by a five-man committee to eliminate the danger that one chief, who might have been pro-Soviet, can install another before he leaves. The successor to Sir Maurice, who retired in 1978, later to be appointed coordinator of security for Northern Ireland, happened to be his former deputy and his recommendation. Members of the committee supported this recommendation to the prime minister, but they expressed concern that their choice was depressingly limited. Others, whom they would have preferred, rejected the post, which is inadequately paid for the enormous responsibility involved.

The same concern was voiced about the new director general of MI5, who was appointed at about the same time. The professional deputy, who might have hoped to succeed the retiring chief, Sir Michael Hanley, was considered to be too young. As a result—and again the field was small—a diplomat from the Foreign Office, Sir Howard Smith, was appointed. Since then, a younger man, who was Smith's deputy and a career security officer, has taken over.

Until recently, the identities of the heads of the Secret Service and MI5 have been withheld from the public as a result of pressure on newspapers suggesting that it was in the interests of national security to do so. This reason was seen to be hollow following a statement to Parliament by Sir Harold Wilson, when prime minister, that national security had never been involved, the implication being that the anonymity had been a matter of personal convenience for those concerned.

Since then, the new dimension of terrorism has provided a more potent reason for anonymity, for the heads of the security services are possible targets. The identity of Sir Howard Smith, however, was disclosed in evidence given to a Parliamentary committee on D-Notices and since published. Jonathan Aitken, the Tory MP for Thanet, pointed out that the current director general had been the ambassador to Moscow and, before leaving Russia, had told the Kremlin of the nature of his new post—with the British government's permission. Sir Howard was appointed in spite of the general convention that nobody who has served in Moscow should be appointed to a senior position in either of the security services. His move was, of course, a triumph for Whitehall, and especially for the Foreign Office, in filling a post that has traditionally gone to MI5 professionals.

During the Parliamentary repercussions of the Blake case, the prime minister, then Harold Macmillan, was required, by pertinent back-bench questioning, to admit that the Secret Service was directly responsible to the Foreign Office. I was told by one of Macmillan's close political friends that Macmillan regarded this admission as one of the most damaging he had ever been forced to make. For such an eminently sensible person, this was a surprising statement, for it has been common knowledge, even among the writers of spy fiction, for many years.

His objection lay in the conclusion, which could obviously be drawn from the association, that the Secret Service makes use of British embassies abroad to house its agents under diplomatic cover. But this again is not only well known but the common practice of all countries. I suspect that as a Briton of the old school he hated having to admit officially to such a deception.

The old-school American politician, Henry Stimson, had done disservice to U.S. intelligence by declaring that espionage was "ungentlemanly," especially when applied to those countries that were not unfriendly. The Foreign Office under the Labour foreign secretary, Michael Stewart, took a similar view and reduced Secret Service operations abroad in places like Libya, which at that time was governed by pro-British King Idris. The result was that when Gadaffi overthrew Idris and set up a revolutionary government, which has enabled Russia to establish major bases in Libya, the British forces then stationed there had no advance warning, and though required to assist Idris under treaty arrangements, failed to do so.

This disinclination to spy on friends did not dissuade the Labour government from instructing the Secret Service to spy on the white government of Mr. Ian Smith in Rhodesia. The eventual result was a most embarrassing situation when Smith discovered that a senior official, operating out of the High Commission in Salisbury, was a British spy and demanded his immediate withdrawal. Under Foreign Office pressure, Smith, who could have made much of the incident, agreed to a cover-up, which was considered to be more important in Britain than in Rhodesia. To account for the spy's sudden return, it was put about that his father was dangerously ill, a subterfuge in which the father, who was hale, had to be involved.

It is inevitable, in any country, that the close association between the Foreign Office and the Secret Service will produce some embarrassing situations, when intelligence agents trip over their cloaks and even fall on their daggers. So efforts, often involving the most blatant lies that sometimes have to be swallowed, are made to hide such situations. The Russians are far and away the most inveterate liars in this connection, if only because they pursue the myth—at least for domestic consumption—that the Soviet Union does not indulge in espionage, which is immoral and practiced only by capitalist imperialists. Still, perhaps the worst example was President Eisenhower's denial that the U2 plane shot down by the Russians had been spying. This had to be smartly followed by his abject admission that photographic espionage had been the plane's purpose after Khrushchev had announced that they had the pilot, alive and able to talk.

The recent public praising in the Russian newspapers of Philby as a Soviet hero is such a rare exception that its purpose has deeply puzzled intelligence chiefs in Britain.

I shall be dealing with some of the strange results of the association between the Foreign Office and Intelligence-gathering in a later chapter. At this stage, it is convenient to deal briefly with the relationship between the Secret Service and the Ministry of Defence.

Under international arrangements, the navy, army, and air force of each major country have officers serving as service attachés accredited to those foreign embassies with which they have diplomatic reciprocity. These men report directly to the Directorate of Defence Intelligence in the Defence Ministry, which has its own director general, who is always a former service chief. These defense attachés are there to send back all the intelligence they can find about the military situation of the country they are in but are required to avoid any indulgence in espionage. As can be imagined, the line is difficult to draw, is sometimes deliberately overstepped, and service attachés are frequently expelled for exceeding their terms of reference or for being accused of doing so.

There is close cooperation between the directorate of Defence Intelligence and the Secret Service, not only on the spot in the various embassies where the officers of both branches meet socially as well as professionally, but through the Joint Intelligence Committee and other coordinating arrangements. Occasionally, the Secret Service feels it necessary to intrude directly into the Defence Ministry, not always with pleasurable results to either, as the following incident demonstrates.

A Red Army officer, who had defected to Egypt, took with him some drawings of what he claimed were Soviet nuclear weapons designed for use in the battlefield. Egyptian intelligence passed them to the British Secret Service to secure a reliable opinion as to whether they were genuine. The Secret Service was anxious to oblige because it might then be given access to the defector to interrogate him on other matters, so an officer took the drawings to a nuclear department of the Defence Ministry. Experts there examined the drawings with interest and made notes but refused to give any opinion. They explained to the Secret Service man that any information they gave might enable Egypt to develop nuclear weapons, and it was the stated policy of successive British governments to oppose any proliferation increasing the number of nuclear powers.

The Secret Service was nevertheless disappointed and

argued that the Egyptians would only take the drawings to the Americans, who would then reap the benefits of any collaboration. A check by the Defence Ministry showed that the Americans had already been given the drawings because the Egyptians wanted a cross-check. The drawings could have been genuine, but the technology they showed was old, so the defector could have been a Soviet plant.

The Defence Ministry is frequently asked for some genuine information that the Secret Service can use as "chicken feed" to establish the credibility of a double agent and in the hope of getting much more in return. Because of nuclear agreements with the United States and the general danger of the subject, such requests are almost invariably refused.

A *contretemps* of an intriguing kind between the Defence Ministry and the Secret Service arose, quite recently, over certain essential security arrangements at the Atomic Weapons Research Establishment at Aldermaston in Berkshire. After the conviction of Klaus Fuchs, the ex-German atomic spy, and the flight of Bruno Pontecorvo, the Italian scientist, Whitehall decreed that access to the most sensitive secrets would have to be restricted to those who were British born of British parents. This ruling now breaches the Race Relations Act, though this implication was not realized when the legislation was introduced. Nevertheless, because of the danger of espionage and sabotage at Aldermaston, it was decided to impose the ruling, which means that most blacks are ruled out of employment there, as are most Southern Irish.

When this local decision was discussed with the then directors general of the Secret Service and of MI5, they agreed with it but warned the Defence Ministry that they could not support it officially because, on paper, it was illegal.

A further stupidity concerning Aldermaston and secret intelligence arose in 1964 when the new Labour government was determined to reduce work on nuclear weapons and, in particular, the amount of money spent on the nuclear deterrent. To strike at the heart of the deterrent, the government set up a secret inquiry under Lord Kings Norton, aimed at examining the work at Aldermaston with a view to reducing it or even closing the station down.

The committee was told everything about Aldermaston and the British weapons being developed there but, on security grounds, was told nothing about the far greater Russian developments because that information was the result of secret intelligence!

A few members of this committee came out in favor of closure, which would have been tantamount to unilateral nuclear disarmament, but the majority, to Sir Harold Wilson's eventual relief, strongly recommended leaving Aldermaston to proceed with its work.

As I believe the events described in this book indicate, both MI5 and the Secret Service are too small for the threat with which they are supposed to deal. The same is now true of Defence Intelligence, which has suffered savage cuts in the succession of defense-spending economies. This weakness and its remedy should be considered by any inquiry into the security services, which would have to include Defence Intelligence.

20
A Hotbed of Cold Feet

The Foreign Office has been described to me by a former member of the security services as "a hotbed of cold feet." What was implied by this stricture was the deep-rooted objection by Foreign Office "mandarins" to taking any resolute action against another country, however offensively it may have behaved, for fear of straining "diplomatic relations."

During the last thirty years, the country that has behaved with the most consistent disregard for diplomatic privilege and general civilized behavior toward Britain and her allies has been the Soviet Union, followed closely by the Czechs and some other Russian satellites. Yet it is to Russia that the Foreign Office defers, in greater degree and with less sound reason, than to any other country.

For purposes that have never been adequately explained in spite of repeated questions in Parliament, Soviet diplomats stationed in Britain enjoy privileges far in excess of those meted out to British diplomats in Moscow. They are allowed greater freedom of movement and employ Russian chauffeurs and Russian domestic staff in the embassy and residences. In Moscow, the British are required to use Russian chauffeurs selected by the KGB and domestic staff heavily penetrated by the KGB, as I shall show.

The foreign offices of other countries, including the United States, Canada, and Australia, also appear to be overborne by Moscow, so that there is no genuine diplomatic reciprocity and the Russians enjoy advantages that the KGB continues to exploit.

Over a period of many years, the Russians were allowed to increase the number of diplomatically accredited staff in London to figures out of all proportion to the size of the British embassy staff in Moscow. In addition, their trade delegations and other nondiplomatic services were steadily boosted to a total of several hundreds. A succession of espionage cases proved that many of the diplomats and the trade delegates were full-time KGB agents sent over for the precise purposes of espionage, subversion, and sabotage. Even the man listed as the doorman at a Soviet establishment abroad can be a commissioned KGB officer, as the Canadian spy trial proved.

It has been repeatedly pointed out to the Foreign Office by security officers that the purpose of these outlandish numbers is to saturate the British defenses that can be mounted by MI5 and Special Branch, both small agencies. Immediately before the last war, there were only about forty MI5 officers to cope with some three hundred Russian agents operating in and around London, which goes some way to explain why the recruitment of so many British spies then went undetected. As regards the current situation, most defectors report that between thirty and sixty percent of all Russians in diplomatic missions and their auxiliary organizations, such as trade delegations, the Tass News Agency, and Aeroflot, are primarily engaged in intelligence operations for the KGB or GRU.

The bloating of all these agencies for subversive purposes became so obvious in the 1960s that newspapers repeatedly drew attention to it but without the smallest effect until 1971. In the autumn of that year, the Conservative government, then headed by Edward Heath, announced the expulsion of ninety Russian diplomats and other officials for subversive and espionage activities against Britain. A further fifteen who happened to be out of the country, mainly on leave in Russia, were refused return entry, making a total of 105.

Shortly afterward it was revealed that the mass expulsion was linked with the defection in London of a Russian KGB officer, Oleg Lyalin, who had been posing as a member of a Soviet trade mission. It was then widely assumed that Lyalin, who had been an officer of the KGB branch formerly known as SMERSH, had given the names of the 105 and that the security authorities had then recommended their expulsion. The truth is that Lyalin, who was relatively low level, did little more than confirm the names already known to MI5 and provide the diplomatic excuse for getting rid of them.

Through a most ingenious system, which cannot be described because it is still in use, MI5 had proof that more

than three hundred of the Russian officials based in London
were grossly abusing their positions to undermine Britain in
various ways. This dangerous situation was brought to the
notice of the foreign secretary, Sir Alec Douglas Home, who
was so appalled that he took the matter up personally with
Andrei Gromyko, his Soviet counterpart. He urged Gromyko
to put a stop to the subversion and eventually, when the
situation grew even worse, warned him that Britain would
have to take action that would result in publicity damaging to
Anglo-Soviet relations.

It is possible that Gromyko took some action inside the
Kremlin, but the Soviet foreign secretary has no influence
over the KGB, contrary to the position prevailing in Britain,
where the Secret Service is firmly under the foreign secretary's control. As I have revealed, Lyalin had been a
defector-in-place for six months before he actually quit the
KGB. In that time, he had disclosed some of the current
plans for his department, which, according to the attorney
general, Sir Peter Rawlinson (now Lord), was responsible for
"the organization of sabotage within the United Kingdom and
the elimination of individuals judged to be enemies of the
U.S.S.R."

These plans included the sabotage, during the twenty-four
hours before a surprise Soviet attack on Britain, of radar
stations, communication centers, and other targets essential
to the nation's defense in war. Lyalin described, in particular,
how he was to be responsible for the blowing up of the
ballistic missile warning system at Fylingdales on the North
Yorkshire moors. He had detailed maps of the site and the
areas where Russian commandos would land from the North
Sea with the necessary explosives.

He told how teams of British traitors had been recruited to
assist in that operation and in the destruction of V-bombers
on nuclear alert at certain airfields. These teams had hidden
caches of weapons and explosives. The subversion squads had
also been equipped with radio receiver transmitters so that
they could receive their action signals from Moscow and
report back on their results. They used them to send one
quick signal to Moscow once a year to ensure that the sets
were working.

In 1980, a Russian transmitting set in a plastic wrapper and
a metal box was accidentally found buried in a field on a

remote hillside in North Wales. It was equipped with preset frequency plugs, all labeled in English, and a mechanism for rapid transmission of messages pricked on to perforated paper tape. The general instructions—on microfilm—were also in English. Inquiries showed that a party of six Russians had booked into a nearby hotel, describing themselves as part of a trade delegation, and had ventured out only at night. Four of those named in the hotel register were among the 105 Soviet agents expelled from Britain in 1971. As the equipment was in such excellent condition, it must have been dug up at intervals and maintained. The security authorities have little doubt that it was the property of a British-manned Soviet subversion unit, probably based in Liverpool.

Lyalin confirmed a plan to sabotage by flooding the Underground railway system in London, which had previously been brought to the attention of the security authorities by a Czech defector, Maj. Gen. Jan Sejna, who had fled to the United States in 1968.

He was unable to give the names of the members of the British fifth columnists, who numbered several hundreds, because he was not to be given them until forty-eight hours before they were due to go into action. The security authorities have identified some of them, but under British law they cannot move until these people commit an offense. The same applies in West Germany where, according to information given to me by a former NATO commander, there are over four hundred known sabotage units ready to assist the Russians.

Lyalin did give the names of two Cypriots who had been recruited by the KGB and sent to England, where they worked as tailors for cover. They were illegal radio operators and were caught with their headphones on. The Fylingdales danger has since been greatly reduced because the installation there has been relegated to being a backup system. The first warnings of an impending or actual attack will come from reconnaissance satellites. The RAF has also been able to take extra precautions to foil the sabotage squads.

Through his contacts with KGB officers posing as officials of Aeroflot, the Russian national airline, Lyalin was able to describe how several Aeroflot civil airliners have been modified for mine laying in the hours immediately before the outbreak of war: Pretending to be off course at night, the airplanes are intended to mine the Clyde estuary, bottling up any American and British submarines still at Holy Loch or Faslane, where they would be easy targets.

The availability of the whole Aeroflot fleet to serve military purposes at short notice has to be taken into account by the NATO defense planners. Unlike the airlines of the West, even those nationally owned, it is nothing less than a subsidiary arm of the Soviet forces.

Lyalin claimed that, in addition to his KGB sabotage network, there was a separate one totally controlled by the GRU—the military side of Soviet intelligence. He could provide no further information, and attempts to uncover it failed. So if it existed, it is probably still in position.

When such details were brought to Heath's attention, he was appalled and asked MI5 for a list of the worst offenders among the Russian officials. He was given 105 names of men against whom there was solid evidence. When MI5 suggested that a high proportion of them should be expelled, he said, "We'll throw them all out." Sir Alec Douglas Home was equally as resolute, but the Foreign Office strongly opposed the move on the grounds that it would prove so damaging to Anglo-Soviet relations "as to ruin *détente*." They would have been prepared to put up with the KGB's covert preparations for war on Britain to avoid "repercussions" against their staff in Moscow.

In fact, the repercussions were negligible because the Kremlin knew that MI5 had the evidence to make a devastating exposure that could be far more damaging than the expulsions. Normally, the Russian ambassador in London demands to know the full reasons why one of his diplomats or trade officials is to be expelled. Expecting this, the foreign secretary had been given detailed evidence against every one of the 105, but the ambassador did not ask him to produce it. Furthermore, the ambassador was told that if tit-for-tat action was taken against any Britons in Moscow, there was an even longer list of Soviet agents who would be expelled. Even after the 105 had gone, there were still some 450 Russian officials left, and many of these were known to be engaged in intelligence operations. Official estimates suggest that only about half of the active spies were expelled.

As an additional disservice to the KGB, and without the blessing of the Foreign Office, the security authorities made sure that a full list of the 105 expelled agents and their true identities—for many of them were in Britain under false names—was circulated to other friendly nations. This should have made it difficult for any of them to restart their activities elsewhere under diplomatic cover, but the Foreign Offices of other Western countries seem to be as "wet" regarding the Kremlin as the British. Several of the expelled agents managed to get into other countries with little delay—two of them, using their proper names, being accepted by Canada.

Whenever it can, the Foreign Office insists that the names of KGB agents expelled for involvement in espionage and subversion should not be divulged, though publication would tend to make them less usable in other parts of the Western world. Efforts, which are usually successful, are made to ensure that during trials neither Russia nor its satellites are mentioned by name, the espionage being for "a foreign power."

In connection with the Volkov Affair, which could have been so valuable to the West if followed up smartly, John Read, the diplomat who was involved, told me that the lack of interest was rooted in "the official attitude that we must, at all costs, accommodate the Russians and do nothing to precipitate East-West hostility. Indeed, reference to ultimate Soviet intentions was likely to provoke the accusation of Fascist tendencies."

This Foreign Office attitude had already resulted in the rejection of most valuable German information in 1943. A German official, who claimed that he had a suitcase full of German Foreign Ministry documents, called at the British legation in Berne, Switzerland, asking to see the military attaché. The attaché dismissed him without examining the material or referring the matter to London. The German then contacted American intelligence in Berne, led by Allen Dulles, who examined the documents and quickly realized they were genuine. With American encouragement, the German continued to supply excellent material that the British Secret Service eventually saw only through the good will and courtesy of the United States.

Michael Straight has told me how he went to see a British Foreign Office official in Washington immediately after the flight of Burgess and Maclean in 1951. He said that he wished to provide information about Burgess, having evidence that he had been a Russian spy for many years. Straight says that the official remarked, "You will have to go to the end of the line and the line stretches all the way round the block." This stupid remark deterred Straight from giving the information that MI5 was unsuccessfully scratching around to secure.

On occasion, the Foreign Office has accepted diplomats known to be KGB officers for a second tour of duty. In the 1960s, determined effort was made by a KGB man, Anatoli Strelnikov, to recruit me by bribery, and after I had reported his efforts to MI5, an attempt was made to have him expelled. Regrettably, this failed because my editor had opened a bureau in Moscow and feared that the Russians would shut it down if he or I played any part in the expulsion of a so-called Soviet diplomat. Nevertheless, the Foreign Office was fully informed by MI5 of Strelnikov's activities. It made no effort, however, to prevent the return of this dangerous character to London after he had served a few years in Moscow.

At about the same time, there was a nasty incident involving KGB men who went unpunished, on Foreign Office insistence, though they had been guilty of assaulting the police. Two Russian intelligence officers had been watching a garage near Clapham Common in London where MI5 cars used to be kept. They wanted the numbers and descriptions of the cars, which were used by the MI5 watchers keeping surveillance on KGB spies. Special Branch policemen were asked to pick them up for questioning, but when approached, the suspects began to fight, and there was a considerable affray in which punches were exchanged with the police, causing injuries on both sides. It was found that the Russians did not have diplomatic immunity and could therefore be charged, but the Foreign Office successfully objected to any prosecution.

In April 1976, two Hungarian diplomats, who were known to be Soviet bloc intelligence officers using their embassy as cover, were seen in a car parked on the private access road to the Royal Ordnance Factory at Burghfield, near Reading, which is involved in the production and maintenance of nuclear weapons, including Polaris missile warheads. This was the only place where a nuclear-weapons convoy, transporting warheads and bombs to and from Burghfield, could be seen and identified as such. After a car chase, they were held by the police, and cameras were found in their possession, though they had disposed of the films by the time they were caught.

There was no doubt in the minds of the security authorities that these Hungarians, who claimed to have friends in the area, had in the past been keeping watch on Burghfield with the intention of securing all the information they could about the nuclear convoys, including the size and nature of their armed guards.

Since the Munich attack on the Israeli Olympic athletes, who were closely guarded yet were overcome by a few determined men prepared to die, the Defence Ministry has taken extreme precautions with the transport of nuclear weapons and explosives. The blackmail problem if terrorists acquired a nuclear weapon would be horrific. Moreover, because of the complexity of modern missile warheads, these often have to be transported by road in a state of near completeness. The details of a nuclear convoy—the size and positions of the armed guard, the nature of the vehicles, and so on—could have been of particular interest to the IRA and other terrorists who are supported by the KGB and its satellite agencies. MI5 therefore wanted full publicity about the Burghfield incident so that the Hungarians could be expelled. The Foreign Office chiefs were horrified when told the details and demanded total suppression of the event because of the danger of a "diplomatic incident." Only when I was informed through an intermediary did MI5 secure the publicity warranted by this blatant breach of diplomatic privilege.

In spite of subsequent questions in Parliament, the offending spies were not expelled, and they were eventually withdrawn only because their cover had been blown by the publicity.

The Russian reaction to comparable situations inside the Soviet Union can be imagined while some measure of the KGB's ruthlessness in a foreign capital, like London, can be gauged from the intense fear experienced by Lyalin after his defection. MI5 seriously believed that an attempt might be made to shoot him in court, or on the way there, if he was to be brought to trial on the drunken driving charge that had prematurely precipitated his defection. Not only did he undergo plastic surgery to change his appearance—arranged and paid for by the security authorities—but MI5 went to the trouble of securing antidotes to all the poisons known to be used by KGB assassins. These were supplied by the Chemical Defence Establishment at Porton, so as to be quickly available if an attempt on Lyalin's life was made.

The comparison with Philby's comfortable situation in Beirut, or Blunt's in London, is instructive.

The Foreign Office seems to be unduly anxious to give the Russians the benefit of all doubts, even in the most serious situations. I have been assured by a former director general of Defence Intelligence that he and his counterpart in the Secret Service repeatedly warned the Foreign Office that the huge buildup of Russian forces on the border with Czechoslovakia in 1968 was not a military exercise but mobilization for an invasion. The Foreign Office chiefs declined to believe it.

More recently, in 1978, intelligence officers based in Hong Kong were able to warn the Foreign Office that Chinese forces were preparing to invade Vietnam in considerable strength "to teach the Vietnamese a lesson." The Foreign Office representatives, both in Hong Kong and in London, refused to believe it. Nor are they prepared to accept intelligence warnings that in the event of a conflict between Russia and China, the port and airport facilities of Hong Kong would be a top-priority target for destruction by the Soviet Red Air Force and the Red Navy, which keeps a carrier on station nearby. Hong Kong is an obvious reinforcement port for military equipment into China, but the Foreign Office refuses to believe that the Russians would attack it.

Over the last twenty years, cooperation between the Secret Service and its Israeli counterpart, the Mossad, has brought incalculable benefit to Britain. The Mossad is arguably the best-informed Secret Service in the Western world, not only about the Middle East but about Russia. I am now informed, reliably, I believe, that in deference to the "Arabists" in the Foreign Office and to the oil-rich Arabs themselves, the Foreign Office has cut off all official contact between the two secret services.

The Foreign Office even overrules the intelligence services on matters beyond its technical competence. When the Post Office Tower was being built in London to transmit messages by microwaves, the Foreign Office was warned by the security authorities that the Russians would probably be able to intercept the messages, especially as the tower would be in the direct line of sight from the top of the Soviet embassy in Kensington Palace Gardens. The Foreign Office replied that after taking technical advice, it was convinced that there would be too many channels for this to be feasible, so when the tower was ready, it was used for the transmission of secret telephone messages.

It was soon found that the Russians were taping all the messages and sending the tapes back to Moscow for analysis there. Of course, most of the messages were ordinary domestic calls, of no consequence to the KGB—what security men call "cabbages and kings"—but their next move showed that they were getting enough valuable material to make the operation worthwhile. They imported a computer analyzer into the London embassy via the "diplomatic bag"—a term that includes large crates as well as leather pouches. This ingenious device recorded only those messages emanating from certain telephone numbers in which the KGB was specially interested.

This was realized at last by the Foreign Office in the 1970s, when the foreign secretary sent an important secret message via the Post Office Tower to the secretary of state in Washington. In a stupidly short space of time, the Russian ambassador was 'round with a complaining document, clearly indicating that the secret message had been intercepted. Only then, when so much had been lost, was it decided to send all such secret messages by undersea cable.

The reason for this soft treatment of the Russians has never been adequately explained, particularly as they and their satellites are afforded diplomatic privileges withheld from countries that are Britain's allies. It cannot be fear of trade reprisals that motivates the Foreign Office because the balance of trade with Britain has long been in Russia's favor, especially since the huge soft-credit facility arranged by Sir Harold Wilson. Some security officers believe that for many years there has been a hard core of pro-Soviet officials in the Foreign Service and at headquarters in London. Some, of course, have turned out to be active spies—the best known case being that of Donald Maclean, though John Cairncross may have been even more damaging.

The particular aspect of the Maclean case, which has

rightly generated so much concern is the way that every
excuse was made for his dreadful conduct—his drunkenness,
his violence, and his boorish manner—which was quite inex-
cusable in a diplomat. The more disreputable he became, the
higher he was promoted. It was well known in the Foreign
Office that he was an intermittent drunkard with psychiatric
instabilities when he was appointed first secretary in the
British embassy in Washington in 1944. After incredibly
irresponsible behavior in Cairo, punctuated by acts of sense-
less violence, he was recalled to London for psychiatric
treatment and immediately afterward promoted to be head of
the American Department in the Foreign Office in London!

Like all ministries, the Foreign Office is responsible for its
own security and it singularly failed to suspect Maclean,
though his behavior, including his occasional homosexuality,
clearly called for scrutiny. The defector Krivitsky had provided proof in 1940—when Russia was assisting Hitler—that
Soviet spies were at work in the Foreign Office, for one of
them was caught, as I have described. That man, King, was a
lowly cypher clerk, but no notice was taken of Krivitsky's
allegation that there was another spy, an Englishman "of
good family . . . an idealist who worked for the Russians without payment." As in the case of Burgess, there was an inbuilt
reluctance even to consider the possibility that a British
diplomat could be a Russian spy.

I have already reported how Maclean was caught only as a
result of the American "Operation Bride," the postwar
deciphering of KGB radio traffic between Washington and
Moscow that had been recorded by U.S. intelligence during
the early 1940s. This produced hard evidence that the Russians
had enjoyed regular access to top-secret messages passing
between Winston Churchill and the U.S. presidents, F. D.
Roosevelt and Harry Truman. The agent responsible was
code-named "Homer," and to begin with, it was not certain if
he had been in the British embassy in Washington or in the
White House or some other American department.

It took the security authorities a year to establish that the
spy had been in the British embassy and must have been one
of the six first secretaries who had been responsible for
encoding and decoding the high-level messages. The deciphered
traffic suggested that the Russians trusted the spy absolutely,

so he had to be ideological. This meant a left-wing background. Arthur Martin traveled thousands of miles to reduce the suspects to two.

What finally pinpointed Maclean was the deciphering of an administrative memo in a KGB message to Moscow that "Homer" needed to travel to New York because his wife was due to have a baby there. Maclean thus became the final suspect only a few days before a decision was taken to interrogate him.

The Foreign Office chiefs were horrified when they had to face the evidence, for it implied that Maclean must not only have given away the British diplomatic codes and cyphers but had betrayed American nuclear secrets, as he had a pass to the Atomic Energy Commission headquarters that allowed him access without an escort, a privilege denied even to J. Edgar Hoover. Their continuing conviction that Maclean was a good man at heart was a crucial factor in enabling him to defect to Russia and so escape interrogation. The interrogation was planned by MI5 for Friday, May 25, but Foreign Office officials assured the security men that it could safely be left until the following Monday because Maclean would never leave his wife when she was so near to expecting another child. For this reason, too, there was absolutely no point in keeping watch on him at his home at Tatsfield, in Surrey. The security officials were assured that Maclean, then head of the American desk, would be in his office as usual on Monday. The MI5 men had also convinced themselves that if Maclean attempted to contact a Soviet intelligence officer, as they hoped he would, he would do so somewhere in London. This belief was based on the fact that Soviet diplomats were not supposed to travel more than thirty miles outside London without permission, but Tatsfield is marginally within that limit, and for all MI5 knew, the Russians could have used an "illegal" agent who would not have been under the travel constraint. Recently, I have discovered that there was a more pressing reason for the absence of surveillance outside London. Hollis restricted the number of watchers available for the operation on the grounds that they were in short supply. I have been assured that if the case officer had been able to secure enough watchers, the surveillance of Maclean would have been continuous.

It was because of the Foreign Office assurance that Maclean

would not flee that MI5 did not bother to have live monitoring of his home, which they had managed to bug with several hidden microphones. The table conversation when Guy Burgess turned up at Tatsfield, in the guise of "Roger Styles" to confuse Mrs. Maclean concerning his true identity, was all recorded but was not heard until the following day, when the tapes were run. As it turned out, the omission was of no consequence because Maclean and Burgess had given no indication that they were going abroad. They may well have assumed that the house was "miked" even if they had not been told so.

It is not impossible that, but for the "Operation Bride" breaks, Maclean could have become a very senior official at the Foreign Office after serving in ambassadorial posts. Philby would then not necessarily have come under suspicion and could have eventually become director general of the Secret Service. What a combination they would have made for their friends in the Kremlin!

While "Operation Bride" led to the detection of Maclean and others, there was one high-level agent mentioned in the radio traffic who has never been identified. One deciphered message from Moscow showed that the Russians had managed to insinuate a spy into a meeting in Washington in 1942 attended by Churchill, Roosevelt, and his aide, Harry Hopkins, to discuss the opening of the Second Front to take some of the German pressure off Russia. The spy, alluded to only as "Agent 19," had reported that Churchill, whose cryptonym in the traffic was "Bear," had said that he wanted both the Germans and Russians to take more casualties before any invasion of Europe, though the main difficulty preventing the early opening of a Second Front was shortage of transport ships.

Strangely, no British record of this discussion, part of the so-called Trident Talks, exists. Searches among Cabinet papers, Churchill's private papers, and diary records produced nothing, though the meeting undoubtedly took place. No effort was made to consult the U.S. records because the likeliest man to have been called into the discussion was a most eminent American, and it was decided that no mention should be made of the possible suspicion against him.

* * *

When Foreign Office officials are asked why they give the KGB such splendid opportunities by having Russian chauffeurs to drive their diplomats in Moscow and Russian servants in the embassy and in the residences there, they plead the needs for economy. The cost of taking over British drivers and servants would be prohibitive, especially when the fares for their holidays were taken into account. The rouble exchange rate is deliberately fixed by the Soviet government to be extremely adverse to foreigners, as a means of securing foreign currency and for other purposes.

The KGB is swift to take every advantage of opportunities. The way in which William Vassall was suborned by a KGB agent, infiltrated into the British embassy in Moscow as interpreter, is already on record. So now is the KGB's attempt in 1968 to blackmail a British ambassador, Sir Geoffrey Harrison, through the wiles of an attractive maid infiltrated into His Excellency's residence, as I indicated in *Inside Story*.

It may be difficult to believe that a career diplomat senior enough to be appointed to head the Moscow embassy could fall for the oldest trick in the world, but that, sadly, is exactly what occurred. The lady, called Galya, indicated her availability for casual sexual encounters, and the ambassador could not resist it, as he admitted. Sure enough, she soon confronted him with photographs of their intimate moments, taken by a hidden KGB cameraman. She said, tearfully, that she was under pressure and that the only way either of them could escape exposure was by providing the KGB with information of value to them.

With a sudden rush of good sense to the head, the ambassador reported his predicament to a senior friend at the Foreign Office in London and was quickly recalled for questioning by MI5's head of counterespionage. His Excellency insisted that he had submitted to only one encounter with Galya, which had taken place in the laundry of the residence on the spur of the moment. He apologized for his stupidity and pleaded "a lapse of his defenses."

Understandably, the security men were horrified by the prospect that the KGB had been able to infiltrate a cameraman into the well-guarded residence, where he could take a whole series of pictures. The entire residence was therefore searched but with no result.

The ambassador, who had remained in London, was inter-rogated again. He persisted in his story until the MI5 officers produced a letter that in spite of his predicament he had just written to Galya in Moscow and that had been intercepted there. It was a letter confessing his infatuation for the house-maid in spite of all that had happened.

He then decided that he had better tell the truth and admitted that he had been having a regular affair with Galya. On one occasion, when he had visited Leningrad, he was surprised to find her outside his hotel. She had explained that she was there purely by coincidence to see her brother, who, as luck would have it, had a flat just around the corner. It so happened, Galya had said enticingly, that the flat would be free for a couple of hours that afternoon if the ambassador was interested. He was.

The flat was a KGB setup, and it was there, not in the laundry, that the pictures had been taken.

The Foreign Office lodged no formal protest with the Kremlin concerning this heinous attempt to blackmail an ambassador. Nor, in spite of his stupidity and lies, did it take any action against the erring envoy, who retired on full pension with the inevitable honors. He must, however, have spent anxious hours wondering whether the KGB might suddenly issue the pictures to the world's press, as they had done in the past to destroy the career of a British member of Parliament.

What had driven the KGB to take this risk? Presumably, they had reason to believe that their subject was susceptible, as they had with Vassall. But they may also have been encouraged by the previous success that they had enjoyed with a Canadian ambassador to Moscow, John Watkins.

Watkins, who was a close friend of the then prime minister of Canada, Lester Pearson, was so well known for his homo-sexuality that Khrushchev was able to mock him about it at a rather drunken dinner party given for visiting Canadian dignitaries in the Crimea. The Royal Canadian Mounted Police were told by two defectors that the KGB had successfully blackmailed Watkins, but they felt unable to move against him until the more direct evidence from a third might become available.

This happened in 1963 when a Russian film script writer, Yuri Krotkov, defected in London while on a visit with a group of Soviet writers. Under interrogation, he confessed that he had been involved in setting up blackmail operations for the KGB, involving both homosexuals and prostitutes. He told how Watkins had been seduced by another man in a room that had been fitted with hidden cameras. The KGB had then shown the incriminating photographs to the ambassador, who was due to return to Canada to a high-level post in Ottawa, as assistant undersecretary of state, where he could influence foreign policy.

After a further foreign assignment as ambassador to Denmark, Watkins, already suffering from high blood pressure, retired to live quietly in Paris. Then, when MI5 reported Krotkov's allegations, he was taken to London for questioning.

The interrogation showed that Watkins had been seen by none other than the ubiquitous Anatoli Gorski, the controller whom Blunt had known as "Henry" and who had been retired from service overseas to Moscow, where he had a cover job as "Professor" Nikitin of the Institute of History. Gorski had explained to Watkins that his masters' requirement was simple. "Use your influence to assist the Soviet Union whenever you can. Steer things our way. We shall be watching."

Watkins admitted his homosexuality but denied that he had been recruited to Soviet intelligence. It may be true that he had not, in the sense that he had agreed to work for the KGB, but he had been seriously compromised and warned what might happen to him if he failed to comply.

There is no evidence that Watkins had ever done much to help the Russians, but he was taken to Montreal for further questioning by a tough Welsh-born interrogator, Jim Bennett. The attempt to extract a confession there ended prematurely in October 1964 with the death of the sixty-two-year-old ex-ambassador from a heart attack during a break between interrogation sessions.

Bennett had recently sued for libel against a Canadian writer, alleging that a spy novel suggested that he had been retired early from Canadian security because he himself was suspect. The case was settled out of court.

Krotkov has also been involved in a complicated, if prosaic, plot to ensnare a French ambassador to Moscow by introducing him to leading Soviet actresses who are required to serve as whores, if the KGB so demands. The ambassador, Maurice

Dejean, a highly sophisticated gentleman succumbed, but the rewards were never reaped because Krotkov told the story to MI5 after he defected in London. Dejean had been set up by the KGB in the most determined way. His chauffeur and his wife's maid were KGB agents. His embassy and private residence were comprehensively bugged, the whole operation being under the control of Gen. Oleg Gribanov, whom I have already mentioned in connection with the Vassall and Nosenko cases. Eventually, Dejean fell for the oldest trick in the blackmail book—the situation in which a husband returns "unexpectedly" to find his wife in a compromising circumstance with her lover.

Soon after Krotkov defected, Dejean, who had been in Moscow for eight years, was recalled to Paris. He was interrogated thoroughly, but no evidence that he had betrayed his country could be established. Nevertheless, he was called to the presence of his friend President de Gualle and summarily dismissed with a bleak "So, Dejean, you enjoy the women do you?"

There is no evidence that the French Foreign Office complained about this attempt to blackmail a senior ambassador and personal friend of the president. So there is little incentive for the KGB to desist from such activities, which often pay rich dividends.

The most surprising aspect of such cases is that men of eminence and experience should fall victim to obvious and pedestrian ploys. But, given congenial circumstances, sex can cut right across both intellect and ambition. So often does this happen that when important businessmen, and particularly those with access to defense secrets, travel behind the Iron Curtain, the Foreign Office or some other ministry may ask them to submit to a briefing by MI5. This usually includes a specific warning about the dangers of sexual compromise.

One such tycoon, a chief of one of Britain's biggest industrial concerns, promised that not only would he take care but would report any attempts to compromise him and even try to pick out the temptress from the rogues' gallery of Soviet seductresses built up by MI5. When he returned from Moscow, where he had stayed in the National Hotel, he reported his experience to his MI5 mentor.

"It was exactly as you predicted. At eleven P.M., there was

a knock on my bedroom door, and there standing in the doorway was a blonde so luscious that I couldn't resist her. But it was all right. I diddled them!"

"What do you mean, you diddled them?" the MI5 man asked, aghast at such complacency.

"I told her to undress in the sitting room while I undressed in the bedroom. When she came in to join me, I had a pillow slip over my head with a couple of eyeholes I had cut in it. I never took it off, so it doesn't matter what the hell they photographed. Boy, I diddled them!"

Since the Vassall case, the Foreign Office has studiously avoided sending homosexuals to Moscow. It might be imagined that following the damage to British interests in America inflicted by Guy Burgess, it would also be diplomatic to avoid posting known homosexual diplomats to Washington. The Foreign Office appears to disagree. A former British ambassador to Washington told me the tragic story of a young man, known to have been a homosexual but believed to have conquered his vice, who was sent out to him. The young diplomat became engaged to an American girl, and feeling that he should tell her of his past problem, he did so, whereupon she broke off the engagement. He was so upset that he got drunk and was picked up by the Washington police for soliciting a male. The FBI reported him to the embassy, and he had to be sent home.

Such a man was clearly blackmailable, and the KGB does not restrict its search for victims to Moscow.

The contempt for diplomatic privilege shown by the KGB in its attempts to suborn ambassadors and other diplomats has always been outweighed by its insolent attitude toward the foreign embassy buildings in Moscow. The bombardment of the American embassy with microwaves in an effort to overhear conversations inside and the mass bugging of rooms there have been widely publicized, but the incredible attention paid to the British embassy has been largely concealed, for understandable reasons so far as the reputation of the Foreign Office is concerned.

The alarming extent of the penetration of the most secret parts of the British embassy in Moscow became apparent only after a fire there in the autumn of 1964, when the large room

allotted to GCHQ, the radio-intercept department of the
Foreign Office, was almost totally destroyed. At first, it was
believed that the fire had been caused by a malfunction of the
fan in an air conditioner, but tests proved that the Russians
had started it by introducing an incendiary device into a duct
leading to the conditioner.

A major detective effort was therefore launched to discover
how the Russians had gained access to this most sensitive and
supposedly most carefully protected section of the embassy.
The answer would have been hilarious, had it not been so
perturbing.

The room was screened off by thick steel bars with a door
secured by an unpickable double-lock system. There were no
windows through which access could be gained, so it had
been assumed that there was no need for a permanent guard
at night, a watchman patrolling every two hours to inspect
the lock being deemed sufficient.

Examination showed that the Russians had been entering
the room regularly at night in between the watchman's
patrols. They had not needed to deal with the lock because
the bolts securing it to the screen had never been properly
installed and were only finger tight. Furthermore, the Russians
had kept them oiled.

As a result, the KGB had been able to read highly secret
cyphers, probably over a long period. The GCHQ technicians
operating various machines in the room were supposed to
turn them back to zero each night, but because of their faith
in the security of the room, they had failed to do this, so that
the KGB men could see, from the readings showing on the
machines, the areas in Russia on which they had been
concentrating.

The KGB's purpose in starting the fire had been to destroy
the room, for when the Russian firemen gained entry, they
set about all the machines and cypher equipment with ham-
mers, destroying them all. The reason for this, which must
have been pressing, was never discovered.

The damage was so great that a new GCHQ room had to
be built, and the security authorities urged that it should be
located in the geometric center of the building so that there
would be no outside walls and no possibility of tunneling
below it. There was believed to be danger from even a deep
tunnel because Soviet technological developments suggested

that the KGB might be able to read messages being encoded by cypher machines simply by recording and analyzing the clatter made by the machines.

The ambassador did not like the idea of the room being in the heart of the building, where it would be inconvenient. After taking technical advice, he ruled that it should be in the basement because he had been assured that if the floor was made of thick concrete, there was no way that it could be penetrated by listening devices. The security authorities point-ed out that Russian scientists might develop a magnetic detector to eavesdrop through thick concrete, but they were told that this danger was remote. So the new room was duly built in the basement.

All appeared to be going well until the impending visit of the British prime minister to Moscow, when a team of "sweepers," equipped with the latest electronic devices, ar-rived from London to make sure that no effective "bugs" could operate in the most secret areas of the embassy, where discussions would be taking place. These areas include a soundproofed security chamber, cantilevered out from the walls, remote from the floor and ceiling, and surrounded by an electronic screen.

One of the sweepers was creeping about inside a wide central heating vent that ran under the new GCHQ room when he saw a tube being slowly pushed through a hole, which had been bored through the side of the vent. He slapped a monkey wrench around it and managed to cut off the head of the tube with a hacksaw while whoever was manipulating it desperately tried to pull it back. The head turned out to be a magnetic detector coil that, as anticipated, the Russians had been using to read the cypher machines through the concrete.

Examination of the vent showed that a series of holes had been drilled to enable each cypher machine to be read. Clearly, the KGB had been particularly keen to read the dispatches that the prime minister would be sending back to colleagues and advisers in London.

The outcome of the episode was the moving of the room nearer to the center of the building at considerable expense.

I can find no evidence of any Foreign Office complaints to the Kremlin about this physical invasion of the British embassy, which, by international convention, is British territory. Any official note might have led to publicity that, in the circumstances, would hardly have redounded to the efficiency of Foreign Office security.

Certainly, after the reelection of the Labour government in 1974, there was even greater effort to placate the Russians in order "to make amends" for the animosity created by the expulsion of the 105 KGB spies and saboteurs three years earlier and to pacify those extremist MPs who believe that Russia can do no wrong.

While James Callaghan was Foreign Secretary, there was a move by MI5 to secure the expulsion of some more KGB men who were misbehaving with more than usual arrogance. The head of the Foreign Office, then Sir Tom Brimelow (now Lord), supported the recommendation but had to tell the director general of MI5, then Sir Martin Furnival Jones, that the Foreign Secretary had turned it down. The security officers felt so strongly about the situation, especially concerning the activities of one very senior officer of the KGB masquerading as a diplomat, that a delegation led by Sir Martin went to see the foreign secretary.

Callaghan explained that he could not afford to offend the Russians at that particular stage. "It would cause a storm," he said, when the details were explained to him, including MI5's suggestion that the KGB men's behavior should be made public.

This was interpreted as meaning that he would be extremely unpopular with a section of the Labour left wing if one or more dangerous Russian spies were thrown out and publicity was given to their offenses. The spies and saboteurs were allowed to remain.

When James Callaghan became prime minister, he had even greater need to avoid offense to his left-wingers, who were steadily increasing both in numbers and influence. Because of the unprecedented publicity concerning Harold Wilson's bad relations with MI5, culminating in suspicions that he himself was under surveillance, Callaghan took steps to amplify and improve his liaison with the heads of MI5 and the Secret Service, a sensible move for which his home secretary, Merlyn Rees, deserves credit. Prime Minister Callaghan was, therefore, well informed of the continuing efforts of the KGB against the United Kingdom and NATO both in furthering the aims of British Communists and in preparing for the eventuality of war. If any effort was made to reduce this threat, there was no public evidence of it, the Foreign Office policy of avoiding anything that would "damage *détente*" continuing unchanged.

It may reasonably be assumed that Mrs. Margaret Thatcher, who established close relations with MI5 and the Secret Service, with Callaghan's agreement, while still in Opposition, would like to be tough with Russian subversives in accord with her "Iron Lady" image. Again, however, there have been no overt signs of a more rigorous attitude, save for her courageous move in drawing public attention to the activities of the KGB through her statement about the recruitment and manipulation of the spy Anthony Blunt. My information is that the Foreign Office permanent staff still call the tune so far as relations with Russia are concerned. Afghanistan apart, that tune means muted.

A trend, which the Foreign Office appears to support and even promote, is that the KGB is no longer recruiting "Establishment" spies, as it did in the thirties when the "climate" was peculiarly favorable because of the Spanish Civil War and the excesses of the Nazis. The danger, these days, is supposed to center on Trotskyists, Socialist workers, and other left-wing militants, of whom Russia is believed to disapprove because they are outside Moscow's control.

The truth is that the KGB is as busy as ever in Britain, exploiting every opportunity not only for espionage but for subversion and sabotage. It will recruit anywhere it can, from "Establishment" figures, including politicians, to other rank soldiers and airmen who may, one day, secure access to military information. Its agents even hang about pubs and discos where servicemen from units of interest to them spend spare time.

Only occasionally does this activity come to light, when a decision has to be taken to prosecute a Briton spying for Russia. The true situation is much more apparent in the United States where suppression of espionage cases by the government is far more difficult because, under the Freedom of Information Act, newspapers serving the public have a right to know the details.

Coupled with the theme that the thirties was a special time not to be repeated is the claim, supported by Whitehall, that the major British spy cases are all "very old and best forgotten" in the interests of better international relations with the Soviet bloc. The KGB and the Kremlin would like nothing more, just as they approved of Harold Wilson's remark that the invasion of Czechoslovakia would be best forgotten. This idea they will no doubt also promote concerning their rape of Afghanistan, once the Western world has become bored with that.

Apologists for the Kremlin even drew attention to its condemnation of the Iranian invasion of the American embassy in Tehran and the seizure of hostages there as evidence of an improved Soviet attitude to diplomatic niceties. Most of the intelligence officers I know construed the Soviet concern rather differently. The last thing the Kremlin wants is any interference with its practice of using its embassies as centers for espionage and subversion activities in lands on its long-term takeover list. The scandals consequent on the defections of Gouzenko in Canada and Petrov in Australia were damaging enough. The seizure of any one of Russia's major embassies would expose an apparatus for illicit action of greater complexity and extent than any fiction writer has imagined.

In view of the intimate connection of the Foreign Office with the gathering and analysis of intelligence and its poor record as regards the use to which that costly information has been put, coupled with its deplorable inefficiency in preventing penetration of its most secret sections by Russian spies, it would be invidious if any inquiry into the efficiency and loyalty of the security services excluded it.

21
Lord of the Spies

In his private evidence to the Franks Committee on the Official Secrets Act, the director general of MI5, then Sir Martin Furnival Jones, stated that 101 members of Parliament were known to be in contact with Russians or other Iron Curtain nationals known to be Soviet bloc intelligence officers. This figure was withheld from the published report of the committee, to which I gave evidence. It referred to 1971, but I am told that the figure has since increased substantially.

Many MPs of both major parties are involved in East-West trade—some of them enjoying considerable financial benefit, which does not always seem to be declared in the MPs' list of outside interests—and so have need to be in touch with Soviet officials and others who could be intelligence officers. Many more MPs are in touch with them for what appear to be social and "cultural" purposes, the latter being a term as much misused by the Russians as the word "peace."

The danger of contacts of any kind was exposed in 1970 by the arrest, trial, and subsequent acquittal of Will Owen, the sixty-eight-year-old Labour MP for Morpeth, on Official Secrets charges. Owen, who headed a travel firm specializing in visits to East Germany, was also a member of Parliament's Estimates Committee, and he was charged with giving Czech intelligence information of a confidential nature. He admitted receiving £2300 from the Czechs, which he had not declared for tax. He agreed that he had lied to a Special Branch officer and admitted that he knew one of his Czech contacts to be a spy, who had, in fact, threatened him.

After disagreements among the jury, Owen, whose counsel admitted that he had behaved dishonorably, was acquitted on the grounds that the information he had supplied had not

been covered by the Official Secrets Act. He was nevertheless ordered to pay £2000 toward his legal costs and was,
presumably, taxed on his illicit earnings.

Full details about the frank espionage activities of Owen,
who died in April 1981, had been published in 1975 by the
Czech defector, Josef Frolik, who had not only given them to
MI5 but put them on record, on oath, to the U.S. Senate
Judiciary Committee. In his book *The Frolik Defection,*
Frolik was restricted to calling Owen by his code name "Lee"
because of the British libel laws. Frolik states that Owen
handed over secret material of the highest military value and
was paid £500 a month as a retainer, spying solely for the
money. "For nearly fifteen years, the little miser met his
handling officer once a week," he recorded. MI5 was convinced, from its surveillance of Owen, for which it managed
to secure special permission, that Frolik's information was
accurate, but it was limited in the evidence it could take into
court for the usual intelligence and legal reasons. The officers
who had investigated Owen were appalled when he escaped
conviction on a legal technicality, and this inhibited them
further from bringing prosecutions against other members of
Parliament.

A more entertaining example of how the KGB manages to
suborn politicians to good purpose is provided by the hitherto
secret life of Tom Driberg, member of Parliament for twenty-
eight years, chairman of the Labour party, and, eventually,
Labour life-peer.

I have recorded how Driberg was recruited, while still a
schoolboy, as an agent on behalf of MI5 to be infiltrated into
the Communist party and how he was expelled when his
duplicity was discovered by the KGB. He continued to serve
MI5 in other intelligence capacities until and after he became
an Idependent MP for Maldon Essex in 1942 and Labour MP
in 1945.

As the KGB can never resist the appeal of recruiting an
MP whatever his past, Harry Pollitt, the general secretary of
the Communist party, who had summarily expelled Driberg,
was asked to try to induce him back. To this end, both were
invited to a party at the Soviet embassy where Pollitt apologized profusely to Driberg for the way he had been expelled
and claimed that he had been given false information. He
urged Driberg to rejoin the party but as a clandestine mem-

ber so that he could function as a crypto-Communist inside Parliament. Pollitt assured him that there were several others already there, though he gave no names.

Driberg demurred at that stage but made the pretence of being keen enough on the idea to meet secretly with Pollitt later. Meanwhile, he reported the whole episode to MI5, where he was advised to do nothing for the time being but to keep the channels to Pollitt open, which he did.

The MI5 chiefs were in no doubt that the Russians knew that Driberg was still working for them. But the Center in Moscow, which had inevitably been consulted, felt that if he was back in the Communist fold, he could be fed a lot of spurious information to mislead British intelligence. There was also the possibility that Driberg, a well-known homosexual, might be blackmailed into working primarily for the KGB.

After Driberg visited Moscow in 1956 to see Guy Burgess about the possibility of writing a book about him, he reported back to MI5 that the Russians had asked him to provide information to them about the internal proceedings, accords, and discords of the Labour party. He was excellently placed to do this, having been elected to the party's National Executive in 1949 and remaining there until his retirement from Parliament in 1974. As Labour was not in office, MI5 had no commitment to it, so it was agreed that Driberg could report what he liked about his own party since no official secrets were involved, provided that he used his connection with the KGB in MI5's interest when this was possible.

The Russians gave Driberg two identical briefcases. When he handed one containing his reports to the Russians in London, they handed him the other containing his payment in banknotes. Under the agreement with the security authorities, Driberg was supposed to give all the money, as well as copies of his reports, to MI5. Over a period of several years, he handed in wads of notes amounting to many thousands of pounds, but there seems to be little doubt that he began to retain more and more of the money for himself.

Driberg reported at length on the private lives of his most senior ministerial colleagues, including some close friends, and on other MPs, men and women, of all parties, given to philandering, as well as on political activities. This material went not only to the Russians, who could use it for recruiting purposes, but to MI5 as well. To swell his information, he lent his flat to parliamentary colleagues, including ministers, for lunchtime trysts. He invariably made subsequent searches, in the hope of discovering the identities of ladies who had been taken there. On one occasion, after lending the flat to a senior colleague, he found an envelope in the handwriting of a woman MP, which he recognized. He then had the effrontery to accuse the colleague concerned of risking damage to the party by causing what could easily have become an open scandal. I have to confess that I know the names of the couple involved in that particular incident. (Politicians and other public figures would be horrified by the extent to which MI5 is informed of their sexual peccadillos by ordinary members of the public.)

Through the Labour party information that Driberg gave to MI5, the security men were able to extend their knowledge of the crypto-Communists in the party machine as well as in Parliament. And the Russians were able to extend their list of those with character weaknesses who might be susceptible to blackmail.

Former Labour party colleagues of Driberg have recently claimed that he could never have been a spy because he had no access to official secrets, but the Russians are just as interested in the kind of information about party politics and personalities, which he was ideally placed to supply.

In the context of Driberg's double-agent effort for MI5 and the KGB, the circumstances that enabled him to write his book *Guy Burgess—Narrative in Dialogue* are intriguing in every sense of the word. What has not been appreciated before is that when Driberg traveled to Moscow to see Burgess, with the intention of preparing the book, he did so with the blessing of both MI5 and the KGB! MI5 knew that the book would be a disinformation exercise, controlled and checked both in the preparation and the proof stage by the KGB. MI5 also knew that Driberg would submit the proofs to it for vetting and that, therefore, it would be party to the KGB operation. But it had a worthwhile purpose in mind.

There had been consternation in MI5 immediately after the weekend of February 11–12, 1956, when Maclean and Burgess had suddenly been produced by the Soviet authorities at a so-called press conference at the National Hotel in Moscow. It was some measure of the paucity of British intelligence behind the Iron Curtain that nothing definite had been heard of them until, in the usual manner, information was provided by a defector. In April 1954, Vladimir Petrov, head of the KGB in Australia, defected and revealed how one of his colleagues, called Kislytsin, had told him about his involvement in transmitting information provided by Burgess and Maclean while he had been serving as a cypher clerk in London, and how he had handled it later when posted to the intelligence archives department in Moscow. Kislytsin had also been concerned with the planning of the escape of the "diplomats" and later of Maclean's wife.

The statement, handed out in English and Russian by Burgess at the "press conference," where no questions were permitted, had clearly been drafted in Russian and could hardly have been less honest. It claimed that the runaways had never been Soviet agents but had left Britain only because they believed from their inside knowledge that Western policies would lead to war and they thought that they could do more to promote East-West understanding in Moscow.

There seemed to be a straightforward reason for the event. Bulganin and Khrushchev, then the joint Soviet leaders, were to visit London within two months to talk about "friendship," and at the dinners and other informal sessions, questions about the "runaway diplomats" might be asked. But inside MI5 there seemed to be near panic.

My first intimation of this was a summons through Rear Admiral Thomson, then secretary of the D-Notice Committee, to his office to meet a representative of MI5. This turned out to be Bernard Hill, the chief legal adviser. Later, Thomson told me that Hill had been asked to see me at the request of Roger Hollis, then still deputy director general.

Hill began by saying, "I am now putting you under the Official Secrets Act," which was nonsense because he had no such powers but indicated the state of his mind and that of others above him. He then said that he and his colleagues had concluded that the theatrical production of Maclean and Burgess was just the prelude to further statements calculated to sow the maximum distrust between Britain and America. The meeting ended with a request that the *Daily Express*, for which I was then defense correspondent, should publish a prominent article warning the public that whatever Maclean

and Burgess might say in the future would be a KGB exercise
and was not to be believed.

That MI5 was so worried made the matter legitimate news,
and we obliged with a splash front-page story headlined
"Beware the Diplomats." It contained a statement made to
me, on Hollis's behalf, to the effect that Maclean and Burgess
would be likely to reappear at press conferences or on
Moscow radio at times when Foreign Office men, whom they
could slander as being pro-Russian, were taking part in
negotiations involving America. No such thing ever occurred.
I am in no doubt that the episode was the start of a continuing MI5 exercise to prevent the embarrassing return of
Burgess to Britain and that the dispatch of Driberg to Moscow
was the next phase of it.

The book that Driberg hurriedly compiled from his talks
in Moscow enabled Burgess to state again that he and Maclean
had not quit Britain because of any deep-laid plot involving
the Russians but purely because they both decided that
Russia was a better place in which to live and to work for
peace. Burgess denied that he had ever been a Comintern or
Russian spy, and Driberg ended the book by stating that he
believed him. This was a blatant lie by Driberg, but it suited
MI5's purpose.

During his questioning of Burgess, Driberg induced him to
recall some details of his brief time in the highly secret,
wartime Special Operations Executive and to name some of
the people who had worked with him. Under instructions
from MI5, he included these in his script, which he then
submitted to MI5 for security vetting. The publishers,
Weidenfeld and Nicolson, were then warned that they risked
prosecution under the Official Secrets Act unless they removed the censored parts, which, in all innocence, they duly
did. Thus was the stage set for the next move in the operation.

A few days before the scheduled publication of the book, I
was telephoned by Admiral Thomson, who said he had been
asked to approach me again by Sir Roger Hollis, by that time
director general of MI5. We lunched together, and the
admiral then told me that MI5 would be grateful if I reported,
with prominence, that it now had evidence that could lead to
the arrest and prosecution of Guy Burgess should he ever

return to Britain. He then explained how, through stupidity on the part of both Burgess and Driberg, the former had committed technical breaches of the Official Secrets Act. At that stage, I had no knowledge of Driberg's connivance in this operation against his old friend.

The details duly appeared in the *Daily Express*, and further prominence for them was afforded by publication of a complaining letter from Driberg with answers from me—supplied by MI5 via Admiral Thomson.

Later, I asked the admiral why Hollis was clutching at such a thin straw, and he replied that the director general was determined to dissuade Burgess from ever returning to Britain. MI5 did not have enough usable evidence against Burgess at that time—none really accrued until the confession of Anthony Blunt in 1964—and the authorities would look foolish if he swanned around London in his old style after helping a known spy, Maclean, to escape.

A later event, in April 1962, of which I am deeply suspicious, enabled Hollis to generate worldwide publicity regarding the inevitable arrest of Burgess and Maclean if ever they set foot on British soil. Defense and crime correspondents of newspapers were quietly told that a tip had been received from Dutch intelligence to the effect that both Burgess and Maclean had been invited to a Communist conference in Cuba and would be touching down at Prestwick Airport on the way. By that time, MI5 had solid evidence against Maclean, and officers there were keener than ever to subject him to tough interrogation, but Hollis was determined to ensure that they would get no such opportunity. He engineered a Home Office statement that warrants were to be issued for the arrest of both men, as they were.

The defectors never moved out of Moscow, and we were told that the tip had proved to be false. The question is whether such a tip ever existed. It seems much more likely that the whole episode was an MI5 disinformation exercise. Maclean was well aware that both MI5 and the CIA must know the extent of his treachery, and it is not conceivable that he ever contemplated returning to Britain. Burgess, the former MI5 agent, was the danger man. He was bored out of his mind in Moscow and desperately wanted to return. Hollis was prepared to go to any lengths to stop him. Understandably, members of the Fluency Committee wondered why. If Hollis was a spy and Maclean had learned of it during his thirteen years of active espionage, that would help to explain why the KGB had been prepared to put Philby and Blunt at risk to get Maclean safely away before he could be interrogated. It would also explain Hollis's determination to prevent the return or arrest of Maclean or Burgess, who might have learned of Hollis's position from Maclean, had he not already known it.

Driberg's book contained enough lies and slanders against MI5 and the political system of the West for the KGB to be pleased with it, while MI5 regarded these as a worthwhile tradeoff to prevent the return of Burgess. Driberg made money out of it while being paid by both the KGB and MI5. So all the participants, save for Burgess himself, who died aged fifty-two, lonely and homesick in Moscow in 1963, were well satisfied.

As with many double agents, Driberg was coming increasingly under MI5 suspicion that he was doing more for the Soviet bloc than he admitted in his regular debriefings. Then, in 1969, the Czech defector, Josef Frolik, who laid information against several Labour MPs, including Will Owen, gave specific information about a senior Labour MP who was a homosexual, had been recruited by Czech intelligence, and had the code name "Crocodile." Frolik described how the Czech intelligence men in London had been smartly censured by the KGB for this adventure because "Crocodile" was already their man. Frolik, who had seen "Crocodile" but did not know his name, identified him as Driberg from a spread of photographs shown to him by MI5.

Driberg was therefore taxed with this information by the MI5 case officer handling him. "Have you ever done anything for the Czechs?" he was asked. "I have written them a few articles," he replied with a shrug. Under questioning, however, he admitted that he had sold the Czechs additional information about the internal squabbles of the Labour party and personal scandals about who was sleeping with whom. "All harmless stuff," he insisted with his usual charm.

He admitted that he had continued to do this while chairman of the Labour party, passing the information to his Czech controller whom he knew only as "Vaclav." Apart from warning him about the danger of giving the Russians any information that had not been passed by MI5 as "chicken feed," there was nothing the security authorities could do or wanted to do, in view of the scandal that open knowledge of the way they had employed the Labour party chairman would create.

My exposure of Driberg's activities in the first edition of this book brought confirmation from several sources. Thus, Mr. Zak Bosnyak, a Yugoslav living in Britain, has revealed how Driberg used him as an unwitting courier to post a letter to the Russian embassy in Belgrade while he was on vacation there.

An opportunity for MI5 to dispense with Driberg's services had arisen during the premiership of Harold Macmillan, who had discovered that several MPs, mainly Tories, were being run by MI5 as agents. The MI5 chiefs were told that this was no longer permissible, and the MPs were all paid off with the exception of Driberg, who refused to desist. He continued to report information to MI5 even after he had been elevated to the lords as Lord Bradwell, being known in MI5 headquarters as "The Lord of the Spies."

Driberg's long relationship with MI5 solves the mystery of why such a notorious homosexual, who was repeatedly caught in the act publicly by the police, was never successfully prosecuted, though the practices to which he admitted in his biography were then serious crimes. He had been given an MI5 telephone number that he gave to police with the request to pass it to Special Branch. This secured his release, and whether the policemen concerned believed that his homosexual acts were "in line of duty" will never be known. (Driberg was prosecuted—and acquitted—on a homosexual charge only once, when two men, insisting on court action, reported him.)

The award of a peerage to such a notorious homosexual, who had admitted to another MP, Woodrow Wyatt, that he had once enjoyed the favors of a House of Commons chef in the members' lavatory, was also a cause for public curiosity. While the award was made by Harold Wilson, ostensibly for Driberg's devotion to the Labour party, it had been requested by his friend Michael Foot. Lady Falkender explained to me that Foot felt sorry for Driberg because he was going blind, a fact confirmed to me by another of his friends, Mervyn Stockwood, the bishop of Southwark. Foot apparently had never asked for an honor on behalf of anybody before, and Wilson felt that he could not refuse him.

Inquiries after Lord Bradwell's death in 1976 convinced MI5 that he had been controlled primarily by the KGB since the end of the war partly because he may have been blackmailed but mainly because he had moved further to the left. The KGB had plenty of incriminating photographs. He had even been caught in a homosexual situation with Burgess when he visited him in Moscow and was shown the photographs as an extra "inducement," as he reported to MI5 on his return. To his friends, Driberg pretended that because his homosexuality was so well known, photographs, however revealing, would be useless as blackmail. In reality, this was far from being the case, as Driberg well knew.

All that the KGB needed to do was to post prints of the pictures to various influential people and to newspapers and magazines. The publicity would have made it impossible for MI5 to continue to support Driberg's immunity from arrest, for his propensity for committing homosexual acts in public places remained an offense. It would also have ended his political career.

Using this crude and ruthless device, in a heterosexual context, the KGB had effectively destroyed the political career of Comdr. Anthony Courtney. Courtney, a most able Tory MP, had the temerity to point out repeatedly in Parliament that the Foreign Office seemed to be psychologically intimidated by the Kremlin in the way it allowed Soviet diplomats concessions that the KGB habitually abused. It was suspected that the embarrassing photographs, taken surreptitiously in a Moscow hotel and involving a Russian woman on MI5's list of KGB seducers, had also been issued to warn somebody else of more value to them what might happen to him if he failed to remain in line. MI5 believes that person was probably Driberg.

It would have been no more than just if Driberg had been betrayed, for the overall verdict on him—in journalism, politics, and intelligence—is that, eventually, he betrayed everybody. His deceitful behavior over so many years hardly justified Michael Foot's *post mortem* tribute that "he never budged from his Socialist convictions."

Another politician whose activities in the intelligence world were vaguely known but surrounded with doubt was Henry Kerby, the Conservative MP for Arundel. It can now be stated with authority that Kerby served for many years as an official agent of MI5, submitting most valuable reports and performing other functions bordering on espionage, which, being of a technical nature and still usable, must remain secret.

After the Macmillan ruling, MI5 was supposed to tell the prime minister of any MPs giving intelligence assistance, but an exception was made in Kerby's case because of his unique usefulness. As he had been born in Russia and spoke the language fluently, he was occasionally used as an interpreter and so gained access to Soviet ministers and other officials. He put these contacts to good use on behalf of the intelligence authorities during his visits to the Soviet Union where, as he put it, he was given "the red carpet treatment." This was not without its dangers because, as happened with Greville Wynne, he could have been seized and put on trial, had it suited the Russians to do so.

Kerby, a large man with a bald, cannonball head and amusing, rubbery features, entered MI5 service through his friendship with "Klop" Ustinov, the father of Peter Ustinov. Klop was a regular MI5 agent, and he and Kerby met through joint friendship with Lord Vansittart, head of the Foreign Office.

In the early part of the Second World War, Ustinov and Kerby were involved in running an aristocratic young German called Baron Wolfgang zu Putlitz, who was in the German embassy in Holland. From 1935 to 1939 Putlitz passed secret information both to the British and the Russians, being at heart really a Soviet agent but prepared to do anything against the Nazis. Through these connections, he also became friendly with Burgess and Blunt, with whom he shared interests.

It was through Putlitz that Winston Churchill, when outside the government, obtained his accurate information about the true strength of the Luftwaffe, which he used to attack Neville Chamberlain in Parliament.

Putlitz's cover was blown early in 1940, almost certainly as a result of a deliberate leak by the Russians, trying to improve their intelligence interchange with the Abwehr during the Nazi-Soviet Pact. Klop Ustinov managed to extricate

him to Britain, where he was put in the care of Anthony
Blunt. He remained in Britain through the war, and as he had
hailed from East Germany and was pro-Soviet, he returned
there. In his interrogation by MI5, Blunt recalled how he,
personally, had taken him to a checkpoint on the East-West
frontier and handed him over.

During Kerby's numerous visits to the Russian embassy,
where he was always an honored guest, as I witnessed
myself, he talent-spotted for MI5 regarding Russians who
might be induced to defect. He seemed to be friendly with so
many Russians that there were some fears inside MI5 that he
might be operating as a double, but the consensus among
those officers who worked with him is that he was entirely
loyal, and while having to make overtures to Russians to
preserve his appearances as a go-between on East-West
trade, he would do anything to undermine the Soviet system.

Kerby was convinced that Philby was a Soviet spy and the
Third Man soon after the Maclean-Burgess defection. As
Philby records in *My Silent War*, Kerby approached him
using his alleged hatred of the Foreign Office as a means of
currying his friendship, for which the spy did not fall.

I became suspicious of Kerby, who was a friend, after he
had obviously induced a Russian diplomat, who was also a
senior KGB officer, to pay attention to me. This man, Anatoli
Strelnikov, eventually offered me money to work for Russia,
and as I was in touch with an MI5 officer throughout the
liaison, I naturally reported Kerby's part in bringing us
together. I was told to forget Kerby's involvement and assumed
that no action would be taken against him because he was an
MP. Recently, I have discovered that he was working under
MI5 instructions, after he had reported I had complained to
him about never being asked to the Soviet embassy.

Concerned about the extramural activities of Strelnikov,
MI5 wanted to get rid of him, and I was to be the stalking
horse, though I did not know it. MI5 was confident that
within a few weeks Strelnikov would proposition me and paid
me the compliment of believing that I would immediately
report him, which I did. The ploy failed, as I have already
recorded, only because my editor declined to report the
events to the Foreign Office, which might have been induced
by MI5 to expel Strelnikov.

As I have reported at length in my book Inside Story,

Kerby was undoubtedly acting as a spy for Harold Wilson and the Labour party inside the Conservative party. He volunteered this service and sent a shoal of letters, many of which I have seen, to Wilson and Wigg, giving details of private Tory meetings, plans, and gossip. Whether this had anything to do with MI5, I have been unable to discover. I have also been unable to find any security official who will admit that he knew anything about it. There is strong evidence that Kerby may have been motivated by frustration at being unrecognized by the award of any honor from his own side and was seeking to secure one from Wilson.

MI5 had been forced to drop Kerby as an official agent after Wilson called his new director general, Martin Furnival Jones, to Downing Street in 1966 and asked, "Are you running any MPs as agents?" Furnival Jones, who knew about Kerby, stalled by answering, "If we are, I will stop it."

When Kerby was told he would have to be dropped, he was extremely disappointed, for he had regarded his work for intelligence and security as being a patriotic service he was proud to perform. He also enjoyed it.

Soon after Wilson first became prime minister in 1964, he decreed that MPs were to be immune from investigation by MI5 without his specific permission, as I have recorded. He also told MI5 that he would not accept the evidence of defectors as a basis for investigation. Since defectors are the main source of *prima facie* evidence, these rulings were tantamount to the granting of immunity to all elected politicians and peers, a situation that to many in the security world is undemocratic, to say the least.

Though several members of Parliament, including former Labour ministers, have been named as Soviet bloc agents by defectors, the only one to be questioned was John Stonehouse, and this was done only briefly in the presence of Harold Wilson. Stonehouse, who had served in the Aviation Ministry and as postmaster general, was the former minister who staged a fake suicide from Miami Beach in 1974 and turned up under an assumed name in Australia, only to be exposed and arrested there, being eventually convicted for fraud. MI5's limited interview with Stonehouse, at which Wilson insisted on being present, produced no further evidence and allowed Wilson to make a statement in Parliament that effectively cleared his former minister of treachery.

I have spoken with Stonehouse about this episode since his release from prison, after his conviction over financial dealings. He agreed that the Czechs would certainly have liked to recruit him as an agent but insisted that there was no way in which they could ever have succeeded.

Nevertheless, MI5 felt cheated by being forbidden to interrogate Stonehouse about the contacts he admitted having made with the Czechs in line of ministerial duty because one of the men who tried to ingratiate himself with Stonehouse was a senior intelligence agent. Once again I was used, without my full knowledge, as a hopeful means of securing publicity about the situation. I was told by a former MI5 officer that a Czech defector, Frantisek August, who had made allegations against Stonehouse to a Senate Judiciary Committee in Washington, would be visiting Britain secretly. It was suggested that I should find him and induce him to talk. I did my best but failed to track him down, though a question to the home secretary in Parliament confirmed that he had been granted a visa to enter the country. For years I wondered why I had been given this interesting tip. Now I know the reason—MI5 wanted to stir up the Stonehouse issue.

Following the defection of August and of his Czech colleague, Josef Frolik, in 1969 information impugning the loyalty of several Labour MPs was laid with MI5, and their identities were established but none could be interrogated. One of them, who was named by Frolik, has since progressed prodigiously in the Labour hierarchy. Frolik reported that the politician concerned was under the control of the KGB, but he was asked, on one occasion, to speak to him at a function and make some trivial-sounding remark that was, in fact, a code phrase. The Czech said that he had been told that the politician would reply with another trite but specific statement, which would be an acknowledgment that he had received the message and understood it. Frolik claimed that the operation had gone exactly as planned.

This and other evidence against British MPs was given by both defectors, under oath, to a U.S. Senate Judiciary Committee but was expunged from its published report.

I understand that Sir Harold Wilson was approached by MI5 and asked if he had ever been "propositioned" by the KGB while in Moscow. He robustly replied that he had not and that his only contact, which had been unpleasant, had been an occasion when he was picked up by the Moscow police for taking a photograph in the street.

It is my intention to produce a book devoted entirely to the left-wing penetration of the Labour party, but, meanwhile, in the context of their trade being treachery, some general observations about certain other MPs and peers are relevant here.

In his evidence to the Franks Committee, Sir Martin Furnival Jones said, "If the Russian Intelligence Service can recruit a back-bench MP and he climbs to a ministerial position, the spy is home and dry." He did not make that remark without case evidence to back it. While MPs are immune from telephone tapping—unless Margaret Thatcher has changed the rules, which I doubt—the Soviet bloc people with whom some of them communicate are not, so details of their conversations are occasionally overheard and recorded. Furthermore, if MI5's watchers who are keeping surveillance on a Soviet bloc intelligence officer happen to see him or overhear him talking with an MP or peer, they are required to report on the meeting.

There is also the evidence of Soviet bloc intelligence officers who continue to defect in far greater numbers than the public suspects. So while MI5 and Special Branch are almost powerless to take any action, there are fat files on more than sixty Labour MPs and on a score or so of Labour peers.

Such files indicate that while some are helpful to the Soviet cause for money, sometimes coupled with threat of blackmail, the majority are ideological agents of influence, giving their assistance because they are secret members of the Communist party.

When people join the Communist party of Great Britain, they are required to make a statement in their own handwriting giving their reasons for wanting to join. If they are accepted, this document is kept with other information about them in a separate folder and provides some degree of hold over them.

The folders on the overt members of the party, who number some thirty thousand, are kept in the headquarters in King Street, Covent Garden, in London. The files on the secret members are kept separately, usually in the house of some highly trusted member, under the closest possible security. Currently, the number of secret members exceeds fifty thousand. This is an indication that the Communist party is far more influential and far more subversive than is generally appreciated.

Some of the secret members either insist on secrecy from the start or are advised to be secret, being what is known inside the party as "beefsteaks"—of indeterminate color outside but deep red inside. Most of them begin as overt members but are later advised to "go underground" and become secret members because in that situation they will be more useful to the cause. If they cannot think of an excuse for doing this, then one is provided for them. They pretend to have turned against communism, using some pretext like the Nazi-Soviet Pact, the savage crushing of the Hungarian Revolution, or an event like the invasion of Czechoslovakia or Afghanistan. Being an organization rooted in deception and fraud, the Communist party encourages its secret members to attack it publicly if that will serve its long-term interest. They are even advised to join anti-Communist organizations, as Philby and Burgess joined the Anglo-German Fellowship, to improve their cover for subversion and espionage. As a result, nobody who has ever joined the Communist party can ever be regarded as being entirely free of suspicion concerning continuing membership. This is hard on those who genuinely revolt against its principles, but the security authorities feel that they must err on the side of safety.

This view received official backing from the post-war Labour government under Attlee, and most of its successors, by the banning of Communists and their close associates from appointments either in government establishments or in industry, where they could have access to secret information. Existing employees and new recruits were given the opportunity to reveal past or present Communist links. Most of those who did not do so were surprised to find that the security authorities knew about their secret membership, in spite of their long years of careful cover-up. There have, of course, been some notable exceptions, one, with whom I was involved, being a guided-missile scientist responsible, at the time, for liaison with American scientists working in that field. His links with communism, which he had never declared, were discovered very late in the day, and he was quietly shunted to nonsecret work.

I am not prepared to reveal just how MI5 knows the identities of the secret members, but though it may come as a shock to certain crypto-Communists in high places, the fact is that it does. I would be surprised if there was a single crypto-Communist in Parliament whose real purpose is not known to MI5.

Though Sir Harold Wilson now seems deeply perturbed by the extremist penetration of the Labour party, he was inclined while in office to dismiss warnings about it by the security authorities. I understand that he was told how an MI5 agent had heard a Russian intelligence officer claim from memory that thirty-one Labour MPs were "full Party members completely on our side and who will do anything to help us." Wilson is said to have dismissed the information as "reds under the beds" propaganda.

Because of the immunity restrictions, all that the security authorities could do to limit the espionage danger was to organize the distribution of secret documents in certain Whitehall departments so that suspect ministers were denied access to specially sensitive information. If questioned about this, they had to deny that it was taking place because it was a technical breach of the immunity, but, nevertheless, it was accomplished to some extent.

When deputy leader of the Labour party in 1961, Lord George-Brown tried hard to secure a list of the crypto-Communist MPs from MI5 so that they could be expelled from the party. He was thwarted in this by the prime minister of the day, Harold Macmillan, who feared repercussions in Parliament if he permitted it.

MI5 has evidence from defectors to the effect that some crypto-Communist MPs are under such close day-to-day control that they are used to ask parliamentary questions calculated to damage the interests either of Britain or her allies. Soviet bloc intelligence officers are detailed to make a close study of Parliament and to make use of its privileges, wherever possible. They will frame an embarrassing question based on intelligence material and induce one crypto-Communist MP to ask it. A second MP will then ask the even more embarrassing supplementary question.

Some of the MPs are even named—by their code-name—in KGB radio traffic. The late Konni Zilliacus was one of them, and Driberg was another. I greatly regret that, at this stage, I am unable to name others who are still alive and shelter behind the libel laws, as it is difficult to induce any intelligence source to appear as a witness, as MI5 itself knows only too well.

This difficulty, coupled with the immunity restrictions, has prevented any action against at least two Labour MPs who are believed to be on the regular payroll of Soviet bloc intelligence. This, of course, makes them effectively agents of the KGB, for apart from their own ideological motives in wanting to overthrow British democracy and establish a Soviet-style system, once they have accepted money, they are driven to take any orders they are given.

A crypto-Communist MP need not have access to secrets to be of great value to Russia as an agent of influence. He or she—the KGB pays particular attention to women—can influence parliamentary and Labour party committees on which they serve. Ministers and junior ministers can pack government advisory committees, on subjects like disarmament and arms control, with left-wingers who are difficult to get rid of when a right-wing government subsequently inherits them.

The attention that the KGB pays to ministers is invariably carefully concealed if it is discovered. During one of the Wilson governments, a quite prominent junior minister was required to resign on "personal grounds" because he was being subjected to attempted KGB blackmail and the prime minister felt that it would be dangerous for him to remain in office. The details would have caused a political scandal, so they were suppressed not only to the benefit of the Labour party but, incidentally, to the KGB. Lord George-Brown has told me how he refused to be party to the cover-up when asked to find a nongovernment post for this man.

More recently, the conviction of Lord Kagan, a long-time, close, personal friend of Sir Harold Wilson, for theft has led to publicity about the way he was courted by the KGB, which would automatically be interested in anyone so close to a prime minister. The first news that MI5 received about Kagan's friendship with a man who was known to be a senior officer of the KGB came from Oleg Lyalin, who defected in London in 1971. Lyalin told the security men that Kagan was on friendly terms with Richardas Vaygauskas, who, like the peer who had made a fortune out of Gannex raincoats, was a Lithuanian. Lyalin confirmed that Vaygauskas, who was a personal friend and exchanged details about his espionage activities with him, was a senior officer of the KGB and eventually he was among the agents expelled from Britain or refused reentry.

Several times during the six months while Lyalin was under MI5 control before physically defecting, he gave details of the Kagan-Vaygauskas relationship. Kagan has admitted that he was friendly with Vaygauskas and that they played chess together on the Russian'sfrequent visits to Kagan's home. But Kagan insists that he had no idea that Vaygauskas was a spy and that Vaygauskas made no attempt to use him as a source of questions to Wilson. According to Wilson, nor did Kagan make any attempt to pump him on anything of political interest to Russia.

Wilson has also stated that Sir Arthur Young, the commissioner of the City of London Police, who died in 1979, was put in touch with Vaygauskas so that he could find out more about Soviet spy networks. What happened, according to my sources, is that Wilson approached Young after he heard of Lyalin's defection and told him about Kagan's relationship with Vaygauskas. Young expressed surprise that he had not gone direct to MI5, and Sir Martin Furnival Jones was furious.

The MI5 case officer in charge of the Vaygauskas and Lyalin inquiries saw Wilson, who told him that he had no idea of Kagan's relationships with Russians except in relation to trading and that he was sure that Kagan was acting in Britain's best interests. According to Wilson, Kagan arranged meetings between Vaygauskas and Young, who, on retiring, accepted a job with Kagan's firm.

Though MI5 retained its interest in the Kagan-Vaygauskas link, Kagan, who was already a knight, was made a peer in Wilson's Resignation Honours. On the advice of Margaret Thatcher, the queen has recently withdrawn the knighthood awarded to Kagan, a very rare recriminatory action. Removal of a peerage would require legislation.

While Kagan was not a member of Parliament until he became a peer and had no official immunity, MI5 had become chary about challenging any of Wilson's friends and associates. It seems that Wilson deeply resented routine inquiries that MI5 made about those who happened to be involved with East-West trade, which he wanted to encourage. He did not like the way MI5 was automatically suspicious of Kagan because he had managed to escape from the Soviet zone after the war even though this might be a standard method of intruding spies in the guise of refugees. The warnings that MI5 gave him about personal friends, including MPs, when he became prime minister are believed to have been the root cause of his dislike and distrust of the organization.

The KGB has always believed in aiming high, and it has scored on some targets of great distinction and value. Some of the names that appeared in the regular KGB radio traffic and have been tracked down as a result of "Operation Bride" beggar belief, though inquiries substantiate their reality. One of them was Eduard Benes, the second president of Czechoslovakia, who suffered a Communist coup d'état for his pains in assisting the KGB. This was perhaps poetic justice, for through his services to Stalin, Benes had been instrumental in touching off the purge in which hundreds of Red Army officers and other Russians were murdered. Heydrich, Hitler's security and intelligence chief, faked a report that the chief of the Red Army's general staff, Marshal Tukachevsky, was collaborating with the German high command to overthrow the Stalin regime. Heydrich used Benes to leak the false information to Stalin, and the great purge followed.

22
Security and
the Unions

Next to the death of Gaitskell in 1963, the event that has been most responsible for accelerating the Labour party's lurch to the left was a decision taken at the Annual Conference of the Labour party in 1973. Until then, it was forbidden for members of the Labour party to belong to, or to give support to, certain organizations known to be offshoots of the Communist party. As Aneurin Bevan, an old-style Labour left-winger, had put it,

> The Communist Party is the sworn, inveterate enemy of the Socialist and Democratic Parties. When it associates with them, it does so as a preliminary to destroying them. The Communist does not look upon the Socialist as an ally in a common cause. He looks upon him as a dupe, as a temporary convenience, and as something to be thrust ruthlessly to one side when he has served his purpose.

Though the Communists had never concealed their loathing of the British style of democracy because they favored a totalitarian system that the voters could never reverse, the Labour party's National Executive was so heavily infiltrated by extremists that in 1973 it was able to induce the conference to abandon the proscribed list of Communist-front organizations.

This move horrified the security authorities, whose prime duty is to prevent subversion by Communists and their associates. Their fears that this would lead to a takeover of

256

the Labour party by extremists, of whom many are known to be secret Communists, have proved to be well founded.

Labour MPs and ministers were not long in appearing openly on Communist party platforms, supporting the scurrilous *Morning Star,* the pro-Soviet newspaper.

Labour party officials and back-bench MPs have declared their support for an amalgamation of the Labour and Communist parties by stating that the differences between them are now "negligible."

Events have moved so quickly that a left-wing demagogue who supports nuclear disarmament by Britain and the weakening of defense relations with the United States—both high-priority Soviet aims—is now leader of the Labour party, in the shape of Michael Foot. After the 1981 local government elections for the Greater London Council, moderate Socialists who had led the Labour party campaign and won it were then immediately voted out of office, their places being taken by left-wing extremists.

In all these moves, extreme left-wing leaders of certain trade unions have played a major role. A few of them, like McGahey of the Mineworkers Union, are open Communists, but many more are on the secret Communist list. They may admit to previous membership, but if so, they claim to have left the party years ago.

The extent to which efforts are made to suborn trade union officials was indicated in the evidence of the two Czech defectors, Frolik and August. They named trade-union leaders alleged to have been recruited when interrogated by the CIA and by the U.S. Senate Judiciary Committee.

Through such people, the Communist party has wielded influence out of all proportion to its size, and in many instances they are working primarily in the interests of the Kremlin. It must always be remembered that, as with KGB agents like Blunt and Philby, Communist trade-union officials are in regular touch with Soviet controllers. They are told what to do, step by step, from Moscow, and they are expected to do it. In 1980, a friend of mine involved in the British construction industry was visited by an MI5 officer to be questioned about one of his manual workers, who happened to be black. When a telephone call showed that the man had been away from work "ill" for three days in the previous week, the MI5 officer revealed that he had, in fact, been in Moscow, his air trip having been paid by the Soviet authorities. The man was an agitator, especially among black workers, and had presumably been in Moscow to report and receive instructions.

One major union leader of recent times was under regular surveillance by MI5 and was seen in contact with Soviet intelligence men. His wife, moreover, is known to have been a Comintern courier. He was present in 1941 at a secret meeting of Communist trade union leaders, at which they reviewed their position after Russia was forced into the war by the German attack. An MI5 agent was also present and reported the full proceedings. Defectors have named him as a KGB agent. Yet both Wilson and Heath forbade any interrogation of this man because, at that time, they wanted no trouble.

Another trade union leader, almost as well known, had occasional meetings with KGB men, specializing in trade union activity, to plan the disruption of the British economy. This plan was partly to promote the spread of communism in Britain but also to reduce living standards so that those prevailing in Russia would not seem so harsh—a deliberate KGB target throughout Western Europe.

Understandably, the Kremlin and its subversion arm, the KGB, pays increasingly close attention to the trade unions of the truly democratic countries where they have power, contrary to their situation in the Soviet Union, where they are merely cyphers. The Trade Union Congress (TUC) and individual unions have gone out of their way to establish close "fraternal relations" with their counterparts behind the Iron Curtain, which are heavily infiltrated and controlled by the KGB. The extent to which Communist unions are run by the state has been brought to public notice by the heroic attempts by Polish workers to gain a modest degree of freedom. The Soviet Union left the Poles in no doubt that, if necessary, it would impose its will by force of arms if the movement for free trade unions went too far for its liking. Yet the Communist-inspired drive to link British trade unions with their East European counterparts-in-name continues—and the attitude of the TUC during the Polish crisis was shameful.

* * *

In 1975 there was a secret meeting in West Germany of Communist trade union leaders from Europe and Britain to discuss tactics for disrupting industry in Western Europe over the following five years. It was sponsored by the Russians, whose main interest it was intended to serve; again, a Western intelligence agent was infiltrated into it. The meeting decided that the motor car and commercial vehicle industry was the most vulnerable to disruption and sabotage and that the British sector offered the softest target. The results, at British Leyland in particular, are there for all to see. The motor industry and its numerous subsidiaries, which provide components and services, are prime employers of labor. Any unofficial strike or wildcat action that creates unemployment and destroys basic industries helps to till the seed bed of communism. One does not need to see the files of MI5 to appreciate that the near-mortal damage to the motor industry has been orchestrated from outside.

This Communist activity had been foreseen by the moderate Labour government under Clement Attlee in 1950. Attlee set up a secret committee, under the late Field Marshal Sir Gerald Templer, to forecast what the British Communists would do after they had failed so miserably to secure representation in Parliament through the ballot box. The Templer Committee questioned many witnesses, including the heads of MI5 and the Secret Service. Its report, which has never been published, concluded that the Communists would concentrate on surreptitious means to achieve influence, and eventually power, through three main targets—the unions, the media, and higher education, meaning the universities and technical institutes. In thirty years, their penetration of all three has progressed inexorably to the point where they can be quite open about it.

There are particular aspects of trade union activity that are causing special concern to the defense chiefs. While the loyalty of the armed forces has never been in doubt, there is less certainty about particular sections of the civilian backup to the nation's defenses. The successful reaction by Britain and NATO to an emergency situation would greatly depend on a few crucial establishments, such as GCHQ intercept stations and decoding sections. These are obvious targets for KGB infiltration, and a few "dissidents" at a critical moment could cripple them. As the employees are members of unions, some dispute could be concocted to give the dissidents an excuse for "downing tools" or "going slow."

The strength of the union in the defense field was demonstrated in the early months of 1981, when civilians employed in the maintenance of Polaris submarines and their warheads walked out at crucial times in furtherance of pay disputes. The unions involved then took widespread retaliation when naval personnel were used to ready the submarines for their essential patrol duties. At the time of writing, three out of the navy's four Polaris submarines are virtually locked in their bases.

Unions responsible for certain workers at the Atomic Weapons Research Establishment at Aldermaston in Berkshire have delayed the production of nuclear explosives there for almost two years, a situation that the Russians must be aware of and appreciate. This is what happened.

After a scare about working with plutonium, the men who operated in the radioactive area refused to enter it unless they were paid special danger money. The civil service refused to pay it because the work was not dangerous, if the precautions were observed, and other workers would have demanded the same increase. To break the deadlock, Margaret Thatcher forced through a deal whereby the men in the radioactive area would receive an extra £15 a week—half of what they had been demanding. The men wanted the money, but their union officials declined the offer because the initiative had come from the government and not from them. In defiance of the Aldermaston shop stewards, the men took the money and returned to work but, in deference to their union, have "gone slow" on the backlog of weapons maintenance work, further delaying the resumption of production.

Fortunately, this has not affected the efficiency of the nuclear deterrent yet because there is enough slack in the program to improve and update the Polaris missile warheads, but it could prove to be serious if the "go slow" continues, and the issue raises doubts about the effects of union action in an emergency.

There is also concern about those post office workers who are involved with security issues, particularly in the event of an emergency, when cable communications would be crucial. Of course, the great majority are loyal, but there are known to be some militants, who may be Communists, among those in key technical positions. Some years ago, men of the post office security unit required to record the telephone conversations of suspects, were vetted, and some were found to have close links with the Communist party. They were duly "purged," but it is far more difficult for the post office to take that action now for a reason that was not appreciated when the government took the steps that created it.

All members of the post office were previously classed as civil servants; as such, those in sensitive positions could be required to undergo positive vetting. With the split-up and reorganization of the post office, they are no longer civil servants, and the unions to which they belong are opposed, on principle, to positive vetting.

The defense chiefs have considered the building of a "hard" communications system under nonunion control for use in an emergency, but the cost has proved prohibitive. As things stand now, communications could be brought to a halt at the height of an emergency by a few post office engineers staging an "industrial dispute."

This situation, and the Communist penetration of the trade unions in general, has greatly stretched the resources of MI5, which has the responsibility for countering them. Also, with the inroads made by the terrorist problem both in Northern Ireland and on the mainland, MI5's resources are now too slim to cope effectively with the KGB.

Incidentally, no member of MI5 or the Secret Service is allowed to belong to a union because of the danger of disruption and infiltration by union officials, who would require access to details of the organizations. Nevertheless, MI5 did once stage what was virtually a sit-down strike.

During Anthony Eden's premiership, a delegation from the Argentine was in London to discuss supplies of meat. The meeting was being held in Lancaster House, and Eden suggested that the anteroom where the Argentinians were to hold their private discussions should be bugged by MI5 to provide some indication of the cheapest price at which they were prepared to settle. Several officers refused to comply on the grounds that the project had nothing to do with the security of the state, and the bugs were never inserted.

23
Should there be
an Inquiry?

Following official disclosures about the treachery of Anthony
Blunt inside MI5, and, previously, about Philby's activities
inside the Secret Service, there were demands in Parliament
for some form of inquiry into both organizations. MPs of all
parties felt that Parliament and the public had need of
reassurance concerning the loyalty, efficiency, and accountability of the two services. I suspect that following the
disclosures in this book, there will be renewed demands for
an inquiry of some kind, though after the debate on the Blunt
case it was decided that none was necessary.

To anyone who has the genuine interests of MI5 and the
Secret Service at heart, as I hope I have, there are basic
objections to an outside inquiry of any kind. As regards MI5,
it is an "illegal" organization, in that it has no basis as a
government department that has ever been authorized and
properly funded by Parliament. Although there is an official
Secret Service vote, the Secret Service is largely in a similar
position. So, insofar as their activities are concerned, especially in the field of counterespionage, the Security Service
can function with effect only by illegal acts, such as entering
premises to search for incriminating documents or for objects
that they can then photograph. Embarrassing legal problems
could be set if they were caught perpetrating a "burglary"
even though, through the judicious use of watchers, communication devices, and other means, this has never happened
and is unlikely to.

On rare occasions, the services need to resort to the hiring
of professional pickpockets to secure keys or documents.
Caretakers and others may have to be bribed to facilitate the

planting of microphones. They may have to exploit the facilities of customs to secure access in luggage to documents, which they wish to photograph. They have frequent need for false pretenses, purporting perhaps to be mechanics to gain entry to a foreign aircraft.

Governments of both the right and the left have seen advantages in retaining this degree of illegality, anomalous though it may seem. So long as MI5 remains "illegal," it cannot be given powers of arrest, so there is no danger that it could become a secret police force and an agency of political repression like the KGB—which has powers of arrest and interrogation exceeding anything available to the British constabulary. As case records described in this book demonstrate, MI5 cannot force or require anybody to be interviewed, much less interrogated. This has enabled people to escape retribution for treachery, for the police cannot be called in to make an arrest until there is evidence of the kind that can be brought into a British court of justice, and, all too often, this is lacking. This inevitably reduces MI5's capacity to catch spies or even to stop known spies from continuing with their activities against the national interest. MI5 is often powerless to prevent a spy leaving the country. It is doubtful, for example, whether it could have stopped Maclean and Burgess from going to France had they been approached and declined to remain in Britain. When these traitors reached Moscow, they drew money from their British bank accounts because, apparently, there were no powers to prevent them from doing so.

My attention was drawn to a further weakness of MI5's position shortly before the big British trade exhibition staged in Moscow in 1961, a weakness that must continue so long as the service remains "illegal." There was considerable concern—justified as it turned out—because MI5 knew that the KGB would do all it could to suborn young technicians, mainly from electronic and engineering firms, attending the exhibition. The firms they represented were for the most part involved in defense projects, and there would be a fair chance that anyone who could be recruited would, one day, find himself concerned with some secret contract. MI5 was therefore most anxious that the visitors to Moscow should first be warned, in as vivid a way as possible, of the dangers of blackmail through gifts and sexual indiscretions, which might be made easy for them. I asked an MI5 officer, who sought my help, why his organization could not warn the visitors or their employers directly. He assured me that this was not feasible because, officially, MI5 did not exist.

To overcome this problem, I was asked to give prominence to a series of actual, and then secret, cases that showed how the KGB operated and how, by making a clean breast of matters at an early stage, its threats could be countered. This seemed a roundabout and uncertain way of issuing a most important official warning, for it was to be limited to the pages of the *Daily Express*, which, in spite of its large circulation, might not be read by those for whom it was intended. Apparently, though, it seemed to work to MI5's satisfaction.

Such weaknesses have been considered preferable to the creation of a legalized Security Service with greater powers, and this remains the view of the government and of MI5 itself.

Over recent years, MI5's powers to carry out routine procedures, such as tapping telephones, has been greatly reduced and controlled, contrary to sensational reports that they have been intensified. While any secretary of state can issue a warrant for the tapping of a suspect's telephone, in practice this is now restricted almost entirely to the home secretary and the foreign secretary. Each time MI5 puts forward a case for the surveillance of a suspect, the home secretary in person has to read the case file, and if he agrees with the proposal, he signs a warrant giving legality to the procedures, which do not include entry to private premises. The foreign secretary is required to observe the same process with regard to surveillance requests made by the Secret Service. Each case is reviewed monthly and only if the counterespionage authorities can substantiate their continuing need is a further warrant issued.

Previously, the security authorities did not require warrants to tap the telephones of foreign diplomats or Soviet bloc embassies, but now they do. Blanket warrants covering organizations rather than individuals are issued for this purpose, but they still have to be reviewed and reissued monthly.

The granting of a warrant for a combined bug and tap, that is, the tapping of a telephone in such a way that it also serves as a live microphone in the room so that conversations there can be recorded on tape even when the telephone is hung up, has been made more stringent.

The installation of taps and microphones is carried out by a special security division of the post office, where controls have also been tightened. The post office invariably refuses to carry out any surveillance work without a warrant except in very rare cases where an immediate tap is necessary before there is time for a warrant to be obtained. In such cases, the warrant still has to be produced within forty-eight hours.

Because it has no powers of arrest, MI5 has to work closely with its arresting arm—Special Branch, the police department that shares with it responsibility for protection of the royal family, as well as counterintelligence against the IRA and other terrorists. Being a "legal" organization, Special Branch has powers to require the post office to tap the telephones of suspected criminals simply by applying to a senior post office official. This power has been given to them because the requirements of the police as a whole in this respect may be so great as to put an impossible administrative burden on the home secretary. In theory, this substantially widens the scope of the security authorities, of which Special Branch must be considered to be a part in any inquiry.

Lord Denning was almost lyrical about the harmony and cooperation between MI5 and Special Branch in his report on the Profumo Affair. No doubt this varies with the personalities involved but in talks at Scotland Yard, I have been given to understand that there is frequent friction. Special Branch complains about having to do too much of the "leg work" in counterespionage operations when its own resources are also overstretched, particularly because of the terrorist threats to the lives of the royal family, senior politicians, and other prominent people.

In its work, MI5 shares with police the power to intercept and read letters, which again can only be done, as a rule, in collaboration with the post office. I am told that the legality of this derives from a royal prerogative dating from the days of Elizabeth I's great Secret Service chief, Sir Francis Walsingham.

In the United States, the clandestine opening of mail is, of course, illegal and when the counterintelligence section of the CIA was discovered to be opening letters from and to the

Soviet Union, this led eventually to the departure of James Angleton and others from the CIA, following contrived publicity about it in 1974.

In the United Kingdom, the task imposed by the authorized opening of letters in the interests of security is enormous, especially when they have to be searched for microdots—photographed messages reduced to such a minute size that they can be camouflaged as punctuation marks. In the past, letters were steamed open and competent "flaps and seals" operators—women being more adept—could open and reseal envelopes without leaving a clue at quite remarkable rates. The operation is now largely automated, the envelopes being slit open, then resealed by a machine that "stitches" the envelope back again, using the fibers of the paper to do so.

Enshrined in the British Official Secrets Act is the further legal right to intercept and read telegrams and cables in the interest of national security. The author was responsible for drawing the public's attention to this in 1967 with extraordinary consequences in Parliament. These led to the setting up of a committee of inquiry under three of the queen's privy councilors to decide whether I and my newspaper had transgressed a semiofficial arrangement between the government and the press whereby certain secret matters remain suppressed. The inquiry reported that we had done no such thing and revealed that the regular practice of reading cables had gone on for forty years. Its report also revealed that senior Whitehall officials had instructed junior officers to lie about the practice in an attempt to preserve its secrecy and make the public believe that I was in error. (Similar decisions may have been taken to discredit the publicity about the much more serious matter of the Hollis Affair.) The security authorities' main purpose in reading private cables is to detect instances where the cable offices, including those of free-enterprise companies like Western Union as well as branches of the post office, are used by foreign embassies and others for sending intelligence messages.

The security authorities are forbidden to tamper with the mail of members of Parliament, including the lords, under the rules introduced by Wilson, which also forbade the tapping of their telephones even when they might be suspect. This has limited their recent activities, particularly in

Northern Ireland, where MI5 is deeply involved, along with the Secret Service. One American senator has long been in the habit of sending packages to a certain Ulster politician, and MI5 was curious to ascertain the contents, suspecting that they might be money. It was decided, however, that this would not only be a contravention of the rules, but the resulting political uproar, if the intervention was discovered, was too dangerous to risk.

In the United Kingdom, and I would guess in most other countries, the security authorities obtain maximum assistance from the customs and immigration control officers, who can so easily manufacture excuses to search baggage and packages in privacy, especially on the grounds of examining them for concealed weapons and explosives. Documents can be quickly photographed and replaced.

The secreting of microphones and other eavesdropping devices unconnected with the telephone system in private homes, offices, and hotels used to be a facility freely available to the counterespionage authorities, but a warrant is now required. (In the case of hotels, ships, aircraft, and similar locations, the permission of the owners is invariably sought and is rarely refused.)

In an ideal world, all privacy should be sacrosanct, but so long as the KGB is so aggressively hostile, the nation's counterforces must have some powers of retaliation. But my latest inquiries convince me that there is probably no country in the world where those powers are now so carefully controlled.

Surprisingly, perhaps, there is some degree of self-restrictive practice inside MI5. A device called the probe microphone enabling an eavesdropper to hear through a party wall, was hailed as a great advance by MI5 surveillance men, but the legal department obstructed its use for a year on the grounds that it constituted trespass!

Much has been made of the fact that facilities have been established so that thousands of telephones can be tapped at the same time. The purpose of this precaution is purely defensive, for use in a war emergency when surveillance of thousands of known suspects would be essential and would be covered, legally, by emergency government powers. I have described how pro-Russian subversion units—of which many members are known, while others would have to be dis-

covered—have been established to sabotage communications
and other essential defense services. Nobody in his right
mind can doubt the wisdom of setting up countermeasures to
defeat them, but the man power to tap thousands of telephones in peacetime would be prohibitive. The tapping and
recording can be automated, but the results have to be
analyzed by MI5 case officers, of whom there are surprisingly
few.

MI5 is the smallest counterespionage organization of any
major military power. Its precise size is an official secret, but
I would be surprised if its numbers exceed two thousand,
including typists and doormen. There are some out-stations,
but most of the staff are based in the new and imposing
headquarters in Curzon Street, where the heart of the operation is the computerized filing system containing quickly
accessible details of about a million individuals, plus a further
million files on organizations and other matters of security
interest.

In his speech in the Blunt debate, Edward Heath suggested
that the hand of the security services should be strengthened.
I would endorse that because as Britain's military inferiority
increases, compared with Russia's, the need for counterintelligence is intensified if limited forces are to be used effectively.
However, I can find no evidence that Heath's government did
anything much to increase the size of MI5.

Successive governments have kept MI5 small by restricting
the money made available to it. This normally increases
annually, save when the security services have to take their
share of government spending cuts but only to keep pace
with inflation. Admittedly, the published figure is not the
true sum, which is larger and hidden in other votes for
purposes of secrecy, but it is still only a tiny fraction of that
available to the KGB.

There is a further disadvantage to the small size of MI5.
Everybody knows everybody else at the officer level, so what
cannot be learned through official channels can often be
gleaned on the "old boy" net. This is a situation that can be
exploited by a spy who manages to gain entry, as both Blunt
and Burgess showed. The same was true of the Secret Service
during the war. Through friendly colleagues, Philby, whose
"need to know" was then restricted to matters affecting Spain
and Portugal, managed to read the "source books" giving the

names of British agents in the Soviet Union, with terrible consequences for them.

Before Sir Percy Sillitoe, the former chief constable, was placed in charge of MI5 in 1946, the organization was totally independent. Its staff was paid in cash, paid no tax, and salaries could be at the whim of the director general. There was an independent auditor to ensure against embezzlement, but no detailed returns were made to the government and recently retired officers can remember how the directors general of both MI5 and the Secret Service had hoards of gold sovereigns, which they could hand out for special operations.

That situation ended when Sillitoe demanded that MI5 be expanded. The Treasury agreed but only on condition that it could impose controls. As a result, MI5 now works largely to civil service rules and pay scales. Retirement is enforced at sixty, while in the Secret Service it is normally required at fifty-five because, by that time, it is virtually certain that an officer's cover will have been blown, making it impossible to send him abroad on intelligence duties. Only in the case of the senior directors is exception made. The pay scales and career structure are not conducive to attract top talent, as was shown by the few candidates prepared to take on the director generalship of either MI5 or the Secret Service when both jobs became vacant recently.

This has not stopped the "Permanent Secretaries Club"—as the chief Whitehall mandarins are collectively called—from trying to grab both jobs for civil servants in need of promotion. When Sir Martin Furnival Jones retired from the director generalship of MI5 in 1974, his natural successor was Michael Hanley, his deputy. The "club" immediately put up its own candidate, a deputy undersecretary at the Home Office, in the hope that it would then have more control over the Security Service. The prime minister, Edward Heath, chose Hanley, but the "club" then came forward with another candidate from the Home Office. They exerted maximum pressure, which was overcome only when Heath was informed that the man being so strongly promoted had been a close friend of both Maclean and Burgess.

I suspect that the "club's" frustration was being expressed when a senior civil servant slyly told me that on Michael Hanley's first visit abroad, to Cyprus, he had torn ligaments in both of his legs and would spend several months in a wheelchair. I kept that secret.

Many civil servants would support a proposition, frequently made in the past and likely to be resurrected, that there should be a ministry for security and intelligence—that is, uniting MI5 and the Secret Service—with a minister responsible to Parliament in control. There is something to be said in theory for such a union. When I telephoned Sir Maurice Oldfield, formerly director general of the Secret Service, when he was appointed controller of security in Northern Ireland, I asked him if he would also be concerned with intelligence there. "The two are inseparable," he replied.

Nevertheless, the objections to such a ministry are legion. MI5 and the Secret Service are already suffering from excessive bureaucracy, and the assumption of responsibility for security by a single ministry would almost certainly make penetration of all the other ministries much easier. Currently, each ministry is responsible for its own security, with a small staff for that purpose. Whitehall and its offshoots are now so vast that a single extra ministry trying to cope with the security problems of all the rest would be unwieldy and almost certainly less effective. Admittedly, the KGB, which is responsible for both security and intelligence, functions like an enormous ministry but succeeds, in spite of that, through its unlimited powers and total immunity from accountability to the Soviet people.

There has been much talk about other ways of making the security and espionage services more accountable to Parliament and to the public, but it is difficult to see how this could be done in view of the degree of secrecy necessary if they are to fulfil their functions. Even those intelligence officers who deplore the way the penetration of MI5 and the Secret Service by the KGB has been concealed, are totally convinced that such organizations cannot operate except in total secrecy. The kind of public inquiry to which the American CIA was subjected following the Watergate Scandal did enormous and probably irreparable damage to the defenses of the Western world, if only by discouraging the assistance given in the past by businessmen and other travelers abroad. No businessman is likely to volunteer valuable intelligence if the name of his commercial organization operating behind the

Iron Curtain is suddenly publicized, enabling the Russians to brand it as a nest of spies, with the consequent arrest of members of its staff, chosen at random by the KGB.

Presumably, any inquiry would concern itself with the efficiency of the secret organizations, and this would not be possible without some critical examination of their methods. The secret methods employed by MI5 and the Secret Service are regarded as being so sensitive that even Sir Derek Rayner, a close friend of the prime minister and cleared for security at every level because of his business-efficiency work in the Defence Ministry and membership of the Security Commission, was barred from access to them. When he was given a free range among the Whitehall departments of state to recommend cost-saving improvements in efficiency, both MI5 and the Secret Service were excluded.

With the increasing reliance on technological advances, which give one side a valuable superiority until they are detected and countered, secrecy concerning methods of countersurveillance and espionage is more vital than ever. Not long ago, the "sweepers," employed by the Foreign Office to search for microphones and other concealed listening devices that might be planted by an adversary, asked MI5 for details of the ingenious ways in which it hides such instruments in its counterespionage operations, hoping that such knowledge would assist them in their work, which has the same end in mind. In the interest of security, MI5 declined to reveal its secrets and when the sweepers induced senior Foreign Office officials to complain on their behalf to the foreign secretary, he upheld MI5's objection. If sweepers, who are cleared for the highest security classifications, cannot safely be told such secrets, how could they be divulged to any lay inquiry board?

As MI5's Jim Skardon maintains after his long experience, the most productive source of intelligence and of leaks is still the wagging tongue. For this reason, any efficient security service limits the number of people permitted access to its secrets on the principle of absolute need to know. Any inquiry would have to infringe this principle, for it also provides a convenient excuse for officials to cover up their failures and embarrassments.

A director general can all too easily convince himself that, concerning some particular event, neither the home secretary nor the prime minister really *needs* to know, a situation that has certainly been exploited in the past. After the Navy Secrets spy trials, Harold Macmillan was assured that no serious leakages of information to the Russians had taken place. He suspected that he was being bamboozled, and he was right. Later, when Adm. Sir Ray Lygo was vice chief of the naval staff, he told me that the leakages had been very severe and their ravages had taken years to repair. There was serious failure to inform Macmillan about the Profumo Affair, while Sir Anthony Eden was kept in the dark about the Crabb naval espionage endeavor and Sir Alec Douglas Home was not told about Blunt.

James Callaghan, when prime minister, was fully briefed on the cases of Hollis and other suspects only after he called in the heads of MI5 and the Secret Service to discuss another matter—an allegation by myself that Sir Harold Wilson had been under surveillance both while in opposition and in office.

In their turn, of course, prime ministers and other politicians have convinced themselves that, particularly as regards spy scandals, the public has had no need to know.

There is a further reason, which is political as well as security orientated, why the need to know principle would have to be rigidly applied concerning methods. Because of the ever-increasing swing toward technical systems of espionage and counterespionage, such as radio interception, code breaking, and reconnaissance satellites, it would be necessary for any inquiry to include an examination of the work of GCHQ, with its huge headquarters at Cheltenham and numerous out-stations. This would not only involve an infringement of secrets of the highest order, but a major difficulty would be created by the fact that the organization runs in close collaboration with the U.S. National Security Agency, which has stations in Britain.

Only those wishing to assist the KGB and its offshoots would want to impair that collaboration, which provides British intelligence with the results of American satellite reconnaissance beyond the financial means of this nation. In this context, the stupidity—or worse—or those Labour politicians who are agitating for the removal of American military bases from British soil deserves the fullest exposure. Not only would the expulsion of the Americans from Britian make the reinforcement of U.S. troops in Europe almost impossible, but it would inevitably deprive the United Kingdom of satellite intelligence.

There is suspicion inside MI5 concerning the efficiency of the security arrangements at GCHQ. It is of major interest to the KGB, yet there is no evidence of recent efforts to insinuate any new recruits there, the implication being that there is sufficient penetration already.

A former senior officer of MI5, who worked at GCHQ for a couple of years after his retirement, has described the security situation there as "a shambles," with people taking out secret papers and few checks at the gate to prevent espionage or sabotage. GCHQ is the heart of British intelligence work, and though its costs are secret, they must run into hundreds of millions of pounds annually.

A further political problem would be created by the close links between the British security services and the CIA. Too close an inquiry would be interpreted as an infringement of Anglo-American agreements on security and intelligence, which require that no joint information shall be passed to any third party without joint agreement.

I have no doubt that left-wing MPs would be delighted to probe the CIA's operations in Britain, which are modest but necessary in view of the huge American investment in bases and other defensive facilities here. In theory, the CIA cannot carry out any counterintelligence operations in Britain without informing MI5, but it is known to have done so.

The KGB's intense interest in Western methods of scientific intelligence gathering, some of which are incredibly ingenious, has been amply demonstrated by the upsurge and success of its espionage effort at establishments, installations, and factories in the United States involving the suborning and recruitment of local-born traitors. In 1977, William Kampiles, a junior watch officer at CIA headquarters in Langley, Virginia, stole a technical manual containing performance details of a highly secret reconnaissance satellite called the KH 11, which has since become popularly known as the "Keyhole" satellite because of its closeup espionage capabilities. The satellite, which cost the American taxpayers hundreds of millions of dollars, can take high-resolution photographs and transmit them instantaneously to ground stations, and was believed to be far in advance of anything available to the Soviet Union. The watch officer, then aged twenty-three, sold the manual to a Soviet agent for three thousand dollars! For this, he was sentenced to forty years imprisonment.

In the recent spy case centered on another CIA officer, David Barnett, sentenced to eighteen years in jail, the KGB controller had been operating as a third secretary in the Soviet embassy in Washington. From Barnett, who had worked for the CIA for twelve years, the KGB received the names of CIA undercover agents and details of CIA operations abroad in return for about $100,000. His most damaging offence had been to sell the Russians an account of Operation Habrink, by which the CIA had secured valuable technical details about new Soviet weapons after they had been supplied to another country. The KGB pressed Barnett to rejoin the CIA, from which he had resigned, or to secure work with the Senate Intelligence Committee. Fortunately, its efforts in both directions failed.

An even more fertile ground for planting agents under diplomatic cover has been opened up and exploited by the KGB in the shape of the UN organization in New York. Several defectors from that organization have listed the spies active there. They include Viktor Lessiovsky, who is now a senior aide to Kurt Waldheim, the secretary general himself. In April 1978, the highest-ranking Soviet officer in the UN, Arkady Shevchenko, sought asylum in the United States and revealed the extent of the Russian conspiracy to manipulate the UN for espionage and subversion. Three months later, the FBI arrested three KGB agents using UN cover to obtain secret plans for American antisubmarine warfare. Soon afterward Vladimir Rezun, a GRU officer posing as a diplomat in the Soviet UN mission in Geneva, defected to London and named five KGB officers working under UN cover in Geneva and New York. Shevchenko stated publicly, "The UN became one of the best places for KGB intelligence activities. The KGB considers the UN the tallest observation tower in the Western world for intelligence activity."

This KGB concentration on the United States does not mean that its efforts against the United Kingdom have consequently been reduced. It is a *canard*, perhaps deriving from Soviet supporters, that Britain, having no defense secrets of any consequence, is no longer a target worth close KGB attention. British defense research, which continues to make a rich contribution to Western defense, still attracts intense KGB interest. Almost every new defector provides evidence that the Soviet bloc embassies and trade missions are infiltrated with intelligence agents who still continue to recruit British traitors.

Leakages of information about British nuclear weapons have been susupected by both the Defence Ministry and MI5 because of information derived from radio intercepts and defectors. Investigations have so far yielded no names, but the information could only have come from a high-level Defence Ministry or Service source.

KGB interest in Britain has, in fact, been enhanced by its intensified activity in the United States. In the event of the military conflict in Europe, which some Kremlin politicians still believe to be inevitable, Britain would be the main reinforcement base for the American forces, without which NATO would have no hope of defensive success. It is therefore a key area—probably *the* key area—for sabotage, subversion, and quick elimination.

Unquestionably, the Soviet leaders would prefer to remove the American component of NATO without the use of military force, and there are relentless political pressures to this end. Andrei Gromyko, the Soviet foreign secretary, is known to have said privately in Moscow that the Soviet government is not much interested in the strategic arms limitation talks (SALT), which are mainly for stringing the Americans along and producing some concessions of value in Russia. For the Kremlin, agreement on a European Security Conference is far more important—as a step toward eliminating U.S. forces from Europe on the spurious grounds that since Russia means no harm, they are no longer needed.

Sadly, the Kremlin's basic intentions are only too apparent—both from its behavior and from the information imparted by defectors, military and political—to divide the Western allies and then to rule.

In this endeavor, NATO has proved to be a productive hunting ground. Several high-ranking West German officers have been suborned, some of them committing suicide when about to face security interrogation. Copies of contingency plans have been stolen from NATO offices. In one instance, of which I have official knowledge, a copy of NATO's entire nuclear targeting plans was removed from the office of the NATO supreme commander, then General Norstad. An RAF officer, who discovered the loss, told me that the document gave the places in Russia and the satellite countries that would be attacked with nuclear bombs in the event of a retaliatory raid, together with details of the squadrons involved and their routes. When he broke the news to Norstad, the supreme commander's reaction was that while he had little doubt that the document was in Moscow, it was perhaps just as well that the Russians should know what to expect if they ever attacked the West. The only necessary action, apart from a general tightening of office security, was to switch the routes.

The KGB's most daring and most productive penetration of the NATO alliance was its planting of the Soviet bloc spy Guenther Guillaume as personal assistant to Willi Brandt, the West German chancellor. When the full extent of his treachery was realized, one of the most senior officials at NATO military headquarters exclaimed, "My God, it's all gone!"

The KGB's Disinformation Department has been incredibly adept at sowing discord among the NATO allies, its most recent resounding success being the distrust of the American neutron bomb that it has implanted in the minds of West Germans, Dutch, and Belgians. The neutron bomb is essentially a counter to an attack by massed tanks, Russia's main weapon in Europe, but the Russians projected it as the capitalist bomb that kills people but preserves buildings. Though so patently fraudulent, this approach led European leaders to object to the presence of the weapon on their soil and induced former President Jimmy Carter to suspend work on it.

With a view to strengthening the United Kingdom's capacity to resist the erosive activities of the KGB, Jonathan Aitken, Tory MP for Thanet, has suggested that a committee of privy councilors could do a "quiet monitoring job" on the security services, reporting in general terms. As Aitken said in the Blunt debate, this would be preferable to a select committee, which would inevitably include "some of the more controversial characters from the back-benches," but even the privy councilors would have to be chosen with great discrimination. There are some among them who are considered unreliable by the security authorities.

In my opinion and in that of experienced security officers whom I have consulted, any inquiry except by people with personal knowledge of security and intelligence operations would be of little use in evaluating the efficiency and loyalty of the security services. This rules out the kind of judicial inquiry carried out into the Profumo Affair by Lord Denning. A judge, used to the rules of evidence and experienced in normal legal cases, is not fitted to give an opinion on counterespionage or intelligence operations that depend on methods quite different from those used by the police.

A tribunal of inquiry such as that set up to investigate the Vassall case, with officers and others giving evidence under oath and subject to the rules of contempt, would be too similar to the post-Watergate investigation into the activities of the CIA to be acceptable in the national interest. I am not greatly impressed by the argument that an inquiry of any kind would seriously damage the morale of the services, for the loyal officers would support anything designed to reduce the risk of harboring traitors and prising out any already there. But of all types of inquiry, a tribunal would be most likely to impair attitudes and morale.

In the Blunt debate, James Callaghan and Merlyn Rees both came out in favor of some kind of limited inquiry, while others, like James Wellbeloved, supported an inquiry wide enough to "clear the air of the stench of treason." Margaret Thatcher won the day with her assurances that an inquiry was unnecessary following improvements in the accountability of MI5 and the Secret Service to ministers, increases in efficiency through better recruiting methods, and intensification of precautions to prevent penetration by traitors. In the last context, Mrs. Thatcher has been urged to announce an amnesty for all the old traitors prepared to come forward, confess their treachery in full, and assist the security authorities to wrap up their cases in return for immunity from prosecution and, hopefully, from publicity. This has so far met with no positive result if only because the publicity given to

the Blunt case as a result of the prime minister's parliamentary disclosure has been off putting to those who know that no
action can be taken against them so long as they decline to
cooperate.

I have established to my satisfaction that Mrs. Thatcher's
assurances are well founded. There is much closer collaboration between MI5 and the Home Office at the highest official
and political levels. When Merlyn Rees was home secretary,
he instituted meetings with the director general of MI5,
which are as regular as those held with the commissioner of
the Metropolitan Police. Meetings between the director general of the Secret Service and the foreign secretary are also
frequent. The prime minister makes it her business to see
both men on occasion, so the days when either chief could
deliberately keep himself aloof from political contact, as
Hollis did, are gone.

With the able assistance of the cabinet secretary, Sir John
Hunt (now Lord), James Callaghan, when prime minister,
revised the recruitment procedures for MI5, bringing them into
line with the improvements instituted in the Secret Service after
the Philby Affair. It was decided to broaden the social classes
from which recruits were sought because MI5 had in the past
been too "incestuous" in this respect and major sources of
former recruits were fast disappearing in the shape of the
ex-members of the colonial and imperial police forces.

Talent spotters from both security services sit in when the
Civil Service Commission interviews candidates for entry to
the civil service as a whole, so that any who seem to be
specially suited by qualifications and temperament for undercover work can be invited to join. Any candidates approaching
the security services on their own initiative, and particularly
those who are persistent, are now regarded as suspect until
fully cleared by passage through positive vetting hoops, which
have been made much more stringent.

Positive vetting means active investigation by trained officers, usually ex-policemen, into the background and activities
of recruits. It has failed to weed out people like William
Vassall in the past, and I have heard security officers say it
would still probably have failed to put suspicion on Philby,
had it been available in his day. It is certainly not as thorough
as the system used in recruitment for the CIA, which in-

volves the use of the polygraph—the so-called lie detector. While the polygraph, which records blood pressure, heartbeat, and surface sweat during questioning, is fallible, I am assured by senior CIA officials that it is a valuable adjunct. It is also undoubtedly a deterrent as the evidence of the recent trail in which David Barnett, a former CIA officer was convicted of espionage, clearly shows. His Soviet controller had urged him to seek permanent re-entry to the CIA but Barnett was reluctant to do so "feeling that he could not pass the polygraph test."

It is commonly believed that officers of the British services would object to the introduction of such a test though when Maurice Oldfield was posted to Washington by the Secret Service he volunteered to undergo a CIA polygraph test to convince the American authorities that, as a bachelor, he had no homosexuality problem.

A further CIA insurance that could improve precautions against penetration of the British services is the principle of random recall. All officers know that they are subject to the possibility of sudden interrogation by security experts simply because their name has come up in the system. The recall includes another polygraph test. In Britain, positive vetting is supposed to be repeated every five years for each individual so having passed once, there is a five-year turn without further check unless suspicion is aroused.

The initial positive vetting process for the security services now takes several months, and nobody is allowed in until these have been satisfactorily completed. So far, this delay has not caused problems, though it has done so at the equally secret Atomic Weapons Establishment at Aldermaston. Some promising recruits there have taken other jobs because the delay in waiting for clearance has been too long. A suggestion that badly needed recruits should be paid during the waiting period has been turned down by the government.

The universities are being used again as recruiting grounds, but in a much less haphazard way than in the thirties, when they were such an easy avenue of entry for spies. University staff, who are themslves cleared as regards political reliability, are briefed by visiting representatives from MI5 and the Secret Service on the types of individual required. The kind of Establishment background that enabled people like Bur-

gess and Philby to penetrate the security screen so easily is
no longer an automatic qualification. The field has been
widened to include people of all social origins, including
some blacks for speical work among non-white communities.

There seems to be a much more pragmatic appreciation of
the supreme importance of the security services in peacetime than existed in the recent past, when lip service was
paid but little else, and they were left to themselves, often
with results regarded as almost derisory. Though Harold
Macmillan was deeply concerned with national security, he
frequently complained to his Cabinet secretary about the
futility and unreliability of many of the intelligence reports
reaching him and, in his diary, was driven to refer to "our so-
called Security Services."

Those ministers, including the prime minister, who are in
closest touch with the security services, believe that their
effectiveness has substantially improved in coping with the
ever-increasing effort being mounted against Britain as a key
member of the NATO alliance by the KGB. The appalling
situation in which senior officials of both MI5 and the Secret
Service were known, or deeply suspected, to be Russian
spies no longer exists. Nevertheless, I find that doubt remains among some politicians and retired members of the
services concerning the possibility that those who were traitors in positions of great influence in the past may have
introduced successors who are still there. That the KGB
would require them to try to do so, there can be no doubt.
Care would have been taken to ensure that any senior spies
in place within the security services served as talent spotters,
providing the names of possible recruits among the more
junior staff. The KGB would then do the recruiting, using
whatever methods it considered necessary. The spies already
in place might also be required to ease the entry of any new
recruits spotted independently by the KGB and to ensure
their allotment to sections of special interest to Russia.

Lord Trend was told by MI5 witnesses that Hollis might
have recruited unidentified Soviet agents into the security
service. That some of them may still be there was suggested
by James Callaghan in his speech during the Blunt debate.
"It is probably true to say that because of the effluxion of time
those concerned in that penetration of the Service have
passed, or are passing out of active service."

As I have said, I can find no evidence of the presence of spies at any high level in the security services, but there may be a case for an inquiry by some group that could reassure the community that "moles" no longer exist at any level. The task of MI5, as publicly stated by Sir Martin Furnival Jones, is worth restating in this context, "the defence of the realm as a whole from external and internal dangers arising from attempts at espionage and sabotage, or from actions of persons and organizations, whether directed from within or without the country, which may be judged to be subversive of the security of the State." In the nuclear age and in the current climate of East-West relations, a traitor in the security services is far more dangerous to many more people than a mass murderer at large. If he happened to be the top man during an attempted coup or a military emergency, such are his powers of command that he could do crucial disservice by ensuring failure to round up the subversion and sabotage units alone.

In discussing this situation with Sir Robert Mark, the former metropolitan police commissioner, he drew a comparison with his force, and particularly the Criminal Investigation Department, when he joined it. It was well known within the force that corruption, in the sense that policemen were taking bribes to protect criminals, was rife. When Mark announced his intention of taking action to root it out, some of his Scotland Yard associates, honest men of good will, strongly advised against it on the grounds that the corruption had gone on for so long that it was accepted practice and that any prosecutions would do irreparable damage to the image of the police.

Mark went ahead, and many policemen, some at very senior levels, were prosecuted and dismissed. Now the public knows that the police force is at least far less corrupt than it was and that any officer taking bribes in the future risks heavy penalties. Nor is there any evidence that morale inside the police service has been damaged by Mark's courageous action, a risk always raised when any far-reaching inquiry into the security services is suggested.

Treachery, for money or ideological motives, is a form of corruption and perhaps the public would be easier in its mind with a reassurance that so far as can possibly be established, the trade of treachery, which has flourished so prolifically in the security services, has been abolished there.

It is essential that any inquiry should not become a McCarthy-type inquisitorial witch hunt, as happened with the CIA, with results of inestimable value to the Kremlin both through the weakening of America's secret defenses and the damage to the image of Western democracy. Nevertheless, if disquietude is to be allayed and confidence restored, full disclosure of the traitorous activites of the past may be necessary.

24
Postscript

The title of the previous chapter was answered by the prime minister on the day this book was first published in Britain when she announced that she was to ask the Security Commission "to review the security procedures and practices currently followed in the public service and to consider what, if any, changes are required." This has been described as Mrs. Thatcher's first policy U-turn because, following the Blunt Affair, she and her government came out so strongly against any such inquiry.

The Security Commission is a standing body called in from time to time to examine breaches of security and to make recommendations arising out of their investigations. At the time of writing, it is headed by Lord Diplock, a judge in his seventies, and he and two other members are to carry out what will be the first independent inquiry in twenty years into the measures taken to prevent penetration by foreign agents.

The prime minister's statement made it clear that the commission's inquiry would not be limited to MI5 and the Secret Service but would cover the Foreign Office, GCHQ, the Defence Ministry, and all relevant departments of state, as the previous chapter suggested that any inquiry should. The inquiry is expected to last at least nine months.

Precautions unprecedented in the publishing trade were taken by the author and the publisher to keep secret the existence of this book and its contents until the newspaper serialization commenced a few days before publication date. No books were sent to booksellers until that day, and none went out to reviewers.

There were two reasons for these measures. First, the book

contained so much that was new that its contents could easily
have been "milked" by the media. Second, I suspected that if
the Cabinet Office or MI5 secured a copy of the text steps
might be taken to have publication suppressed under the
Official Secrets Act. I knew that it would be obvious that
much of the material could only have originated from within
the security services and that technical breaches of the Official Secrets Act, which can be used—journalists would say
misused—to cover material going back before World War I
must have occurred.

Three days before publication day, the managing director of
Sidgwick and Jackson, the house publishing the book, received
a personal request by telephone from Sir Robert Armstrong,
the secretary of the Cabinet. He said that the prime minister
needed a copy of the book so that she could be in a position
to make a statement about it with the least possible delay if
pressed to do so in Parliament. Sir Robert thought such
pressure was likely in view of what had already appeared in
the *Daily Mail*, which had begun serialization of the book.

In view of our fears concerning possible suppression, I
suggested that this request should be granted only if Sir
Robert undertook, in writing, not to prevent or to delay
publication. I did not think that he would be in a position to
give such an undertaking. Nevertheless, he did so in a letter
to the publisher dated March 23. This letter, which was not
marked "personal" or "confidential," also contained an assurance that the book would not go outside Sir Robert's office or
the prime minister's. The explanation for this surprising
alacrity was soon provided by friends who kept me informed
of what was happening in Whitehall. Through its secret
resources, MI5 had secured a copy of the text at least a week
in advance and probably well before that. I know that a
former director general of MI5 and a former Cabinet secretary were shown the script and given time to read it well
before publication day and had given their views on it.

I was not unduly surprised by this discovery, for I had
surmised that former security and intelligence officers to
whom I had written for advice or approached personally
would have reported the events back to their old offices.
Scores of people connected with Whitehall and Westminster
knew that I was contemplating some publication or other
about the Hollis Affair and had been for some years. Jonathan

Aitken had alerted the prime minister and the Cabinet Office to the fact that journalists were actively investigating the suspicions that had arisen in MI5 concerning both Hollis and Mitchell.

If Downing Street already had access to the script of *Their Trade is Treachery*, why had the Cabinet secretary so urgently requested a copy for the prime minister? To forestall a barrage of individual parliamentary questions about points in the book, especially those concerning Driberg and other former and existing MPs, Mrs. Thatcher was determined to clear the problem away on the first day of the book's publication by announcing the Security Commission inquiry. I have no doubt that the Cabinet Office received a copy of the text as soon as MI5 secured it and that a brief was made available to the prime minister then. Without a copy of the book provided by the publisher, it would have become obvious that the text had been obtained surreptitiously and its source had to be covered. There was the further point that the Cabinet Office would want to ensure that no last-minute changes had been made in the text before publication, though I regard it as probable that MI5 had also secured an advance copy of the bound volume.

If there had been serious breaches of the Official Secrets Act really damaging to national security, it would have been the government's duty to prevent them by warning myself and the publisher before the book appeared. That it did not do so after reading the text, implies that ministers and their advisers took a decision on the security issues. Sir Robert Armstrong's quick agreement not to prevent or interfere with publication could only have meant that it had already been decided that there were no realistic grounds for proceedings under the Official Secrets Act at that stage or that it would be impolitic to institute them. This, presumably, was also the reason why the *Daily Mail* received no complaint from the secretary of the D-Notice Committee drawing attention to the D-Notice specifically referring to intelligence and security matters.

Recent interviews I have had with Jonathan Aitken show that he and his own excellent MI5 source, whose identity is known to the government, stand firm on the original evidence that Aitken submitted to Mrs. Thatcher early in 1980. They both accept, as I now do, that Lord Trend declared Hollis not guilty for want of sufficient corroborated evidence to the contrary, though his innocence could not be proved, either. I happen to know, however, that Aitken's informant, who could not have been closer to the action, believes Hollis to have been guilty and to have been "cleared" as Philby was "cleared" in 1955. I also know that his account of such cases as those of Driberg, Ellis, Cairncross, and others would be very similar to mine. I can say in all honesty that I have never met or spoken with this man, whose loyalty is beyond question. His evidence, therefore, is quite independent from mine.

Much was made by newspapers of the fact that, in answer to a parliamentary question, the prime minister stated that an official inquiry was being made into the sources of my information for this book. Journalists who consulted No. 10 Downing Street were told that the inquiry was being conducted by MI5. That has proved to be the case. I know of former members of MI5 and the Secret Service who have been interviewed about specific matters in this book that, according to one of them, "read as though they were straight out of the official files." To date, nobody has asked to question me, suggesting that the inquiry is internal for MI5's own purposes. A similar inquiry stimulated by a series of parliamentary questions took place consequent to the publication of my previous book *Inside Story* in 1978, with no result affecting the author.

So far, the main result of the inquiry has been to deter present and former members of MI5 and the Secret Service from publicly confirming what I have written, which several of them could do, as Mrs. Thatcher has been informed. I do, however, have the private satisfaction of knowing that those interviewed confirmed their belief in almost everything stated in this book.

The impending publication of *Their Trade is Treachery* would appear to have put the prime minister in a difficult position because though none of the suspicious events that I record occurred during her premiership, she felt responsible for defending the reputation of the security services as well as she could. There were several politically explosive ingredients in the book, of which the most dangerous was the Hollis Affair, about which the public was ignorant. There was no way that Mrs. Thatcher could deny the main disclosures that Hollis, when director general of MI5, had been deeply

suspected over several years by his own colleagues of being a
KGB agent, that he had been interrogated, had failed to clear
himself, and that, a year after his death, a further inquiry by
Lord Trend had been unable to establish his innocence.

Whatever the results of the Trend Inquiry, it would have
been virtually impossible for the prime minister to have
admitted that Hollis had been a spy or to have given any
other result beyond the statement that he had been "cleared."
The consequences internationally would have been too damaging.

Shortly after the prime minister's statement, a privy councilor who had read the Trend Report gave me a verbal
summary of it. Since then, information from others, including
a senior minister in the present government and others from
previous governments, have confirmed that summary and
expanded on it. The main point that I have established
beyond all doubt is that no new evidence whatever accrued
to Lord Trend during his inquiry. Recalling a statement that
Mrs. Thatcher made about this book, I can say with certainty
that the Trend Report contained no information that was new
to the security authorities who had carried out the original
inquiries into the Hollis Affair.

To summarize, it would seem, then, that in cricket par-
lance all that Trend was able to do was to give an umpire's
verdict on an appeal by a hostile bowling side insisting that
Hollis was "out." After an agonizing, year-long deliberation,
during which he consulted other "umpires," like Sir Dick
White, he gave Hollis the benefit of the doubt with a "not
out" verdict. It is a verdict that could still be shown to be
mistaken, though this seems unlikely because of the age of
the case. The only certainty in my mind is that if evidence
disputing the verdict ever arrives in MI5 or in any other
secret department, it will be withheld there from the public,
as almost everything else in this book was, unless some
investigative writer with prime source contacts chances to
uncover it.

It is the opinion of former senior officers of MI5, the Secret
Service, and the CIA that Mrs. Thatcher went unnecessarily
far in trying to convince the public that Hollis had been
effectively cleared of ever having been a KGB agent. So her
position, as well as that of the officials who advised her, could
be at risk. She might have been more cautious had she taken

the opportunity of a first-hand rundown on the Hollis case by a senior member of the Fluency Committee when this was offered to her in a letter sent to her by Jonathan Aitken early in 1980. Presumably, she declined that offer on the advice of officials who may not have wished her to receive a first-hand rundown but to put her faith in the Trend Report, which casts doubt on the motives of some of the investigation officers.

Mrs. Thatcher's rejection of a first-hand rundown surprised me because I am aware of her deep personal interest in security and intelligence affairs. While she was still in Opposition, as leader of the Conservative party, I saw her with the precise purpose of suggesting that she should be regularly given first-hand briefings on such matters by Sir Maurice Oldfield, then head of the Secret Service. Sir Maurice had asked me to approach her, as protocol forbade him to do so. She seized on the offer, provided that she could first secure the agreement of the prime minister, then James Callaghan, which she duly did. Mrs. Thatcher and Sir Maurice became firm friends.

Though Mrs. Thatcher did her best for Hollis in her statement, she "damned him with no praise," as one politician described it. There was no suggestion that he had been an able public servant whose reputation was being traduced. In private, ministers have expressed the opinion that Hollis's behavior in office was due to incompetence rather than treachery. One law officer has been reported to me as saying that Hollis was "indecisive, ineffectual, and bumbling." It is extremely unlikely, however, that a professional as discerning as Sir Dick White would have recommended a bumbling incompetent either to be his deputy or, later, to succeed him in the top job. When incompetence benefits an adversary on such a scale and over such a long period, deliberate action is a more acceptable explanation.

In other respects, the brief prepared for Mrs. Thatcher and read by her to Parliament was an above-standard example of the Whitehall art of news management. It included the statement that the book contained no information "new to the security authorities." Considering that most of the information, which was entirely new to the public, had originated from the security authorities, this was, in its way, a compliment, but those who prepared the brief and are well versed in the idiosyncrasies of Fleet Street foresaw that those news-

papers envious of the *Daily Mail's* exclusive acquisition of the
serial rights would misconstrue the phrase as meaning that
the book contained nothing new, period.

The brief then went on to suggest that the investigation of
Hollis had been almost a routine procedure, one among many
inquiries into various leads. In fact, Hollis was the first
director general of MI5 to fall under any suspicion whatever.
Nobody anywhere near that rank, in either MI5 or the Secret
Service, had ever been investigated before, and the brief was
careful to avoid confirming that the deputy director, Graham
Mitchell, had been suspected at the same time. The situation
had been quite unprecedented, but the prime minister was
required to do all she could to play it down.

In doing this, she was also led to claim that the leads
pointing to Hollis could be attributed to Philby or Blunt, a
statement that, as I have explained, is certainly false and her
advisers may come to regret. To recall but one example, Blunt
convinced his interrogators, who were not particularly disposed to believe all he told them, that he could not possibly
have been the wartime spy inside MI5 with the code name
"Elli." Nor could "Elli" have been Philby, who was not in
MI5. "Elli" could, however, have been Hollis.

The suggestion that Hollis's behavior after the end of the
war was not the subject of inquiry by the security authorities
is so patently false as to throw doubt on the rest of the
statement. Apart from the fact that I know that the Fluency
Committee continued their inquiries with increasing intensity
until his retirement in late 1965 and afterward until his recall
for interrogation in 1970, it is inconceivable that if the KGB
had managed to recruit Hollis during the war years, they
would have left him alone when he became deputy director
and then director general. It is difficult to avoid the conclusion that the statement prepared by officials for Mrs. Thatcher
was angled to suggest that all the suspicions originated forty
years ago or more in what has been described as "the
poisoned past" covering the activities of the proven spies,
Burgess, Maclean, Philby, and Blunt.

The serious problems in MI5, which are not explicable
unless there was a spy at a high level there, did not disappear
after Blunt and Philby left. They did appear to cease when
Hollis retired.

During the many interviews I have given about the contents of this book, I have been asked repeatedly if I believe that Hollis was a spy. I have taken the view that as the circumstances are so complex, the facts should be allowed to speak for themselves. I have to say, however, that I am not impressed by the final decision of Lord Trend virtually to exonerate Hollis or by the government's decision to accept the verdict as final. The evidence that there was a high-level "mole" in MI5 not only during the war but up to the middle 1960s seems more compelling to me the more that I study it. Trend's decision that this evidence did not incriminate Hollis does not dispose of it. If Hollis was not guilty, who was? It would seem to be unlikely now, because of the passage of time and people, that there will ever be a satisfactory answer to this question.

Before accepting the Trend Report as the final answer on the Hollis Affair, I suggest that readers should recall the "clearance" of Philby by the then foreign secretary, Harold Macmillan, in 1955. This followed the publication of a brief and uninformative official report on the defection of Burgess and Maclean calculated to give the impression that neither had been important spies, though the damage that had been inflicted by Maclean was already well understood. Philby was "cleared" because, in spite of the suspicion against him, there was no evidence that could have been brought into a British court. Unless a suspect confesses, there hardly ever is. Had Philby accepted the immunity to prosecution on offer to him eight years later in Beirut, this "clearance" would have continued so far as the public was concerned.

Philby himself may have something to say about Hollis if he ever completes the book he is thought to be writing, though of course this would be another KGB-controlled exercise and his statements would need expert analysis.

Mrs. Thatcher referred to other "distortions" and "inaccuracies" in this book but declined to identify any of them. In such a context, a "distortion" is an interpretation of which Whitehall disapproves. As regards "inaccuracies," nobody who was close to the action has been able to point to any, save for the final rendering of the Trend Report and an odd date, which has since been corrected. On the contrary, confirmatory information has flowed in from witnesses; as a result, I have not only been able to expand the original material but to identify people concerned.

The events that followed in Parliament immediately after the conclusion of the prime minister's statement were peculiar, to say the least. Michael Foot, the Labour leader, who had been advised of the contents of the prime minister's statement in advance, seized on the opportunity to stifle questions about Driberg, his former friend and Socialist colleague, by referring to the unidentified "inaccuracies." In fact, every aspect of the Driberg Affair, as stated in this book, is correct.

The speaker then permitted only eight back-bench MPs among the many who wished to ask questions to do so. Those whom he selected to speak proved to be noncontroversial. One of them even suggested that I had been the victim of a KGB disinformation exercise: as I then pointed out in a letter to the *Times*, if that had been so, then many of my informants, who included former prime ministers, home secretaries, foreign secretaries, defense and intelligence chiefs, must have been working for the KGB.

The most extraordinary parliamentary result of the prime minister's statement was the attitude of MPs of all parties in desisting from asking any parliamentary questions on the numerous issues raised by the book's disclosures. Normally, back-bench MPs seize on any controversial question that will get their names into the newspapers or, better still, on radio and television. Yet they took the view that once the prime minister had announced the setting up of the Security Commission's inquiry, no further questions need to be asked until it has reported. This was quite unjustified because the prime minister's statement made it clear that the Security Commission would not be investigating the specific allegations in this book but only examining the precautions being taken now against further penetration of secret departments by foreign intelligence agents.

My inquiries suggest that the Conservative MPs, who have an ingrained objection to making any criticism of the security and intelligence services, remained quiet in support of the prime minister. Those of the left were too embarrassed by the disclosures about Driberg, their former party chairman, and other Labour MPs to pursue any of the issues, especially when the party was beset with a crucial struggle for power between the moderates and the Communist-inclined far left.

I am confident that the situation would have been very

different in the United States, where the issues would have been more thoroughly discussed and investigated. If the Watergate scandal or anything like it had occurred in Britain, it is unlikely that it would have been fully exposed as it was in America because neither Parliament nor the press would have pursued it to conclusion. Both would have become bored with it. As Sir Harold Wilson said, "A week is a long time in politics." So it is in British journalism.

At the individual level, the reaction of those who knew the spies and suspects I name for the first time has been, almost universally "The allegation must be false because had this person been a spy I would have known it." Normally intelligent and perceptive people wrote to newspapers denying the evidence about their friends without offering any rebuttal beyond their gut feelings. Even Michael Foot dismissed the information about Driberg's activities on the grounds that had it been true, it would have leaked years ago. In fact, the security services have been very efficient at keeping their secrets from the public, if not from the enemy. KGB agents have proved even more adept. The two wives with whom Philby spent most of his adult life had no inkling that he was a spy. Neither did the family or friends of Colonel Ellis, John Cairncross, or Anthony Blunt, save for those who were helping them.

The case histories outlined in this book demonstrate that anybody can turn out to be spy. Who would have thought that Burgess, the habitual drunkard and pouncing homosexual, could keep a secret? Blunt, the sensitive esthete, Philby, the affable guy, Maclean, the polished diplomat during office hours, Cairncross, the unremarkable civil servant, Ellis, the former soldier, and others whom I cannot name yet because of the libel laws, all were traitors; in my view, there is no worse crime. A mass murderer can take a score of lives, but in a nuclear age the traitor can endanger the lives of millions.

The attitude of former colleagues of those MI5 and Secret Service officers who proved to be traitors is particularly intriguing. One would imagine that there would be no sympathy for the man who has been systematically undermining a protective organization in the interests of an alien country. It was this reasonable belief that provoked Colonel Ellis's daughter into declaring that her father could not have been a spy because Sir Maurice Oldfield, while head of the Secret Service, had sent a congratulatory cable on the occasion of the colonel's eightieth birthday. Yet shortly before Sir Maurice died, at his hospital bedside, I discussed the Ellis case with him and he knew all about his confession of spying for the Germans. Another Secret Service officer who knew all about Ellis's guilt and confirmed it independently to me told me that he had admonished Oldfield for being so forgiving toward such a traitor.

Few of Blunt's former colleagues among those I have met wanted to take revenge on him. I sincerely believe that if a memorial service were eventually to be held for Kim Philby, there would be a fair turn-out of those former colleagues still alive.

It would seem that those who have spent years inside the shadowy world of deception and counterdeception come to appreciate the dangers of being "netted" or compromised and having escaped themselves, feel sympathy for those who were less fortunate.

As I anticipated, I have been censured for naming dead men who cannot defend themselves, yet it would have been quite legitimate for me to have embarked on a biography of Sir Roger Hollis, for example. If, while pursuing the necessary researches, I had learned about what must have been the most traumatic years of his life, culminating in his interrogation as a suspected KGB agent, would I have been justified in suppressing it in the book because he was no longer around to defend himself? Many biographers have faced a similar problem and have resolved it by honestly telling all.

As regards the others whose treachery has been proved, the damage they must have caused to their own countries and to their countries' allies calls for public censure, whatever the hurt to their relatives.

The damage that must have accrued to the United Kingdom through the Soviet penetration of the British security and intelligence services is all too obvious. Anything that weakens Britain's defense capabilities also automatically damages NATO as a whole. In addition, the Soviet spies operating against Britain also inflicted specific damage on particular allies, the United States being unquestionably the most important in this respect.

While the need to know principle was generally applied on both sides of the Atlantic—so much so that Robert Kennedy, when attorney general, had great difficulty in inducing John McCone, then CIA chief, to show him certain CIA documents—the relationship concerning the mutual interchange of secret information on intelligence and counterintelligence was so intimate that little was withheld for long. As a result, there can be no doubt that Philby, Maclean, Blunt, and others betrayed many American secrets and prejudiced many American operations: Philby and Maclean were the most damaging known spies in that respect because of their close connections with U.S. interests while working in Washington.

Maclean did far more than supply the Russians with diplomatic and political information concerning secret Anglo-American exchanges on the North Atlantic Pact and other matters concerning the creation of NATO. He was at meetings concerned with secret nuclear affairs, such as the availability of uranium ores, and had a pass to the headquarters of the Atomic Energy Commission, providing the privilege of entry to various departments without need for an escort.

In spite of Mrs. Thatcher's attempts to allay public disquiet in Britain following the disclosures in this book, most of the MI5 and Secret Service officers of my acquaintance, who were in the midst of affairs at the relevant time, remain convinced that there was a "mole" at a high level in MI5. I find that this is also the firm view of former CIA officers who were serving at the height of the fears entertained by the Fluency Committee. As George Carver put it to me, "Many things not explicable become so if there was a spy at high level in MI5."

If Hollis was the culprit, his activities, spread over nearly thirty years, must have been extremely damaging both to Britain and the United States. There is one possible aspect that might have had enormous impact on the efficiency of the CIA and the FBI: as books like David Martin's *Wilderness of Mirrors* have pointed out, James Angleton became convinced that the CIA had been penetrated by one or more Soviet "moles" inserted by the KGB. This belief arose from statements by defectors who had proved their good faith, like Anatoli Golitsin, but also from definite instances of leakages of highly secret information to the other side as evidenced by radio intercepts and other feedback sources. While some low-level "moles" were detected and rooted out, those at a high level, if they ever existed, were never found. David Martin and others have suggested that the belief in the existence of such high-level "moles" was the result of a KGB disinformation exercise designed to cause distrust and disruption in the CIA.

There is no doubt that the "mole hunt" led to the departure of totally innocent officers from the CIA, and this has been recognized by the rehabilitation of some of them through financial arrangements organized by Congress.

Some of Angleton's many friends and admirers in the British secret services believe that his possibly excessive suspicion is a reaction to his completely misplaced trust in Philby when the latter was liaison man in Washington but the judgment of almost everybody else was equally at fault in that respect. This suspicion, looked on by others to have been too Machiavellian, appears to have been the prime cause of Angleton's resignation following a move by William Colby, then Director of the CIA, to secure it. As a result, it has even been suggested that Golitsin was really a loyal KGB officer posing as a defector to promote the suspicions inside the CIA and so undermine it.

My inquiries convince me that Golitsin provided so much information that proved to be correct and thereby did so much damage to the Soviet cause that he was a genuine defector. This is also the view of George Carver, who has read the documents concerning Golitsin's record and has a reputation, both inside and outside the CIA, for perceptive and objective judgment. The Senate Intelligence Committee appears to agree. Its members take the view that Golitsin's factual knowledge was excellent. It was his analysis of raw intelligence that was often faulty.

He also suffered from the fault of all defectors that as they begin to dredge deep in their memories, their recall is often in error, and they may even begin to convince themselves that old suspicions that they entertained or heard about were facts. At worst, they may be driven to invent things to convince their interrogators that they are still of value. This problem was excellently described to me by Sir Maurice Oldfield, a wine lover, when we were celebrating his retirement from the Secret Service over dinner. "The first pressings from a defector almost always have the most body. The third pressings are suspect."

Golitsin gave information concerning a "mole" in the CIA's Directorate for Plans who had sent certain reports, which he had seen and partly remembered. The defector also said that he knew that the "mole" had contacted a KGB controller in London on a date that he also recalled. This led to the identification of a suspect against whom nothing could ever be proved but who was nevertheless required to leave the agency.

While the suspected high-level "moles" in the CIA may, in fact, have been mythical, the hemorrhage of secrets was very real. So could it be possible that the leakages of CIA information really orginated in MI5, to which it had been passed on this interchange of information basis? I put this possibility to James Angleton in writing, but he declined to comment on it. George Carver thinks that some leakage of CIA information could have occurred this way but by no means all of it.

I have established that Golitsin had little to contribute about the existence of any high-level "mole" in MI5 when he was debriefed in London. He had no information to offer concerning Hollis. Though Fluency Committee files with Hollis's name blanked out were shown to him, he could offer no guidance.

While U.S. interests have undoubtedly been damaged by British treachery and incompetence, some share of the blame lies on the American side. Fuchs, the atomic spy, did most of his spying in the United States using American nationals like Harry Gold as couriers. Maclean and Philby were both contacting their Soviet case officers regularly while in Washington, under the nose of the FBI. There have been some very bad all-American security breaches, which probably damaged British as well as NATO interests. The worse of these was perpetrated by Sgt. Robert Lee Johnson of the U.S. Army, when he enabled the KGB to see documents that he had rifled from Armed Forces Courier Center near Paris in the early 1960s. William Martin and Bernon Mitchell, the National Security Agency officers who defected to Russia in 1960, may have been as damaging as Burgess and Maclean.

I have already mentioned some more recent American instances of KGB penetration from which no Western intelligence agency of consequence has been free. It is partly because of such home-grown cases that the U.S. authorities have been so forgiving about British lapses, but there are other, more practical reasons. British intelligence and counterintelligence still make their contributions, and the American authorities find them valuable.

Denigrators of the British Secret Service delight in telling a true story that originated with the Rev. Halsey Colchester, a former Secret Service officer who felt the call of religion and left to take Holy Orders in 1972. While serving as a prison visitor, he talked with a thief who mentioned that he came from the Elephant and Castle, in South London. Colchester remarked that he, too, had worked there. "Were you in Century House?" the convict asked, referring to the Secret Service Headquarters, which is located in that area. When Colchester admitted that he was, the thief said, "I thought I recognized you. I was often in and out of Century House—as a laborer, doing repair work or pretending to. All you need to get into Century House is to carry a ladder and a bag of tools. But it was a waste of time. There's nothing in Century House worth nicking."

In fact, there is plenty in Century House that the KGB would like to steal, for agents on the ground are still important. Satellites can reveal little about the long-term political and military intentions of an adversary. An agent or a defector-in-place can. More important, the United Kingdom provides territorial facilities for intercept installations for the National Security Agency, which runs in close harness with Britain's counterpart, Government Communications Headquarters. There are also, of course, nuclear and air-base facilities considered essential for the quick reinforcement of the American forces based in Europe.

Britain benefits most, perhaps, through the regular receipt of U.S. reconnaissance satellite photographs and other information, having no such capability of her own. Except for occasions immediately after a security lapse when feelings on either side may run high, my experience over many years indicates that both the British and American defense authorities find the joint interchange to be crucial to the Western alliance and are loath to do anything to disrupt it. A potent sign of its value is the continuing effort made by the Soviet Union to drive any kind of wedge between Britain and America, their current efforts being concentrated on encouraging the disruptive activities of militant politicians of Britain's far left, who are making the Expulsion of American installations a plank in their political platform.

Farther north, the reaction in Canada to this book was intense because of the close relations between the Canadian and British security and intelligence authorities, and because of specific instances of apparent treachery involving Canada.

Attention focused itself on aspects of the Canadian spy trials and other events consequent on the defection of the Soviet cypher clerk, Igor Gouzenko, from the Russian Embassy in Ottawa in 1945. Gouzenko is still alive, still in hiding, and, after thirty-six years, still afraid of being assassinated by the KGB.

Some newspapers were at particular pains to confirm or deny that Gouzenko had been interviewed by Hollis on behalf of MI5 as I assert. It was quickly proved that Hollis had been sent to Ottawa, and as I have described, Gouzenko is convinced that Hollis questioned him and submitted a false report to London. Nevertheless, Sir William Stephenson, "The Man called Intrepid," whom I have mentioned in connection with the Ellis case, denied that Hollis had ever actually interrogated Gouzenko. Sir William had been intimately involved in preventing Gouzenko from falling into the hands of the Russians, who were searching for him, but his memory is no longer reliable. He is eighty-five and has suffered two serious strokes.

The controversy has been complicated by the discovery that a number of crucial documents dealing with the Gouzenko defection are missing from the Canadian archives. In addition the Canadian government has pursued a hush-up policy on the subject. The confidential papers of the Report of the Royal Commission set up to investigate the espionage ring disclosed by Gouzenko were due for publication in 1977 under the usual thirty years classification rule but the Trudeau government decided to keep them secret for a further ten years. There have also been questions in the Canadian Parliament suggesting political collusion between the British and Canadian governments over information relating to the Hollis Affair.

The official Canadian reticence may be partly due to diplomatic pressure from the British government and its

security services because full disclosure would damage the
reputations of certain people who are still alive. There is
certainly such reluctance on the part of the Canadian authorities on the grounds that official disclosure could damage
Canadian reputations. For this reason it seems unlikely that a
counterespionage operation called "Operation Featherbed"
mounted between 1958 and 1972 will ever be officially reported
as it is believed to name many prominent agents of Soviet
influence.

For differing reasons various individuals in both Britain and
Canada have gone out of their way to throw doubt on the
Hollis connection with the Gouzenko revelations by attacking
my information, which had not been made public before, that
Gouzenko warned Hollis about a Soviet spy inside MI5 with
the GRU code-name "Elli." Much has been made of the fact
that one of the members of the Canadian spy ring, an
Englishwoman called Kathleen Willsher, also had the code
name "Elli" or "Ellie." It has been argued that the Russians
would never have given the same cryptonym to two spies. Yet
this has often been Soviet practice when the spies belonged
to different rings and could easily be differentiated in radio
traffic by some prefix or number. The source book on the spy
Richard Sorge by Sir William Deakin and G. R. Storry
describes how the Red Army's spy ring in China in the 1930s
contained two agents each code-named "Alex," these being
referred to in the index of the book as "Shanghai Alex" and
plain "Alex." The British atomic spy, Nunn May, who was in
the Canadian spy ring, was given the cryptonym "Alek." At
the same time, in the Lucy Ring in Switzerland, the Russians
had a spy called "Alex."

"Alex," "Alek," and "Elli" are conveniently short names to
transmit by radio, and the Russians at the Center in Moscow
would not be likely to confuse a man known as "Elli" working
inside MI5 in Britain with a woman called "Elli" sitting in the
registry in the High Commission in Ottawa.

Gouzenko did not mention the name "Elli" when he wrote
his memoirs. The Canadian authorities would not have allowed him to do so, any more than they would have let him
name Hollis for, in those days the identities of members of the
security and Intelligence services were held secret.

However, when interviewed in Canada recently by the

Toronto Globe and Mail, Gouzenko recalled that the MI5 spy had indeed also been called "Elli." As I have recorded, he gave the same assurance to me.

I have little doubt that Canada continues to be of special interest to the KGB because as the former Soviet spy, Alexander Foote, has described it, Canada is "the Clapham Junction of espionage—a way into the United States or a way out into Europe." The Russians have found it all too easy to secure false Canadian passports for their spies. Rudolph Abel, who had so many other names, entered the United States via Canada on a Canadian passport, though he was a Soviet citizen of British birth. Lonsdale, the alias of Konon Molody, assumed the identity of a dead Canadian of that name.

On the other side of the world, publication of my findings caused an immediate media and political sensation in Australia and New Zealand because of the connections of Hollis and Ellis with the security and intelligence services of those countries.

Communist activity in Australia became increasingly threatening in the years immediately after World War II, with Communist-controlled unions inflicting great and deliberate damage to the economy. Australia had been singled out by the Stalin regime for political penetration, and the KGB was enjoying increasing success. The prime minister of the day, Ben Chifley, therefore set up the Australian Security Intelligence Organization (ASIO) to counter the Communist drive, which was so obviously being assisted by money and professional expertise from Moscow. Britain's interest was intensified because of postwar decisions to transfer a great deal of military research on missiles, aircraft, and nuclear weapons to Australia, which had the space for such work to be carried out remote from towns and, therefore, in greater secrecy. It was a grandiose concept, which was to come to little beyond vast, wasteful expenditure, but in the early 1950s, great hopes were placed in it.

Sir Percy Sillitoe, the director general of MI5, was sent out to Australia to convince Chifley that ASIO should be set up along the same lines as MI5. To assist in this endeavor, to which Chifley agreed, MI5 officers were dispatched from London, and among them was Roger Hollis. Understandably, much was made of Hollis's part when news of the deep suspicions concerning him reached the Australian newspapers. Hollis had not only given advice but had hand-picked some of the key officers for the Australian service. There was reasonable concern as to whether some of these had been selected because they were KGB agents.

There was a further reason why the setting up of an effective counterintelligence service in Australia was essential to Britain's interests. The American "Bride" traffic had turned up the names of Soviet agents working in Australian government services. These agents were clearly being controlled from the Soviet embassy in Canberra, which was securing secret information from the Department of External Affairs and other sources. Following this discovery, the United States was opposed to sharing certain sensitive secrets with Britain in case some of them might be passed to Australia because of the joint British-Australian defense ventures. By helping Australia to establish ASIO on a sound basis, the British government hoped to convince the Americans that the Australians were more secure.

If Hollis had been a Soviet "mole," then the establishment of ASIO was also in the KGB's interest because any improved flow of American secrets to Britain meant that some of it would filter through to him and to any "moles" he might have insinuated into ASIO.

It soon transpired that Hollis had performed a similar service for New Zealand when that country set up a security organization in 1957. Of the original nineteen officers in the New Zealand Secret Intelligence Service, seven were said to have been recommended by Hollis and were British.

The revelation that the Australian-born British Secret Service officer, Charles "Dick" Ellis, had confessed to spying for Germany and was believed to have been recruited by the KGB, also caused a furor in Australia, but, sadly, the arrows were directed there at the wrong target. As readers of this book can see, I reported that Ellis, after apparently taking fright in Britain in 1953, returned to Australia and secured employment with the Australian Secret Intelligence Service (ASIS). Due to misreporting, the widely read newspaper *The Australian* stated that he had joined ASIO. Understandably, Sir Charles Spry, the retired director of ASIO, denied ever having recruited Ellis without, of course, adding that he had been recruited by ASIS. Eventually, I induced *The Australian* to print the true facts, and I put them on political record by informing the prime minister, Mr. Malcom Fraser. By that time, however, many people had been misled about Ellis, which only added to the controversy.

Further public argument ensued over my claim that the KGB had almost certainly been forewarned of the defection of Vladimir Petrov from the Soviet embassy in Canberra and had missed detaining him by only a few hours. Some retired security officers hotly denied that there had been any leak to the KGB, but a former prime minister of Australia, Sir William McMahon, settled the issue by informing Parliament that the Russians had indeed been "tipped off" about the defection. When asked if Hollis could have been the source, Sir William replied that it was possible but that he did not know. As this book indicates, the tip could have come from Philby via Ellis, who had been told of the impending defection in good faith by Sir Charles Spry.

While this book has brought me hostile criticism, particularly for making disclosures likely to bring the British security and intelligence services into disrepute both at home and abroad, I remain unrepentant. Those foreign services close to the British, like the CIA, the FBI, and the Canadian and Australian counterparts, have known about most of the matters exposed here. So, obviously, have the KGB and the GRU. It is only the public from whom the facts have been withheld, and I decline to accept the official line that skeletons that might "frighten the children" should be left in cupboards.

What really matters, from all Western points of view, is that the lessons learned from the calamities of the past should be fully applied to the present. I am confident that MI5 and the Secret Service are currently clean at the top and in good hands. I expect the inquiry by the Security Commission to endorse that belief when it duly reports, though with such a resourceful and relentless adversary there will never be grounds for complacency.

The Security Commission is also likely to confirm that physical security, particularly relating to the control of documents, has been tightened to the limits of practical stringency. A recent expression of this improvement was the behavior of Secret Service officials following the untimely death of their old chief, Sir Maurice Oldfield. They were into his

hospital bedroom and his flat, removing every scrap of paper
that might be of interest to prying eyes.

The book has also brought me quite a few compliments and
one, in particular, that I cherish. During my inquiries, I was
able to confirm that both MI5 and the Secret Service have
recruited journalists to their paid service over the years. I do
not blame the secret agencies for doing this: foreign correspondents, in particular, are well placed to secure information
and perform other intelligence services. But I do think that
the journalists place themselves in an invidious position,
which must limit their professional scope, when they accept
money.

During my long journalistic career, I performed several
important services for MI5 and the Defence Ministry, as I
confessed in my book *Inside Story*, though never for money,
and none was ever offered. I therefore took the opportunity
of asking a former MI5 officer why his organization had never
tried to recruit me to the payroll. "We thought about it, but
decided that we would be unable to control you," he replied.
That was a compliment indeed!

Index

305

Carver, George, 134, 295–296
Castro, Fidel, 187
Central Intelligence Agency. See CIA
Chamberlain, Neville, 246
Chemical Defense Establishment, 221
Chiang Kai-shek, 49
Chifley, Ben, 60, 300
China, invasion of Vietnam, 221
Chisholm, Rory, 185
Churchill, Winston, 64, 131, 156, 173, 192, 223, 225, 246
CIA, 3–4, 14, 147, 302
   and Burgess and Maclean, defection of, 132–133, 142
   "Climber" operation, 22–23
   entrants, screening of, 278–280
   and "Fifth Man," 162
   and Goleniewski, Michal, 177–178
   and Golitsin, Anatoli, debriefing of, 13, 18, 21, 72–73
   Hollis Affair and, 97, 102, 287
   KGB infiltration of, 102–103, 273–274, 294–295
   and McCarthy, Joseph, 150, 282
   MI5 and, 273
   Operation Habrink, 274
   and Penkovsky, Oleg, 183, 189
   Watergate Scandal, effects on, 270, 277
Civil Service Commission, 278
Clarke, Richard Otto, 15
Climate of Treason, The (Boyle), 132
"Climber," CIA/Secret Service operation, 22–23
Cockburn, Claud, 47, 97
Cockerill, A.W., 55
Cohen, Andrew, 166, 168
Colby, William, 295

Colchester, Halsey, 297
Comintern, 108
Committee of Five, 103
Coote, Colin, 30–31
Costello, Paddy, 167
Courtney, Anthony, 245
Crabb, Commander, 65–67
Creighton, Gordon W., 139
Cripps, Stafford, 56
Crossman, Richard, 149
Cuban Missile crisis, 83, 186–187
Cunningham, Charles, 148
Czechoslovakia, 221, 235
   intelligence operations of, 236, 243, 249
   invasion of, 251

Daily Mail, 284, 285, 289
Deakin, William, 299
Defense, Ministry of, 210–212, 283
deGaulle, Charles, 229
Dejean, Maurice, 228–229
Denning, Lord, 81–83, 85–86, 90–91, 174–175, 265
Deutsch, Arnold, 23
Diaries (Crossman), 149
Dilhorne, Lord, 88, 91, 182
Diplock, Lord, 283
D-Notice Committee, 24, 30–31, 182, 208, 285
Dobb, Maurice, 108, 110
Dolnytsin, Anatoli, 30–31. See also Golitsin, Anatoli
Dreadnought (British nuclear submarine), 69
Driberg, Tom, 47, 64, 80, 115–116, 135, 237–245, 285–286, 291–292
Dulles, Allen, 218
Dutch intelligence, 242

ABOUT THE AUTHOR

CHAPMAN PINCHER began his professional life as a scientist, continuing in that capacity in World War II with his involvement in secret weapons work. For more than thirty years he dominated Fleet Street as an investigative journalist through his close friendships with statesmen, Civil Servants, Defence and Intelligence chiefs.

He now concentrates on writing documentary books and novels based on secret information he was unable to use fully while in Fleet Street, or has gathered since through his continuing high-level contacts.

While writing for the *Daily Express*, where he specialized in defence and politics, he was nominated Reporter of the Year in 1964 for a major Intelligence coup—the exchange of the KGB spy, Gordon Lonsdale, for the British businessman, Greville Wynne—and Reporter of the Decade in 1967, following his triumph over the Government in the major political and security scandal known as "The D-Notice Affair."

He was recently elected a Fellow of King's College, London where he had originally studied zoology and botany, and receive an honorary Doctor of Letters of Newcastle-upon-Tyne University.

Married with two children, his hobbies are fishing, shooting, listening to music, and ferreting in any area where he thinks important information is being suppressed.

**Give them
the pleasure of choosing**

Book Tokens can be bought
and exchanged at most
bookshops in Great Britain
and Ireland.